The
Enlightenment

Recent Titles in
Greenwood Guides to Historic Events, 1500–1900

The Second Great Awakening and the Transcendentalists
Barry Hankins

The Age of Napoleon
Susan P. Conner

The American Civil War
Cole C. Kingseed

The Scientific Revolution and the Foundations of Modern Science
Wilbur Applebaum

The Mexican War
David S. Heidler and Jeanne T. Heidler

The Abolitionist Movement
Claudine L. Ferrell

Maritime Exploration in the Age of Discovery, 1415–1800
Ronald S. Love

The Trail of Tears and Indian Removal
Amy H. Sturgis

Darwin's *The Origin of Species*
Keith Francis

The Age of Romanticism
Joanne Schneider

The Reformation Era
Robert D. Linder

Slave Revolts
Johannes Postma

The Enlightenment

RONALD S. LOVE

Greenwood Guides to Historic Events, 1500–1900
Marsha L. Frey and Linda S. Frey, Series Editors

GREENWOOD PRESS
Westport, Connecticut • London

Library of Congress Cataloging-in-Publication Data

Love, Ronald S., 1955–2008.
  The Enlightenment / Ronald S. Love.
     p. cm.—(Greenwood guides to historic events, 1500–1900, ISSN 1538-442X)
  Includes bibliographical references and index.
  ISBN 978-0-313-34243-1 (alk. paper)
  1. Enlightenment. I. Title.
B802.L69 2008
940.2′5—dc22   2008028522

British Library Cataloguing in Publication Data is available.

Library of Congress Catalog Card Number: 2008028522
ISBN: 978-0-313-34243-1
ISSN: 1538-442X

First published in 2008

Greenwood Press, 88 Post Road West, Westport, CT 06881
An imprint of Greenwood Publishing Group, Inc.
www.greenwood.com

Printed in the United States of America

The paper used in this book complies with the
Permanent Paper Standard issued by the National
Information Standards Organization (Z39.48–1984).

10 9 8 7 6 5 4 3 2 1

For Mel and Nancy Steely, Aran and Elaine MacKinnon,
and Glenn and Beth Ames.
They have proved to be my friends, indeed.

CONTENTS

Series Foreword by Linda S. Frey and Marsha L. Frey   ix

Preface   xiii

Acknowledgments   xv

Chronology of Events   xvii

Chapter 1   Historical Overview: Preliminaries, Principles,
and Preconceptions   1

Chapter 2   Science and the Triumph of Reason: Newton, Locke,
and a New Philosophy   25

Chapter 3   The *Philosophes*, the Church, and Christianity   47

Chapter 4   The *Philosophes*, Political Thought, and Enlightened
Despotism   75

Chapter 5   The Alternative Vision of Montesquieu and Rousseau   101

Biographies   113

Primary Documents   143

Glossary of Selected Terms   181

Annotated Bibliography   187

Index   205

Photographs follow page 112.

SERIES FOREWORD

American statesman Adlai Stevenson stated, "We can chart our future clearly and wisely only when we know the path which has led to the present." This series, Greenwood Guides to Historic Events, 1500–1900, is designed to illuminate that path by focusing on events from 1500 to 1900 that have shaped the world. The years 1500 to 1900 include what historians call the early modern period (1500 to 1789, the onset of the French Revolution) and part of the modern period (1789 to 1900).

In 1500, an acceleration of key trends marked the beginnings of an interdependent world and the posing of seminal questions that changed the nature and terms of intellectual debate. The series closes with 1900, the inauguration of the twentieth century. This period witnessed profound economic, social, political, cultural, religious, and military changes. An industrial and technological revolution transformed the modes of production, marked the transition from a rural to an urban economy, and ultimately raised the standard of living. Social classes and distinctions shifted. The emergence of the territorial and later the national state altered man's relations with and view of political authority. The shattering of the religious unity of the Roman Catholic world in Europe marked the rise of a new pluralism. Military revolutions changed the nature of warfare. The books in this series emphasize the complexity and diversity of the human tapestry and include political, economic, social, intellectual, military, and cultural topics. Some of the authors focus on events in U.S. history such as the Salem witchcraft trials, the American Revolution, the abolitionist movement, and the Civil War. Others analyze European topics, such as the Reformation and Counter-Reformation and the French Revolution. Still others bridge cultures and continents by examining the voyages of discovery, the Atlantic slave trade, and the Age of Imperialism. Some focus on intellectual questions that have shaped the modern world such as Charles Darwin's *Origin of Species*, or on turning points such as the Age of Romanticism. Others examine defining economic, religious, or legal events or issues such as the building of the railroads, the Second Great Awakening, and abolitionism. Heroes (e.g., Meriwether Lewis and William Clark), scientists (e.g., Darwin), military leaders (e.g., Napoleon Bonaparte), poets (e.g., Lord Byron) stride across the pages. Many of these events were seminal in that they marked profound changes or turning points. The Scientific Revolution, for example, changed the way individuals viewed themselves and their world.

The authors, acknowledged experts in their fields, synthesize key events, set developments within the larger historical context, and, most important, present well-balanced, well-written accounts that integrate the most recent scholarship in the field.

The topics were chosen by an advisory board composed of historians, high school history teachers, and school librarians to support the curriculum and meet student research needs. The volumes are designed to serve as resources for student research and to provide clearly written interpretations of topics central to the secondary school and lower-level undergraduate history curriculum. Each author outlines a basic chronology to guide the reader through often-confusing events and presents a historical overview to set those events within a narrative framework. Three to five topical chapters underscore critical aspects of the event. In the final chapter the author examines the impact and consequences of the event. Biographical sketches furnish background on the lives and contributions of the players who strut across the stage. Ten to fifteen primary documents, ranging from letters to diary entries, song lyrics, proclamations, and posters, cast light on the event, provide material for student essays, and stimulate critical engagement with the sources. Introductions identify the authors of the documents and the main issues. In some cases a glossary of selected terms is provided as a guide to the reader. Each work contains an annotated bibliography of recommended books, articles, CD-ROMs, Internet sites, videos, and films that set the materials within the historical debate.

Reading these works can lead to a more sophisticated understanding of the events and debates that have shaped the modern world and can stimulate a more active engagement with the issues that still affect us. It has been a particularly enriching experience to work closely with such dedicated professionals. We have come to know and value even more highly the authors in this series and our editors at Greenwood, particularly Kevin Ohe and Michael Hermann. In many cases they have become more than colleagues; they have become friends. To them and to future historians we dedicated this series.

Linda S. Frey
University of Montana

Marsha L. Frey
Kansas State University

PREFACE

During the 18th century, the conviction began to spread throughout articulate sectors of European society that social and political change and reform were both possible and desirable. The movement of ideas that fostered such thinking among people is called the "Enlightenment." Its leading voices combined confidence in the human mind inspired by the 17th-century Scientific Revolution, and faith in the power of rational criticism to challenge the intellectual authority of tradition, the Christian past, and the institutional church. These writers, called *philosophes*, stood convinced that human beings could comprehend the operation of physical nature and mold it to the ends of material and moral improvement. Indeed, the rationality of the physical universe became a standard against which the customs and traditions of society could be measured and criticized. Such criticism penetrated deeply into many segments of contemporary society, politics, and religious opinion. The implication of all of this was that humans could improve their life in this so-called "veil of tears" by their own efforts.

But the Enlightenment was less an event than it was a set of attitudes that developed throughout the 18th century. At is core was criticism, a growing questioning of traditional institutions, customs, and morals. Consequently, Enlightenment writers explored virtually every aspect of social, political, and economic life. They sought to encourage economic development and the spread of prosperity. They wrote in favor of legal reform and supported the "radical" idea of religious toleration. They were highly critical of the militarism that characterized so much of European life during the mid-century wars. Yet, they were practical enough to recognize that warfare was a common feature of human civilization. In short, these writers championed the improvement of human life, the human condition, and human morals. And while there has always been potential for this kind of development, not until the 18th century were these various attitudes brought together to create an optimism about life. The idea of progress (in a secular sense, meaning hope for a better future) was the real turning point. And its two key ingredients were *reason* and *nature*, the underlying elements of the Scientific Revolution.

ACKNOWLEDGMENTS

Professor Ron Love tragically passed away in the midst of finishing this volume. We can therefore thank, only in a general way, those who have assisted him in completing this work. In particular, though, we acknowledge the generous assistance of his friend, Aran MacKinnon, and his brother, Dave, in locating Ron's notes and drafts. Thanks are also due the Library of Congress for their invaluable assistance in providing illustrations. His close friend and former graduate student, Melissa Stock, has compiled the bibliography, and the series editors have finished the work Ron had begun on the documents and the biographical sketches. Sarah Davis, our assistant, has been indefatigable in aiding us in the completion of Ron's last work. Professor Love, a greatly admired professor of history and rigorous and prolific scholar, specialized in early modern France. He will be missed by many: his family, his friends, his students, and especially his colleagues. He was a man of great wit, unfailing generosity, and original mind who never hesitated to attack courageously the unthinking orthodoxies of the profession. He made a difference in our lives—and in the lives of many.

Chronology of Events

1678	Richard Simon (1638–1712) published *Histoire critique du Vieux Testament* (*Critical History of the Old Testament*).
1679	Death of English philosopher Thomas Hobbes.
1684	Giovanni Marana (1642–1693) published his *Letters Writ by a Turkish Spy*.
1685	Louis XIV revoked the Edict of Nantes, ending limited religious toleration in France; French Huguenot immigrants were welcomed in England, Brandenburg-Prussia, and the Dutch United Provinces.
1687	Isaac Newton published *Principia mathematica* (*Mathematical Principles of Natural Philosophy*), in which he introduces the theory of universal gravitation.
1688	The Glorious Revolution erupted in England.
	Aphra Behn published her novel *Oroonoko*.
1689	John Locke's *Letter on Toleration* is published without his knowledge.
	Birth of Charles-Louis de Secondat, the future baron de Montesquieu and *philosophe*.
1690	John Locke published *Essay on Human Understanding* and *Two Treatises of Government*.
1693	John Locke published *Some Thoughts Concerning Education*.
1694	François-Marie Arouet, subsequently known as Voltaire and the leading *philosophe* of his day, was born in Paris.

1695	John Locke published *The Reasonableness of Christianity*.
1696	John Toland published *Christianity Not Mysterious*.
1697	Pierre Bayle published the *Dictionnaire historique et critique* (*Critical and Historical Dictionary*).
1702	The War of the Spanish Succession erupted in Europe.
	William III died and Queen Anne ascended the British throne.
1704	Isaac Newton published his work on *Opticks*.
	Death of John Locke.
1706	Death of Pierre Bayle.
1707	Birth of Georges-Louis Leclerc, comte de Buffon, the future scientist and *philosophe*.
1709	Birth of Julien Offray de La Mettrie, the future doctor and *philosophe*.
1710	Gottfried Leibniz published *Essais de Théodicée sur la bonté de Dieu, la liberté de l'homme et l'origine du mal* (*Essays of Theodicy on the Goodness of God, the Liberty of Man, and the Origin of Evil*), in which he introduced his doctrine of Optimism.
1711	Birth of David Hume, the future Scottish philosopher.
1712	Birth of Jean-Jacques Rousseau, the future *philosophe*.
	Death of Richard Simon.
1713	The peace treaty of Utrecht was signed, concluding the War of the Spanish Succession between France and Great Britain.
	Birth of Denis Diderot, the future *philosophe* and chief editor of the *Encyclopédie*.
1714	The peace treaties of Rastatt and Baden were signed between France and Austria, concluding the last of the fighting over the Spanish Succession.
	Death of Queen Anne and succession of George, Elector of Hanover, to the British throne as George I.
	Gottfried Leibniz published his book, *Monadologie*.

1715	Louis XIV died and was succeeded by Louis XV as a minor king; the regency of the duc d'Orléans was established.
	Birth of Claude Adrien Helvétius, the future *philosophe*.
	Abbé Étienne Bonnot de Condillac, the future *philosophe*, was born in Dauphiny, France.
1716	Death of Gottfried Wilhelm Leibniz.
	Charles-Louis de Secondat inherited his title as baron de Montesquieu and his judicial office as deputy president of the *parlement* of Bordeaux, a position he relinquished in 1728.
1717	Birth of Jean-le-Rond d'Alembert, the future *philosophe*.
	François-Marie Arouet was arrested and imprisoned in the Bastille for offending the duc d'Orléans, the French regent.
1718	François-Marie Arouet premiered his play *Oedipus* and subsequently adopted the pen name Voltaire.
1721	The baron de Montesquieu published the *Lettres persanes* (*Persian Letters*).
1723	Birth of baron d'Holbach, the future *philosophe*.
1724	Birth of Immanuel Kant, the future German philosopher.
1726	Voltaire was arrested and confined in the Bastille for a second time over the Rohan affair; he embarked for England upon his release in May.
	Jonathan Swift published *Gulliver's Travels*.
1727	Death of George I and accession of George II to the British throne.
	Death of Sir Isaac Newton.
1729	Voltaire returned to France from his three-year exile in England.
1732	Pierre-Augustin Caron de Beaumarchais, the future playwright, was born.
1734	The poet Alexander Pope published the *Essay on Man*.

	The War of the Polish Succession erupted, ending in 1735.
	Voltaire published the *Lettres anglaises ou philosophiques* (*Philosophical Letters on the English Nation*).
1736	Voltaire and Madame du Châtelet jointly published the *Éléments de la philosophie de Newton* (*Elements of the Philosophy of Newton*).
1739	David Hume began publication of *A Treatise of Human Nature*.
	The War of Jenkins' Ear erupted between Great Britain and Spain.
1740	Frederick II (the Great), an "Enlightened despot," ascended the throne of Prussia; he published the *Anti-Machiavel*.
	Maria-Theresa ascended the throne of the Habsburg Empire, which inaugurated the War of the Austrian Succession.
	James Boswell was born in Edinburgh, Scotland.
1743	Birth of Marie-Jean-Antoine-Nicolas Caritat, marquis de Condorcet, the future *philosophe*.
1746	Abbé de Condillac published his *Essay on the Origins of Human Knowledge*.
	Lima, Peru, was damaged severely by an earthquake.
1747	Denis Diderot became chief editor of the proposed *Encyclopédie*.
1748	The baron de Montesquieu published his masterpiece, *De l'esprit des lois* (*The Spirit of the Laws*).
	Julien Offray de La Mettrie published *L'Homme machine* (*Man the Machine*).
	Peace was signed at Aix-la-Chapelle, ending the War for the Austrian Succession.
	David Hume published his *Enquiry Concerning Human Understanding*.
1749	Denis Diderot published the *Lettre sur les aveugles à l'usage pour ceux qui voient* (*Letter on the Blind for the Use of Those Who Can See*).

Comte de Buffon began his *Histoire naturelle* (*Natural History*), which he completed in 1788.

Death of Voltaire's mistress, the marquise du Châtelet.

Henry Fielding published his novel *The History of Tom Jones, A Foundling*.

1750   Jean-Jacques Rousseau published his *Discours sur les lettres et les arts* (*Discourse on Letters and the Arts*).

Voltaire accepted the invitation of King Frederick II for an extended visit to Prussia.

1751   Denis Diderot invited Jean-le-Rond d'Alembert to assume joint editorship of the *Encyclopédie*.

Jean-le-Rond d'Alembert wrote the *Discourse préliminaire* (*Preliminary Discourse*) for Volume I of the *Encyclopédie*, which began publication.

Death of Julien Offray de La Mettrie.

1753   Tobias Smollett published his novel, *The Adventures of Ferdinand Count Fathom*.

After quarreling bitterly with Frederick II, Voltaire left Prussia and returned to France.

1754   Abbé de Condillac published his *Traité des sensations* (*Treatise on Sensations*).

1755   The Portuguese city of Lisbon was devastated by an earthquake on November 1.

Jean-Jacques Rousseau published his *Discours sur les origines et les fondations de l'inégalité* (*Discourse on the Origins and Foundations of Inequality*).

Death of the baron de Montesquieu.

1756   The Seven Years' War erupted in Europe.

Voltaire published his poem on the Lisbon earthquake.

The marquise du Châtelet's translation of Newton's *Principia mathematica*, which was published posthumously.

1758   Claude Adrien Helvétius published his book, *De l'esprit* (*On the Spirit*).

1759	Voltaire published *Candide ou l'optimism* (*Candide or Optimism*).
	Samuel Johnson published *Rasselas, Prince of Abyssinia*.
	The Jesuits were expelled from Portugal.
1760	Death of George II and accession of George III to the British throne.
1761	Jean-Jacques Rousseau published *La nouvelle Héloïse* (*The New Heloise*).
1762	Death of Empress Elizabeth of Russia and the accession of Peter III (December).
	Jean-Jacques Rousseau published *Émile* and *Le contrat social* (*The Social Contract*); he subsequently renounced his Swiss citizenship when the political authorities in his native Geneve condemned *The Social Contract*.
	Jean Calas was executed in Toulouse on false charges; the dead man was finally exonerated and his sentence rescinded in 1765.
	Peter III was deposed and murdered in a palace coup, paving the way for his wife, Catherine II (the Great), an "Enlightened despot," to usurp the Russian throne and begin her personal reign.
1763	Voltaire published his *Traité sur la tolérance* (*A Treatise on Toleration*).
	The Peace of Paris was signed, ending the Seven Years' War.
1764	Voltaire published his *Dictionaire philosophique* (*Philosophical Dictionary*).
	Stanislaw Augustus Poniatowsky, an "Enlightened despot," was elected king of Poland.
1765	Joseph II, an "Enlightened despot," became Holy Roman Emperor and began to rule the Habsburg Empire jointly with his mother, Empress Maria-Theresa.
1767	The Jesuits were expelled from Spain.
1769	Denis Diderot wrote *Le Rève d'Alembert* (*D'Alembert's Dream*).

1770	The baron d'Holbach published his book, *Système de la Nature* (*The System of Nature*).
1771	Louis XV exiled the judges of the *parlement* of Paris, to Voltaire's satisfaction, for obstructing a general reform of the royal finances.
	Death of Claude Adrien Helvétius.
1773	The dangerous and widespread Pugachev Rebellion erupted in Russia and was ruthlessly suppressed by Catherine II.
1774	Louis V died of smallpox and his grandson ascended the French throne as Louis XVI.
	The judges of the *parlement* of Paris were recalled from exile.
1775	Beaumarchais' play, *The Barber of Seville*, had its premiere.
	Catherine II began far-reaching reform of provincial administration in Russia.
1776	The Declaration of Independence was issued, officially beginning the American War for Independence.
	Adam Smith published *An Inquiry into the Nature and Causes of the Wealth of Nations*.
	Death of David Hume.
1778	France entered the American War of Independence in support of the rebels, a decision that proved disastrous to French finances and helped to lay the basis for the revolution.
	Death of Voltaire during his last visit to Paris.
	Death of Jean-Jacques Rousseau.
1779	Publication of *Dialogues Concerning Natural Religion* by David Hume.
1780	Death of the Abbé de Condillac.
	Death of Maria-Theresa, empress of Austria, leaving Joseph II in sole control of the Habsburg Empire.
1781	Serfdom was abolished in Austria by Emperor Joseph II, who also issued an edict of religious toleration.

1783   A peace treaty was signed at Versailles between Great Britain, France, and the American colonies, ending the American War for Independence.

The death of Jean-le-Rond d'Alembert.

1784   Beaumarchais' play *The Marriage of Figaro* had its premiere and was quickly banned from further performance.

Death of Denis Diderot.

1785   Immanuel Kant published "Was ist Aufklärung?" ("What is Enlightenment?").

Catherine II issued charters to the Russian nobility and towns.

1786   Wolfgang Amadeus Mozart premiered his opera, *Marriage of Figaro*, based on the play by Beaumarchais of the same name.

Death of Frederick II (the Great) of Prussia.

1788   Death of the comte de Buffon.

1789   The meeting of the French Estates General opened at Versailles in May.

Fall of the Bastille (July 14).

Abbé Sieyès published *Qu'est-ce que le Tiers État?* (*What is the Third Estate?*).

Death of the baron d'Holbach.

1790   Edmund Burke published the *Reflections on the Revolution in France*.

Death of Emperor Joseph II.

1792   The constitutional monarchy was abolished in France (September 22), and the new French Republic was declared.

1793   King Louis XVI (on January 21) and Queen Marie Antoinette (October 16) were executed in Paris by the revolutionaries.

Reign of Terror began in France (October).

The members of the Girondin Party were executed (October), including Madame Roland.

English radical William Godwin published *Political Justice.*

1794   The Thermidorian Reaction (June) brought the fall of Maximilian Robespierre, ending the Reign of Terror.

Death in prison by suicide of the marquis de Condorcet.

1795   The Directory government assumed power in France.

The posthumous publication of the marquis de Condorcet's book, *Tableau historique des progrès de l'esprit humain* (*Historical Table of the Progress of the Human Mind*).

The death of James Boswell.

1796   Death of Catherine II (the Great) of Russia.

1798   Death of Stanislaw Augustus Poniatowsky, former king of Poland.

1799   Napolean Bonaparte overthrew the French Directory, the first step toward his military dictatorship of France.

Death of playwright Pierre-Augustin Caron de Beaumarchais.

CHAPTER 1

Historical Overview: Preliminaries, Principles, and Preconceptions

The enlightened age we live in demands of writers greater cultivation of reason.

—Voltaire, 1764

During the interval between the First and Second World Wars, the foreign correspondent for the New York *Evening World*, Pierre van Paassen, moved his home-away-from-home to the small French village of Bourg-en-Forêt from the city of Paris in 1929. A Dutchman by birth and a naturalized Canadian citizen, Van Paassen was also a reporter of rare qualities, possessing among others a graceful writing style, keen intuition, and acute powers of observation, to which were joined a world view of extraordinary breadth and sympathetic understanding. Yet his transition to village life from the hustle and bustle of one of the globe's great capitals was more than a change of residence, he recalled; it "was like another world." Although time and tempest had left their mark on the decrepit houses, the weather-worn stone church, the sagging roofs, and peeling paint of his new abode, "life had remained untouched by the tumult with which the modern metropolis seeks to hide its secret anguish."[1] The peasant folk among whom Van Paassen lived for the next decade possessed little, but feared nothing, neither futurity, death, nor life itself. He marveled:

> And yet they had a remarkably clear conception of the problems of our time, and did not hesitate to take definite stands when occasion demanded it. Their rule was *to cultivate their own*

gardens. I think that the serenity of their existence ... resided in
the fact that they insisted on being men before social beings.
They were individualists. They were content to be human. Thus
they had retained something of that fundamental dignity which
is the sole condition of happiness because it is both our physio-
logical norm and the law of nature.[2]

It was not accidental that Pierre van Paassen evoked the idea of
cultivating one's own garden, the final words in the 1759 novel, *Candide*, by François-Marie Arouet, better known as Voltaire (1694–1778)
(see Document 5), whose name is all but synonymous with the eighteenth-century intellectual movement known as the Enlightenment.
For *Candide* was one of the first secular books introduced to and read
by a sixteen-year-old Van Paassen,[3] and surely one of the most influential in forming his adult perceptions of the world. Hence, it is not surprising that in his description of the tranquility of life and the essential
contentment that prevailed in Bourg-en-Forêt, he summoned up the
fundamental principles associated with the Enlightenment as defined
by Voltaire: respect for human dignity and individuality, and the pursuit of happiness, all of which proceeded from man's basic nature in
relation to natural law.

Connected also to these principles was a conviction that began to
enter into the minds of educated people across the length and breadth
of eighteenth-century Europe from London to St. Petersburg that
change was something to embrace, not fear, and that old ideas, institutions, social relationships, and perceptions of man's place in the world
could and should be reformed. Prompted by the remarkable achievements of the Scientific Revolution of the previous century, the leading
spokesmen (or *philosophes*) of the developing Enlightenment combined their new confidence in the power of human reason with an
equal confidence in rational criticism to defy the authority of tradition,
which was entrenched most stubbornly in two institutions (see Documents 3 and 4). The first was privilege, in which social status inherited
by blood was more significant than individual merit; the second was
Christian theology, Christian history, and the Christian Church, meaning usually but not exclusively the Catholic Church, in which the
depravity of man after the Fall and his inability to cleanse himself of
original sin without the divine grace of God were emphasized. The
power of tradition that continued to hold popular mentality in thrall
was to these thinkers the source of ignorance, injustice, inequality,
complacency, and superstition; it was regarded therefore as the chief
impediment to progress in the human condition.

A major component of this fresh mode of thinking among the
spokesmen of the new movement was the conviction that if human

beings had the capacity to grasp the operations or laws of physical nature through reason and education, then they could caress or coerce those laws to the material and moral benefit of all mankind. For "it is at least as important to make men better," wrote Denis Diderot (1713–1784), Voltaire's contemporary and a prominent *philosophe* in his own right, "as it is to make them less ignorant."[4] Consequently, the rational character of physical nature, a concept derived chiefly from the work of the great English mathematician Sir Isaac Newton (1642–1727), became the litmus test for long-hallowed social customs, accepted traditions, and established patterns of thought, which were analyzed and criticized in terms of their consistency with nature's laws. Such scrutiny, founded upon reason, was applied over time to every conceivable aspect of eighteenth-century culture—political, religious, social, and economic. The *philosophes* championed, for example, reform of the laws, free speech, and the even more radical notion of liberty of conscience. And although realists who recognized that warfare was a common feature of human history and civilization, they bitterly opposed the militarism in Europe of their own day. The Enlightenment "saw no area, in fact, to which reason, properly conducted, could not attain."[5] From such intense scrutiny (which Diderot defined as "the spirit of doubt")[6] and the criticism that followed from it, there emerged among these men the important, even revolutionary implication that human beings no longer had to accept their "assigned" lot in life according to ages-old ideas and social structures. They could uplift their condition by their own efforts. Therein lay the key to progress in human dignity, human happiness, and the general improvement of human life.

It is interesting, however, that many historians cannot agree on precisely what the Enlightenment was or when it started, though there is greater consensus as to its goals and effects.[7] In textbooks and specialized histories on the subject, there is a wide range of interpretation. To some scholars, the Enlightenment movement emerged out of the scientific and intellectual achievements of the seventeenth century as a natural outgrowth, and thus represented "the transfer into general philosophy, particularly political and social thought, of the intellectual revolution that had already taken place in the physical sciences." Its most prominent characteristic was, consequently, "the emergence of an informed body of public opinion, critical of the prevailing political system, that existed outside the corridors of power."[8] For others, the Enlightenment was "a set of attitudes" (rather than ideas) at whose core was criticism; namely, "a questioning of traditional institutions, customs and morals." Hence, for this group of scholars, the great thinkers of the movement were "not so much philosophers as savants"; that is, "knowledgeable popularizers whose skills [and, one should add, major contributions] were in simplifying and publicizing a hodge-podge of new views."[9] Still others see the Enlightenment as a "period of contagious intellectual energy and enthusiastic quest for knowledge," during which its leaders believed that "their role was to bring light and progress to the world through the application of reason to their reflections on the nature of mankind," and that their primary goal was to extend their ideas "to a general reading public."[10] As for the chronological origins of the movement, the dates vary from as early as 1680 to as late as 1748.

Part of the reason for the different interpretations and dates of origin for the Enlightenment may be that during the eighteenth century itself, the movement "meant very different things in different parts of the continent and even as between different individuals in the same country."[11] It also penetrated different regions of Europe at different times, starting earliest in England and France, before extending steadily across central and southern Europe to Italy and Germany, and finally to Russia. Furthermore, though most of the *philosophes* came from bourgeois or even more humble backgrounds, a few were noblemen. Some of the Enlightenment's leading proponents were also important crowned heads, the so-called "Enlightened Despots," such as Frederick II "the Great" of Prussia, Joseph II of Austria-Hungary, and Catherine II "the Great" of Russia, even if their responsibilities and actions as monarchs often contradicted their claims to live and rule in accordance with the ideas of the new movement that they too embraced.

At the same time, the work of the *philosophes* took different forms depending upon the region in which they lived and worked. These forms ranged from a moderate position that sought more gradual change and reform, as in Great Britain—the birth place of the Enlightenment, where free speech and representative government reigned under a constitutional monarchy—to "radical and aggressive criticism" that was "contemptuous of the past and particularly of the religious assumptions which had done so much to shape the history of Christian Europe."[12] That attitude prevailed in France, where censorship, privilege, and absolute monarchy were the order of the day. If, as one modern scholar has suggested, the Enlightenment had less the scientist's passion to know than the schoolmaster's passion to teach, then it was also in France that the movement "exhibited most clearly its tendency and power to become ... popular and didactic"[13] through the publication of books that criticized existing beliefs and institutions often through the use of satire. "Ridicule overcomes everything," quipped Voltaire, "It is the most powerful of weapons."[14] In the German states, by contrast, the work of the *philosophes* was more muted and tended to be more serious, erudite, and academic in scope.[15] At the same time,

Enlightenment ideas took root quickly in some kingdoms, where they spread rapidly and influenced public opinion profoundly among articulate segments of society, including even some of those who had the power to affect political decision-making. Elsewhere, the same ideas had far less impact, for in such places the educated groups were smaller in size and thus weaker, and in any case "were protected against radical intellectual challenge by strong feelings of self-interest or powerful religious influences."[16]

A further complication was that neither the movement nor the *philosophes* themselves reflected a single set of ideas or a single current of thought. As free thinkers, social critics, and writers of talent rather than philosophers in any formal sense, they were men of their times, deeply embedded (notes historian Peter Gay) "in the texture of their society," and who had been shaped by many of the same influences. They shared, for example, "with literate Christians a religious education, a love for the classics of Rome and [in France, at least] French literature, and an affection for the pleasure of cultivated leisure."[17] Writing of his first encounter with Voltaire, for example, the famous eighteenth-century gossip and gad-about, James Boswell (1740–1795), recalled his reception at Voltaire's château de Ferny, where the great man entertained "with the elegance of a real prince."[18] Furthermore, because they wished to distinguish themselves from their colleagues, they were not inclined to abolish all distinctions in society, and in public they often defended one "orthodox party" against another.[19] "Men of letters," wrote Edmund Burke in 1790, "fond of distinguishing themselves, are rarely averse to innovation" that could bring fame, fortune, or both.[20] Because he lived in almost perpetual want of money himself, Denis Diderot, for example, could not understand why Jean-Jacques Rousseau (1712–1778)—a near contemporary of Voltaire whose name is just as inseparable from the Enlightenment—declined the offer of a royal pension, despite Rousseau's own confession that his "greatest misfortune has ever been inability to resist flattery, and I have always regretted yielding to it."[21]

Yet notwithstanding certain commonalities of background, outlook, and even personal or literary ambition, the *philosophes* never presented a united front nor, as a result, ever developed "a coherent political program or a consistent line of political tactics"[22] (see Documents 6 through 12). They never worked easily together, writes Peter Gay; and because they quarreled frequently (the bitter feud between Voltaire and Rousseau being only the most famous example), they hardly presented a "harmonious portrait of a friendly debate within a philosophical family."[23] As the contemporary English novelist Tobias Smollett (1721–1771) pointed out, these men lived, after all, "in a censorious age; and an author cannot take too much precaution to anticipate the prejudice, misapprehension, and temerity of malice, ignorance, and presumption."[24] To be sure, on occasion the *philosophes* could rise to each other's defense, as Voltaire did when Diderot came under official fire for publishing the great *Encyclopedia* (see Document 2) seen by many as the crowning achievement of the age, though Voltaire himself had very little faith in the project, despite his claims to the contrary. He also defended Rousseau's right to freedom of expression when the publication in 1762 of his rival's great work, *The Social Contract*, excited fierce opposition, even though Voltaire personally despised the book (see Documents 8 through 12). Rousseau in his turn had earlier interceded on Diderot's behalf when the latter's *Lettre sur les Aveugles à l'usage pour ceux qui voient* (*A Letter on the Blind for the Use of Those Who Can See*), published in 1748, landed the author "in the donjon of Vincennes." Rousseau appealed directly to Madame de Pompadour, the French king's mistress and a woman sympathetic to the new current of ideas.[25]

For the most part, however, the *philosophes* worked independently of each other, though they read (and criticized!) each other's work and only occasionally collaborated. They were nonetheless aware of the divisions among them and equally conscious of the danger that disunity sometimes posed to their personal safety, the publication of their books, and the survival of the intellectual movement in which they were all engaged. Voltaire, for one, frequently expressed his distress at seeing a powerful opposition united to crush the *philosophes*, "while the *philosophes* calmly let themselves be slaughtered one after another."[26] Precisely because of the divisions within their small community, he complained, this "little flock [of thinkers] is eating at one another while the wolves come and devour it."[27] Rousseau expressed similar bewilderment at the petty jealousies and intellectual rivalries that perpetually divided his colleagues.[28]

Yet however disunited, however quarrelsome, or however critical of each other, the *philosophes* composed a "party of humanity" (a term coined by Peter Gay) which claimed a common role, even a mission to change society, and their works should be read with that spirit in mind. They were, in effect, a very different breed of intellectual whose activity did not constitute a mere philosophical exercise, though it was partly that; above all, their activity constituted political involvement, meaning to be *engagé* (i.e., engaged in the world). The ultimate aim of this engagement was *bienfaissance universelle*, or the "universal good."[29] Under that common goal fell the reform of society, social mores, patterns of thought, and structures of government for the benefit of human liberty, which included "freedom from arbitrary power, freedom of speech, freedom of trade, freedom to realize one's talents, freedom of aesthetic response, freedom, in a word, of moral man to make his way in the world."[30]

To achieve those ends, the *philosophes* placed supreme confidence in the power of man's reason and basic common sense as an operative force "to dispel the obscuring clouds of ignorance and mystery [i.e., prejudice and superstition] which weighed upon the human spirit" and impeded human liberty in all its forms. Reason and common sense were thus the means "to render men at once happier, and morally and spiritually better."[31] Or to put it differently, reason was exalted by the *philosophes* and their disciples as the natural sovereign of a free people. From that mutual confidence emerged a new belief, ironically not held by many of the leading *philosophes*, but nonetheless apparent toward the end of the eighteenth century, "that all human beings can attain here on this earth a state of perfection hitherto in the West thought to be possible only for Christians in a state of grace, and for them only after death."[32] That view helped to fuel the early idealistic period of the French Revolution that erupted in 1789 at the century's end, which conservative thinker Edmund Burke (1729–1797) dismissed sneeringly as a "philosophical revolution" that had upset the old order of society by a "new empire of light and reason," but in the "splendor of these triumphs of the rights of man" had also lost "all natural sense of [moral] wrong and right."[33]

There had always been a potential for improvement in the human condition along ethical and material lines, of course. Similar ideas had been expressed, after all, by the Renaissance humanists. In their own opposition to the predominance of ancient or biblical authority in the realms of philosophy and science, at least, they had turned to the examination of nature and developed in the process "a new spirit of realism in politics and the study of society."[34] During the Reformation, the same challenge was opposed to religious doctrine and institutional forms, specifically the monolithic structure of the Catholic Church and the preeminence of papal authority.[35] But not until the late seventeenth and early eighteenth centuries were these various attitudes toward traditional authority, society, patterns of thought, politics, religious belief, and human creativity brought together. This combination resulted in the creation of a new sense of optimism about life, even if the *philosophes* themselves were not particularly optimistic. What prevented them from slipping into "pessimism or pious resignation," writes Peter Gay, was their constant engagement, inexhaustible energy, and deep antagonism to "the Christian doctrines of man's depravity."[36] It was, however, the idea of progress, meaning hope for a better future in a secular (as opposed to a spiritual) sense, which was the real turning point. This concept was derived from, and depended upon, the ancient Greek emphasis on man as a thinking being and the Christian idea of God as active in history and the ethical life. For without the concept of an ethical, rational human being, there could be no concept of progress for the better.

The two keys that unlocked this novel idea were reason (including the notion of basic common sense) and nature. The same two elements also underlaid the Scientific Revolution, which had begun to unfold in the sixteenth century, but had become fully developed during the seventeenth century as a result of the work and achievements of such giants as Johann Kepler, Sir Francis Bacon, René Descartes, Galileo Galilei, and above all Sir Isaac Newton. It became clear to the *philosophes* of the subsequent Enlightenment, based upon the remarkable discoveries of the previous century, that just as there are natural laws that govern physical nature and the universe, there is a "natural" way in which human beings function. The *philosophes* similarly became convinced that all men had the potential for reason, an idea that grew out of the philosophy of the great English thinker, John Locke (1632–1704). So if, according to this idea, human beings are also rational beings, then through the application of their reason they could discover the natural laws of the physical world and of human nature, too.

Several preconditions made the Enlightenment possible as an intellectual movement for reform. The first is that the long period from 1648, the end of the Thirty Years' War, to 1789, the eve of the French Revolution, was an age of relative political and social stability. To be sure, wars were still fought for reasons of state, dynastic interest, and commercial or imperial advantage, but these conflicts were conducted in a far more orderly and limited fashion than ever before, especially in contrast to the brutality and chaos of the wars of religion that had been so devastating in the sixteenth and early seventeenth centuries. This new stability was provided by the emerging nation-state, and with it "the development of more professional forms of government" that combined both personal (i.e., monarchical) and impersonal (i.e., bureaucratic) elements, in which governance "had ceased to be a partnership between rulers and great magnates whose birth conferred offices as well as economic power and social status."[37]

That evolution is usually, but not always, associated with the triumph of royal absolutism, writes historian Norman Hampson, though Great Britain—with its constitutional monarchy and representative body of parliament—was an obvious exception, as were the republican United Provinces of the Dutch Netherlands. In any case, since the early reign of French king Louis XIV (r.1643–1715) and even before his succession to the throne of his fathers, the states of western Europe, at least, had increasingly asserted themselves "as impersonal forces" with their "own machinery directed by … professional servants," whose positions depended upon royal favor alone, and whose power was commensurate with the effectiveness of the administrative mechanism that they oversaw.[38] In the process, the state had acquired a monopoly on all political functions from domestic policy and taxation to foreign affairs, including an exclusive right to wage war. The monarchs themselves were aware of this transition. Unlike his predecessors, who had spoken of "*my* state," Louis XIV had slowly but surely "subordinated himself to the procedures of his government" and, in the last two decades of his life, began to refer increasingly to "*the* state" and to himself as its first servant.[39] In fact, by the time he died in 1715, the idea of France as an organic entity had so taken hold in his own mind that he declared to those attending his deathbed, "I am leaving you, but the State will always remain." "Be faithfully attached to it," he admonished further, "and let your example serve all my other subjects. Be united and in accord: this is the unity and strength of a State."[40] Frederick II of Prussia later expressed many of the same sentiments.

A second precondition for the Enlightenment was economic stability, together with increasing prosperity. These advances had developed also to a large degree under the protection of the state, as did a corresponding growth in size of a bourgeois society devoted to commerce. Though the European economy was still overwhelmingly agricultural, and industry remained traditional in its methods,[41] most kingdoms in the early eighteenth century were producing slightly larger quantities of food than were required for mere subsistence, a process enhanced by the introduction of new kinds of crops, different methods of farming, and better animal husbandry over time, which yielded surplus goods that could be sold not just in the local or domestic market, but in foreign markets, too. Maritime commerce was also on the rise, as the global trade in everything from Indonesian spices to Indian cotton, Chinese tea, American tobacco, Caribbean sugar, and African slaves increased dramatically in volume.

The result of these agricultural and commercial developments was, in part, a slow but steady growth in European population, owing to better nutrition and the decline of certain diseases such as plague, as well as the increase in the number of men who acquired wealth and a new degree of status from trade. Together with such professionals as lawyers, doctors, financiers, and civil servants—all city dwellers— these men of commerce formed an ever larger body of bourgeois who set the standards of urban culture and over time began to demand greater equality of status with the hereditary nobility (their social betters) and a role in the political decision-making process in proportion to their wealth, growing importance, and economic influence. The Enlightenment was largely a bourgeois phenomenon, after all, and most of its leading spokesmen (e.g., Voltaire, Diderot, Rousseau, David Hume, and Adam Smith, to name just a few) came from bourgeois or petty bourgeois origins. These men, and the movement itself, advocated individual rights, and openly attacked the traditional emphasis on heredity by blood and social privilege accorded to the aristocracy, who owed their dignity (sneered Tobias Smollett) "to the circumstances of their birth, and are consecrated from the cradle for the purposes of greatness, merely because they are the accidental children of wealth."[42] In fact, without the existence of an increasingly rich, numerous, vocal, and self-conscious bourgeoisie, eighteenth-century society would have been very different than it was, and the Enlightenment could not have occurred as it did. For without the bourgeoisie, the *philosophes* "could hardly have existed," writes historian Franklin Baumer, and without the *philosophes* "the bourgeoisie must have lacked assurance and a philosophical basis."[43]

A third precondition for the intellectual movement was the erosion of religion or religious authority, specifically of Catholic Christianity, provoked by generations of scholars, religious reformers, and scientists since the Renaissance. The humanism of the fourteenth and fifteenth centuries focused in part upon deriving a lay ethic from the literary classics of ancient Rome that was suitable to "modern" times and secular life. This search was not a movement away from religion, for the humanists were neither anti-religious, skeptical, nor atheist in any sense. At a time, however, when the Catholic Church had become spiritually bankrupt and a corrupt papacy had lost the ethical leadership of Christianity, humanism offered an alternative pagan morality that paralleled Christian morality. Partly from this pursuit had emerged the concept of "civic humanism" that stressed the active life and good citizenship in secular society. But because the humanists conceived of man in a religious sense as a being of elevated status, having been created (according to the book of Genesis) in the image of God, he was endowed with certain potentialities that allowed him to chart his own moral course through life. The highest expression of this challenge to the traditional view of human depravity after the Fall of Adam is Pico della Mirandola's famous *Oration on the Dignity of Man* (1486), in which he argued that God had given human beings "neither fixed abode, form, nor function," and moreover that "human actions, not thoughts, determine man's nature."[44]

Subsequently, in the sixteenth and seventeenth centuries scholars began to focus their attention on Christianity. In the process, their work steadily (if inadvertently) undermined the religious traditions of

European society and thus weakened Christianity's hold on many artic-ular people (see Documents 16 through 19). The earliest steps in this direction were not critical, but rather conservative, as Christian humanists and "historians" such as Martin Luther undertook biblical translations for the benefit of a wider reading audience, in order to increase knowledge of the Christian past. This in turn led to critical study of the sacred texts by others, starting with the compilation of more scholarly editions of the Gospels based on the original languages, the attempt to define key words in scripture, and the effort to reconcile inconsistencies that appeared too often among various versions of the Bible but which had crept in by mistake or clerical error as the texts were reproduced and passed down from generation to generation.[45] This biblical scrutiny culminated in such analytical works as Richard Simon's *Critical History of the Old Testament* (1679) and Pierre Bayle's *Historical and Critical Dictionary* (1697), which only fueled the grow-ing skepticism with respect to the historical accuracy of scripture, as both works revealed omissions, transpositions, implausibilities, and contradictions that undermined the value of the Bible as revealed truth and exposed much religious doctrine "as ludicrous superstition."[46]

Scientific discovery only contributed to the new skepticism. De-spite the fact that all, or almost all, the men engaged in the various branches of "natural philosophy" (as the sciences were still called) were sincere Christians who believed deeply that their discoveries "glorified God by revealing the unsuspected grandeur of his Crea-tion,"[47] their findings nevertheless chipped away at the foundations of Judeo-Christian tradition backed by ancient Greek authority. The heli-ocentric theory of the solar system proposed in 1543 by Nicolas Coper-nicus, and steadily developed by other European scientists over the next century and a half, had very important implications for the theo-logical relationship between man and nature. For if the earth were the center, writes Norman Hampson, then man was the "Lord of the uni-verse" in accordance with ancient Greek belief and Christian doctrine. If, however, man merely inhabited one planet orbiting a local star, then it was a short step to conceive of similar planets and solar systems scat-tered across the heavens.[48]

At the same time, the perfection of God's Creation was steadily undermined. Johann Kepler demonstrated, for example, that the plan-ets orbited the sun in an ellipse, not a perfect circle, while Galileo's tel-escope revealed not just imperfections on the moon's surface and sunspots, but also Jupiter's moons. This discovery proved that the earth was not the center of the universe, around which the planetary system was supposed to pivot. Newton's universal theory of gravitation further contributed to that displacement by demonstrating through advanced mathematics that there was, in fact, no center at all. Compounding the growing rupture between reason and revelation was the discovery of fossil evidence, which made it clear that early life-forms had disappeared, only to be replaced by new ones. But neither phenomenon was accounted for in the scriptures, nor could they be explained away by reference to the great flood. Nevertheless, most scientists still believed that scientific discovery and religious orthodoxy were not incompatible, despite the mounting evidence, but could be reconciled. To that end, in 1614, Galileo published *The Authority of Scripture*, while René Descartes illustrated his whole approach to inductive reasoning in the *Discourse on Method* (1637) by "proving" the existence of God. Even Newton devoted much of his considerable intellectual energy to biblical studies during his later life. Yet the fact remained that by 1700, Christianity no longer enjoyed its former invincibility.

A fourth and final precondition for the Enlightenment was the process of maritime exploration and expansion around the globe, starting in the early fifteenth century, which had provided Europeans with direct exposure to non-Western, non-Christian societies that often appeared more civilized and advanced than their own. This contact helped not only to nourish the growing skepticism about Christianity already evident from scientific endeavor, but also to pose "disturbing contradictions to Europe's ethnocentric confidence and sense of superiority" in terms of culture.[49] The publication of travel literature (see Documents 26 through 30), which began as a trickle in the early sixteenth century but by the late seventeenth century had become a flood, was vital to these changing attitudes. As the *National Geographic* of their day, these accounts provided a reading audience in Europe with vicarious experience of the wider world, which broadened their minds with respect to geography, ethnography, and anthropology. The knowledge, in particular, that there existed several high cultures, especially in Asia, that owed nothing to the Judeo-Christian or Greco-Roman heritage made Europeans more self-reflective in a way that served to inspire a new sense of cultural relativism,[50] as contemporary Europeans "came to appreciate that difference *a priori* did not constitute inferiority or superiority."[51] English novelist Sarah Fielding (1710–1768) made a similar observation when she wrote in 1744 "that the Customs and Manners of Nations, related chiefly to Ceremonies, … have nothing to do with the Hearts of Men."[52]

On the contrary, Europeans looking outward and discovering around the globe "a vast agglomeration of non-Christian values, [and] a huge block of humanity which had constructed its moral system, its concept of truth, on lines particularly its own," compelled articulate men and women to reconsider their fundamental concepts of the Western world "as a result of the conditions in which [the same ideals] were seen to operate in far-off countries," and to recognize that they no longer could take their old perceptions for granted.[53] Or, as Simon de La Loubère expressed it more succinctly in his 1691 relation of Siam, "so true it is that the Phantasies [i.e., social mores and cultural patterns], even they which seem to be most natural, do greatly consist in Custom."[54]

To be sure, those who traveled abroad and published accounts of their experiences upon their return still carried the baggage of their own culture, especially in terms of their Christian faith (which they saw as the engine for moral advancement) and the achievements of Western science and technology (which they saw as the engine for material progress). These twin pillars of early modern Europe constituted for them the most striking contrast with the rest of the world of their day. Whether laymen or ecclesiastics, these authors were, after all, people of their time and place. Yet the depth of their observations on the societies they experienced reveals a profound recognition of the essential structures of these cultures and a sincere endeavor to gauge them according to indigenous standards, not European, in a manner that transcended a description of mere superficialities.[55] Commenting specifically on human virtue and vice, for example, English novelist Lawrence Sterne (1713–1768) observed that

> there is a balance ... of good and bad everywhere; and nothing but the knowing it is so can emancipate one half of the world from the prepossessions which it holds against the other—that the advantage of travel ... was by seeing a great deal both of men and manners; it taught us mutual toleration; and mutual toleration ... taught us mutual love.[56]

Nor were these authors of travel literature reluctant to draw unfavorable comparisons critical of European custom. In writing about the superstitious nature of the Siamese people, for example, and their belief in such notions as lucky and unlucky days, Simon de La Loubère quickly reminded his readers that this "Folly [also] ... is perhaps too much tolerated amongst Christians; witness the Almanac of *Milan*, to which so many persons do now give in to blind belief."[57] He also praised the simplicity of Siamese life in contrast to European materialism, as well as some of their other cultural practices, such as child-rearing. The Jesuit priest, Philippe Avril, was similarly able to set aside his antagonism to Christendom's traditional enemy, Islam, in order to praise Muslim devotion to piety and prayer. In fact, he wrote in 1685 while traveling through the Near East on caravan, only the Turks retired "three or four times a day from the gross of the Body" to pray. This humility he contrasted sharply with the general laxity observable among his fellow Christians who, he scolded, "are so far from believing such a holy Practice to be a Duty, that they think it a shame to pray to God, that Worship is so justly due to him."[58] On the whole, early modern globe-trotters were well aware of the beneficial effects of travel as a solvent upon long-hallowed truths, biases and established precepts. "One of the greatest advantages that a traveler brings back from his journeys," the chevalier d'Arvieux wrote in 1673, after an extensive tour of North Africa and the Near East, "is that he rejects the prejudices which he imbibed in his own country against foreigners, something that those who never leave will ever accomplish."[59]

Not only were contemporary Europeans fascinated, therefore, by the published accounts of new places, exotic varieties of plants and animals, strange social customs, different systems of government, and capacities for mass warfare beyond mere commercial opportunity.[60] But some non-Western nations were also acknowledged as archetypes for their social organization and benign rule, a view which had particular appeal among the *philosophes*, "who used such travel literature to blast apart old preconceptions about European society itself."[61] China, "which equals all of Europe in greatness" (wrote a seventeenth-century contemporary) but "has proudly done without the rest of the world until now,"[62] became the particular "model state" seen to possess, among other attributes, "unique and effective governmental and educational institutions; examinations for public office; state-supported schools; social services; and courier systems."[63] René Descartes, for one, used the example of China (with Persia) to argue that social customs vary, and that "it seemed to me that the most useful [course] would be to adapt my behaviour to that of those with whom I would have to live."[64] Other writers, such as Voltaire, idealized China and especially Confucius' teachings, which were equated "with the pagan values of ancient Rome," and thus usable as evidence that the *philosophes'* "secular values were no less politically effective than Chinese ones."[65] At the same time, it astonished most Europeans, who were convinced on the basis of biblical chronology that the world had been created about 4004 BC, that the Chinese, Egyptians, and Babylonians traced their own histories well back beyond that date. Equally disturbing was the possibility revealed by Egyptian records that the early Hebrews might have borrowed many of their beliefs from Egypt, as opposed to direct divine inspiration as had always been believed.[66]

Contact with so-called "primitive" (as opposed to "civilized") societies was just as disturbing to European self-perceptions and inspired the idea of the "Noble Savage"; that is, uncivilized men who are basically good, living in the pristine state of nature. This concept had been developing ever since the mid-sixteenth century, when Franciscan Father Bartholomé de Las Casas contrasted the Central American Indians as "gentle lambs, imbued by the Creator with all the qualities" of innocence, simplicity, honesty, and loyalty, with the Spanish conquistadors, whom he characterized as "ravening wolves" who "fell upon the fold."[67] French author Michel de Montaigne picked up this idea in his essay "On Cannibals" (1580), in which he wrote that the native Brazilians "are still governed by natural laws and ... are in such a state of purity that it sometimes saddens me to think we did not learn of them earlier."[68] In his account of Guiana (1596), Sir Walter Raleigh echoed similar views of the native peoples, of whom he wrote that "in all my life either in the Indies or in Europe did I ever behold a more goodly or better favored people, or more manly."[69] Perhaps the highest expression of the "noble savage" concept applied to a "primitive" culture, however, is found in the journal of the Pacific voyage by Count Louis-Antoine de Bougainville in 1767–1968 (see Document 30). Enchanted by the tranquil island and placid people of Tahiti, which he described in idyllic terms, the French count concluded, "Lawmakers and philosophers, come and see here all that your imagination has not been able even to dream up.... It is a true Utopia."[70]

From such idealized accounts of genuine people and societies, it was a very short step to the invention of imaginary peoples and societies in fictional travel literature, used for the specific purpose of criticizing European customs and culture. Already prior to the eighteenth century, works of this kind were in circulation. In his *Letters Writ by a Turkish Spy* (1684), Giovanni Marana used the literary device of a series of briefs written by a foreign visitor to France to satirize contemporary politics, religion, social mores, and values—a device later copied to great effect by the baron de Montesquieu (1689–1755) in his most famous book, *The Persian Letters* (1721; see Document 28). In her 1688 novel *Oroonoko*, the story of an enlightened native prince from an imaginary African kingdom enslaved by barbaric Europeans, author Aphra Behn anticipated a similar novel, *Rasselas, Prince of Abyssinia* (1759) by Samuel Johnson, and also foreshadowed the ideas of natural man as expressed later by Rousseau. Perhaps the most famous work of this kind of fiction is *Gulliver's Travels* (1729) by Jonathan Swift, which depicts a pilgrimage (writes a modern literary critic) "that brings one face to face with the Yahoo image of man."[71] Far from accepting that man was a reasonable being by nature, Swift believed that he was only capable of reason, and that man's passions—above all his self-love—were the "real facts of human existence."[72] To a greater or lesser degree, the authors of these works used imaginary people or fictional voyages to exotic places to exemplify the virtues they thought were lacking in European culture, or to criticize that culture from the satirical viewpoint of fictitious foreign observers who visited Europe. Hence, it is entirely probable that the Enlightenment could not have developed as it did without the existence of non-Christian, non-Western peoples—savage or sophisticated, real or imagined—on which to base the "Noble Savage" concept in contemporary thought or to criticize European values by comparison to those developed in other high cultures independently of a Greco-Roman, Judeo-Christian heritage.

Altogether, the preconditions from which the Enlightenment evolved, notes Peter Gay, laid the foundation for the rapid advance in secularism and secularist ideas during the eighteenth century. Travel literature, he observes, "offered the spectacle of happy and civilized non-Christian cultures," while the transformation in government under the emergent nation-state and "the demands of international politics forged secular rather than sectarian alliances." At the same time, the growing European economy "stimulated the desire for worldly goods" and with it the demand for a greater bourgeois voice in political decision-making; meanwhile, the great discoveries of the Scientific Revolution "suggested the appalling possibility of a universe without God."[73] In short, writes Robert Caponigri, the emergence of secularism, or at least secularist culture, presented a sharp contrast to the religious culture that had characterized western civilization prior to 1700. Through the simple force of reason, the Enlightenment "rejected religion's readiness to recognize some principles beyond the immediate order of experience and life" that claimed "ultimately to represent some transcendent principle [i.e., God] and to draw their power from it."[74] What the Enlightenment did, in other words, was to transfer European attitudes "from a transcendent to an immanent principle—not God, but humanity; not eternal truths, but immanent reason itself; not the sanction of the law, but the intrinsic reasonableness of law—as an object worthy of esteem."[75]

Consequently, argues historian Crane Brinton, "with the eighteenth century we are in many ways in modern times."[76] For it is to the Enlightenment, adds John Merriman, that one can trace the origin of the belief, in terms of political structures and relationships, "that people should be ruled by law, not rulers, that a separation of powers ought to exist within government in order to prevent the accumulation of too much power in one or a few hands, the concept of popular sovereignty, and the assumption that it is the responsibility of rulers to look after the welfare of the people."[77] Belief in the intrinsic value of human freedom, humanity's natural goodness, man's capacity for material and moral improvement (i.e., progress), and the superiority of knowledge arrived at through reason and reflection, not revelation and received truths,[78] also formed part of the new equation in philosophical and religious terms.

Owed as well to the Enlightenment was a vast increase not necessarily in the size of the reading public, but rather in the emergence of an informed body of public opinion. "There is no question," asserts Crane Brinton, "about the fact of the spread of ideas in some form among many thousands who could not be numbered among the intellectuals or ruling classes in any restricted sense of the term."[79] Across western Europe in particular, a powerful print culture developed in the eighteenth century for the exchange of ideas, based upon the publication not just of books, but also of newspapers, cheap pamphlets, periodicals, journals, broadsheets, and novels that circulated widely. Lending libraries, literary societies, and salons, which fostered "a spirit of conversation,"[80] assisted in this process, as did a considerable increase in levels of popular literacy and public discussion. Only Edmund Burke's "swinish herd"—that is, the uneducated masses— remained completely unlettered. The most significant aspect of the new print culture, however, was the existence in Great Britain, France, the United Provinces, and other countries of contemporary Europe "of a strong, literate middle class, numbering several millions and devoted to the ideas of the Enlightenment."[81]

Yet it took time for the movement to reach its full stride, and for that reason it is divided customarily by scholars into three phases of development, though the lives of the *philosophes* themselves often spanned at least two, if not all three stages. For with very few exceptions, such as Voltaire (1694–1778) and Montesquieu (1689–1755), almost all of them were born, lived out their lives, and died during the eighteenth century. In any case, the first phase of the Enlightenment, which encompassed the generation of Voltaire and Montesquieu, was a moderate phase that covered the first half of the eighteenth century. The *philosophes* who were active in this period were most directly influenced by the effects of the Scientific Revolution, as well as the current of taste established during the reign of Louis XIV. These men adhered to the values of restraint, decorum, social and aesthetic equilibrium, though at the same time they opposed enforced conformity to the ideals or structures of such entities as the institutionalized church. The *philosophes* of this stage were also skilled satirists who poked fun at those aspects of eighteenth-century culture that they despised, whether religious, political, military, intellectual, or economic.[82]

The second phase, called by some the "high Enlightenment,"[83] by consensus began in 1748, after the publication of the baron de Montesquieu's book *The Spirit of the Laws*, which is widely regarded by

historians as the greatest sociological work of the moderate first generation. Even Voltaire, who could be stingy with his praise, considered
Montesquieu's work to be "full of great maxims." "The author always
thinks and causes others to think," Voltaire observed, "his imagination
causes mine to run forth.... It must be confessed that few people have as
much wit as he, and his lofty boldness must please all who think
freely."[84] In essence, *The Spirit of the Laws* "revolutionized mens' conception of history by showing the interrelation of social, geographical,
political, economic, and religious forces," and could be considered,
therefore, as the starting point of modern sociology.[85] His object was to
demonstrate the way in which these social forces confined men in a kind
of straightjacket of conventional thinking, thus shackling their reason.

It was almost a matter of consequence, therefore, that the generation of *philosophes*, whose work was most prominent after 1748—
including that of Rousseau, Diderot, Julien Offray de La Mettrie, David
Hume, Adam Smith, Claude-Adrien Helvétius, and the baron
d'Holbach, to name just a few—tended mostly to be radical in their
views and opinions. Their primary interest was religion, and their own
confessions of "faith" ranged from mild deism (essentially the belief
that the world had been created as a great mechanism by God, but
afterward there was no further need for God's providential intervention
in it) to outright materialism and atheism. Atheism in this case was
not, however, a form of skepticism; rather, it was a positive belief in
the universe as a great machine governed only by natural, physical
laws.[86] Yet, the second generation took interest also in human behavior
and conditional reflexes, going to the extent (as did La Mettrie, a doc-
tor by profession; see Documents 19 and 21) of seeing man himself as
a kind of biological machine. In economic thought, meanwhile, they
defended unfettered free competition, defined by Adam Smith (1723–
1790) as "*laissez-faire.*"

By the third phase of the movement, which began traditionally
with the deaths of Voltaire and Rousseau in 1778, the two elements
that characterized the later Enlightenment—namely, the "rational-
classical" and "sentimental-romantic"—were fully developed. Afterward, they worked in tandem to discredit the Old Regime in Europe
during the critical years just prior to the French Revolution of 1789.[87]
But, notes John Merriman, the major preoccupation was with the emo-
tions and passions of mankind.[88] At all events, reason and sentiment
combined during this stage of the Enlightenment in the works of such
individuals as Immanuel Kant (1724–1904; see Document 1) and the
Marquis de Condorcet (1743–1794) to mold a view of man as both
naturally virtuous and naturally rational—a being whose "heart and ...
head were both sound."[89] This was also the stage when several

monarchs, the Enlightened Despots, applied the *philosophes'* principle "that rulers work for the good of their subjects," even if their efforts more often resulted in the reorganization of their states to enhance royal authority.[90] Hence Voltaire's earlier shifting views of Frederick II of Prussia, from praise for the man he called the "Marcus Aurelius of the north" and a monarch informed by the new ideals, to disappointment that "the king has altered the man, and now he relishes despotic power, as much as a Mustapha, a Selim, or a Suleiman," all Turkish sultans.[91] Hence also Voltaire's more favorable (though mistaken) prediction of a bright future for young King Louis XVI, who succeeded to the French throne in 1774. The new monarch, wrote the aging *philosophe*, had given himself over "to reason and [had braved] the outcries of prejudice and nonsense." "That gives me a high opinion of the age of Louis XVI," continued Voltaire:

> It seems to me that he was born prudent and firm. Therefore he will be a great king. Happy are those who are twenty [years old] and who will long relish the sweet pleasure of his reign![92]

Despite Voltaire's vision of a promising future for his native country, the result perhaps of wishful thinking, the third phase of the Enlightenment actually witnessed the diffusion of ideas that helped to undermine confidence in, and respect for, the French monarchy, "and thus indirectly contributed to the French Revolution."[93] "The Bourbon [dynasty] is by no means a cruel race," observed Lawrence Sterne in 1768, "they may be misled by other people." But, he also noted, "there is a mildness in their blood."[94] To find the origins of the Enlightenment, however, one must look first to England in the late seventeenth century, and only then to France, which in time became the center of the intellectual movement during the eighteenth century.

Notes

1. Pierre van Paassen, *Days of Our Years* (New York: Hillman-Curl, Inc., 1939), 210.

2. Ibid. (Emphasis added.)

3. Ibid., 18, 19. He was introduced to the book by his uncle, a landscape painter with "an enthusiastic and sensitive nature."

4. Denis Diderot, *Rameau's Nephew and Other Works*, Jacques Barzun and Ralph H. Bowen, trans. and eds. (Indianapolis: The Bobbs-Merrill Company, Inc., 1956), 300.

5. A. Robert Caponigri, *Philosophy from the Renaissance to the Romantic Age* (Notre Dame: University of Notre Dame Press, 1963), 277.

6. Diderot, *Rameau's Nephew*, 288.

7. For a good, general introduction to the conflicting views among some writers from the eighteenth century to the present, see Dena Goodman and Kathleen Willman, eds., *The Enlightenment* (Boston: Houghton Mifflin Company, 2004), 9–39.

8. Thomas F.X. Noble, Barry S. Strauss, *et al.*, *Western Civilization: The Continuing Experiment*, 2nd ed. (Boston: Houghton Mifflin Company, 1998), 659, 660.

9. Mark Kishlansky, Patrick Geary, and Patricia O'Brien, *Civilization in the West*, 2nd ed. (New York: Harper Collins College Publishers, 1995), 578.

10. John Merriman, *A History of Modern Europe, from the Renaissance to the Present* (New York: W.W. Norton & Company, 1996), 399.

11. M.S. Anderson, *Europe in the Eighteenth Century, 1713–1783*, 3rd ed. (London: Longman, 1987), 408.

12. Ibid.

13. Caponigri, 272, 275.

14. Voltaire to Jean Le rond d'Alembert, June 26, 1766, Richard A. Brooks, trans. and ed., *The Selected Letters of Voltaire* (New York: New York University Press, 1973), 264.

15. Caponigri, 275.

16. Anderson, 408.

17. Peter Gay, *The Party of Humanity: Essays in the French Enlightenment* (New York: W.W. Norton & Company, Inc., 1959), 119.

18. Frank Brady and Frederick A. Pottle, eds., *Boswell on the Grand Tour: Italy, Corsica and France, 1765–1766* (New York: McGraw-Hill Book Company, Inc., 1955), 196.

19. Gay, *Party of Humanity*, 119.

20. Edmund Burke, *Reflections on the Revolution in France*, H.D. Mahoney, ed. (New York: Macmillan Publishing company, 1955), 126.

21. Jean-Jacques Rousseau, *The Confessions* (Ware, Hertfordshire: Woodsworth Editions Ltd., 1996), 360, 370.

22. Gay, *Party of Humanity*, 119.

23. Ibid., 116.

24. Tobias Smollett, *The Adventures of Ferdinand Count Fathom*, Paul-Gabriel Boucé, ed. (London: Penguin Books, 1990), 42–3.

25. Rousseau, *Confessions*, 336.

26. Voltaire to Jean-le-Rond d'Alembert, April 25, 1760, Voltaire, *Selected Letters*, 209.

27. Voltaire to Jean-le-Rond d'Alembert, March 19, 1761, Ibid., 219.

28. See, for example, Rousseau's remarks on 376, 386, 443–4, in his *Confessions*.

29. For a good discussion of the origins and application of this term, see Norman Hampson, *The Enlightenment* (Harmondsworth, Middlesex: Penguin Books, 1968), 79–83.

30. Peter Gay, *The Enlightenment: An Interpretation, Volume I: The Rise of Modern Paganism* (New York: Alfred A. Knopf, 1967), 3.

31. Caponigri, 272.

32. Crane Brinton, *Ideas and Men: The Story of Western Thought* (Englewood Cliffs, NJ: Prentice Hall, Inc., 1950), 289.

33. Burke, 87, 93, 152.

34. Caponigri, 273.

35. Ibid.

36. Gay, *Party of Humanity*, 114–5.

37. Hampson, 48–9.

38. Ibid.

39. John B. Wolf, *Louis XIV* (New York: W.W. Norton & Company, Inc., 1968), 379.

40. Quoted in Ibid., 618.

41. Hampson, 45, 46.

12. Smollett, *Count Fathom*, 16.

43. Franklin Baumer, *Main Currents of Western Thought* (New Haven, CT: Yale University Press, 1978), 365.

44. Ernst Breisach, *Renaissance Europe, 1300–1517* (New York: The Macmillan Company, 1973), 318. For a good general discussion of humanism and civic life, see 318–21.

45. A. Lloyd Moote, *The Seventeenth Century: Europe in Ferment* (Lexington, Mass.: D.C. Heath and Company, 1970), 400–1.

46. George A. Rothrock and Tom B. Jones, *Europe: A Brief History*, 2 vols., 2nd ed. (Chicago: Rand McNally College Publishing Company, 1975) vol. I, 341–2.

47. Hampson, 24.

48. Ibid.

49. Rothrock and Jones, 340.

50. Glenn J. Ames and Ronald S. Love, eds., *Distant Lands and Diverse Cultures: The French Experience in Asia, 1600–1700* (Westport, CT: Praeger Press, 2003), xvii.

51. Glenn J. Ames and Ronald S. Love, eds., *Distant Lands and Diverse Cultures: The French Experience in Asia, 1600–1700* (Westport, CT: Praeger Press, 2003), xvii.

52. Sarah Fielding, *The Adventures of David Simple*, Malcolm Kelsall, ed. (Oxford: Oxford University Press, 1987), 27.

53. Paul Hazard, *The European Mind, 1680–1715*, trans. J. Lewis May (Harmondsworth, Middlesex: Penguin Books Ltd., 1964), 25–6, 45; first published under the title, *La Crise de la conscience européene* (Paris: 1935.) See also Lach, vol. I, bk. 2, 835.

54. Simon de La Loubère, *A New Historical Relation of the Kingdom of Siam* (London: 1693; facsimile reprint, Singapore: Oxford University Press, 1986), 27.

55. Ames and Love, xvii.

56. Lawrence Sterne, *A Sentimental Journey through France and Italy*, Graham Petrie, ed. (Harmondsworth, Middlesex: Penguin Books, 1967), 84–5.

57. La Loubère, 66.

58. Philippe Avril, S.J., *Travels into Divers Parts of Europe and Asia, Undertaken by the French King's Order to Discover a new Way by Land into China* (London: 1693), 44.

59. Chevalier d'Arvieux, *Mémoires du Chevalier d'Arvieux, Envoyé Extraordinaire du Roy à la Porte, Consul d'Alep, d'Alger, de Tripoli, & autres Echelles du Levant*, 6 vols. (Paris: 1735) III, 15–6.

60. Donald F. Lach, *Asia in the Making of Europe* (Chicago: University of Chicago Press, 1965) vol. I, bk. 2, 835.

61. Ronald S. Love, "Simon de la Loubère: French Views of Siam in the 1680s," in Glenn J. Ames and Ronald S. Love, *Distant Lands and Diverse Cultures: The French Experience in Asia, 1600–1700* (Westport, CT: Praeger Press, 2003) 282; Lach, *Asia in the Making of Europe*, vol. I, bk. 2, 835.

62. Jacques de Bourges, *Relation du Voyage de Monseigneur l'Évèque de Béryte, Vicaire Apostolique du Royaume de la Cochinchine, Par la Turquie, la Perse, les Indes, &c. jusqu'au royaume de Siam, & autres lieux*, 2nd ed. (Paris: Denys Bechet, 1668), iii–iv.

63. Lach, *Asia in the Making of Europe*, vol. II, bk. 2, 835.

64. René Descartes, *Discourse on Method and the Meditations*, F.E. Sutcliffe, trans. (London: Penguin Books, 1968), 45.

65. Hampson, 26.

66. Rothrock and Jones, 341.

67. Bartolomé de Las Casas, *A Short Account of the Destruction of the Indies*, Nigel Griffen, trans. and ed. (London: Penguin Books, 1992), 9, 11.

68. Michel de Montaigne, *Essays*, J.M. Cohen, trans. (London: Penguin Books, 1958), 109–10.

69. Sir Walter Raleigh, *Selected Writings*, Gerald Hammond, ed. (Harmondsworth, Middlesex: Penguin Books, 1984), 95.

70. John Dunmore, trans. and ed., *The Pacific Journal of Louis-Antoine de Bougainville, 1767–1768* (London: Hakluyt Society, 2002), 72–3.

71. Jonathan Swift, *A Selection of His Works*, Philip Pinkus, ed. (Toronto: The Macmillan Company of Canada Ltd., 1965), xx.

72. Ibid., xxix.

73. Gay, *Party of Humanity*, 120–1.

74. Caponigri, 278.

75. Ibid.

76. Brinton, 293.

77. Merriman, 401.

78. Ibid., 400–1.

79. Brinton, 293.

80. Baumer, *Main Currents of Western Thought*, 364.

81. Brinton, 293.

82. Ibid., 291.

83. Merriman, 399–400.

84. Voltaire to Charles-Emmanuel de Crussel, duc d'Uzès, September 14, 1751, Voltaire, *Selected Letters*, 164.

85. Hampson, 114–5.

86. Bainton, 291.

87. Ibid., 292.

88. Merriman, 400.

89. Bainton, 292.

90. Merriman, 400.

91. Voltaire to Jean-Baptiste de Boyers, marquis d'Argens, October 2, 1740; and to Sir Everard Fawkener, June 1742, Voltaire, *Selected Letters*, 84–5, 98–9.

92. Voltaire to Louise-Florence Pétroville de Tardin d'Esclavelles d'Épinay, July 8, 1774, Ibid., 301.

93. Merriman, 400.

94. Sterne, *Sentimental Journey*, 28.

CHAPTER 2

SCIENCE AND THE TRIUMPH OF REASON: NEWTON, LOCKE, AND A NEW PHILOSOPHY

Nature and Nature's laws lay hid in night, God said, Let Newton Be! And all was light.

—Alexander Pope, 1727

Like the term "Renaissance," writes intellectual historian Robert Caponigri, the term "Enlightenment" belongs first and foremost to the history of culture. It points to fundamental change "in the controlling disposition of mind and spirit" from which the cultural patterns of Europe "flowed, were expressed and realized." Such change also involved a subtle interaction between the old and the new that produced a slow process of transformation from which a novel philosophy developed as a separate dimension "of the complex cultural pattern" of the eighteenth century.[1] For that reason, adds Peter Gay, ideas and the philosophies they inspire ought to be viewed as multi-dimensional "social products." They are "conceived, elaborated, and modified amid a specific set of historical circumstances," and reflect such things as contemporary social realities, caste structures, and new pressures induced by changing patterns of thought or taste. Because ideas, in short, are not "independent, unchanging entities," concludes Gay, but must be placed within the context of the age and culture that produced them, the historian "must not merely understand ideas through their civilization, but also civilizations through their ideas."[2]

This interconnection of culture and ideas was integral to the period of the Enlightenment. Yet the eighteenth century was not a great

philosophical age, as the previous century had been, even if philosophy occupied "an enormous, even dominant place" in the culture of
the day,[3] and also served as the primary vehicle through which the
philosophes attacked obsolete social, religious, and intellectual perspectives that, they asserted, continued to hamper human progress. The
reason for this deep confidence in the effects of philosophical inquiry
(by which the *philosophes* really meant the mobilization of sound
thinking for the sake of right thinking) was simple, as explained by
Rousseau in a manner that reflected an almost scientific approach to
the realm of thought. "Physicians and Philosophers," he wrote, "differing entirely from theologians, only admit that to be true which they
are able to explain, and make their understanding the measure of what
is possible."[4] "Philosophy knows only rules that are grounded in the
nature of things," echoed Denis Diderot, "and this nature is eternal and
immutable."[5] The study of philosophy was thus characterized by
Madam Roland (1754–1793) later in the century, as she reflected on
her adolescent exposure to the currents of contemporary thought,
"the science of behavior and the foundation of happiness, [which]
became the sole object of my reading and observation."[6] Hence, added
Voltaire, there "are only two types of happiness in this world: that of
fools who become stupidly intoxicated with their fanatical illusions
and that of philosophers." "It is impossible," he asserted,

> for a thinking person to want to explore the first kind of happi-
> ness which is based on a state of stupidity. The more one is
> enlightened, the more one enjoys life. Nothing is sweeter than
> to laugh at the foolishness of men and to laugh with reason.[7]

But even if the Enlightenment itself never espoused "a profound
conception of philosophy" comparable to the intellectual ferment of
the previous century, the ideas to which it gave expression were fresh,
persistent, and influential in ways "quite beyond their intrinsic
strength."[8] Moreover, the *philosophes* were conscious of the effect their
ideas produced. "I see the progress which the mind, eloquence and philosophy have made in this century," wrote an aging Voltaire in later life:

> By developing their right judgment people have divested them-
> selves of their prejudices.... Philosophy is bringing about a
> bright new day.... Philosophy causes virtue to be loved by mak-
> ing fanaticism detested, and if I dare say so, it is avenging God
> for the insults of superstition.[9]

But perhaps the highest expression of contemporary confidence in philosophy to reform society by evoking the principles of reason and

nature (or natural law), the twin foundations of Enlightenment thought, was enunciated by Denis Diderot. He wrote:

> Today, when philosophy is advancing with gigantic strides, when it is bringing under its sway all the matters that are its proper concern, when its tone is the dominant one, and when we are beginning to shake off the yoke of authority and tradition in order to hold fast to the laws of reason, there is scarcely a single elementary or dogmatic book which satisfies us entirely. We find that these works are put together out of the production of a few men and are not founded upon the truths of nature. We dare to raise doubts about the infallibility of Aristotle and Plato, and the time has come when the works that still enjoy the highest reputation will begin to lose some of their great prestige or even fall into complete oblivion.... Such are the consequences of the progress of reason, an advance that will overthrow so many old idols and perhaps restore to their pedestals some statues that have been cast down.[10]

From Diderot's explanation of philosophy as the key solvent on the power of tradition and ancient authority in the pursuit of social progress (see Document 2), it is evident that the *philosophes* were fundamentally humanitarian in their attitudes. "They had no sense of the reality of another world," observes Franklin Baumer, "no interest in plumbing spiritual depths."[11] Theirs was a purely secular world, and the moral and material improvements they sought in the human condition were defined in purely secular terms. They would certainly have agreed, therefore, with Alexander Pope (or perhaps he would have agreed with them), when the great English poet wrote in his *Essay on Man* (1733–1734): "Know then thyself, presume not God to scan; / The proper study of mankind is man."[12] If, consequently, man and man's world had become the measure of all things, as Pope's famous couplet asserted, then the Enlightenment represented "the profound secularization ... of Western thought," in which political and economic thinking was stripped of religious overtones, while even morality no longer required religious sanction.[13] Secularization was the product, in turn, of the efforts by the *philosophes* "to extend to man and society the methods and laws of the natural scientists," wherein lay their chief claim to originality.[14]

Predominant among the natural scientists to whom the *philosophes* turned for inspiration was Sir Isaac Newton. He and his fellow Englishman, the philosopher John Locke (1632–1704), were the leading intellectual forerunners of the Enlightenment. Newton's formulation of the laws of universal gravitation, first published in his great work *Principia Mathematica* (*The Mathematical Principles of Natural Philosophy*) in 1687, exemplified the powers of the human mind. His example and his scientific works encouraged Europeans at the close of the seventeenth century and during the opening decades of the eighteenth to approach the study of nature directly and to avoid metaphysical speculation and supernaturalism. Furthermore, though Newton had formulated general laws upon which to ground his theory of gravitation in particular, he always insisted on a foundation of specific empirical evidence to support those laws. Thus, empirical experience served as a constant check on his rational speculation.

Newton called his general laws the "Rules of Reasoning," and they appear in Book II of *Principia*.[15] His rules were a response, in part, to the essential question asked in the seventeenth and eighteenth centuries, "How can men know anything, and what kind of system of knowledge is necessary?" Newton's general laws provided an answer to the various degrees of skepticism that question had generated. Moreover, the Rules of Reasoning provided a link between the rules of nature and the rules of politics, demonstrating to the *philosophes*, for example, the necessity of toleration in both a religious and a secular sense. Wrote Newton in Rule I: "We are to admit no more causes of natural things than such as are both true and sufficient to explain their appearances." In other words, because nature does nothing in vain, one needs only to know enough causes to explain the appearances of natural phenomena.

The second rule is perhaps more important than the first: "Therefore to the same natural effects we must, as far as possible, assign the same causes." This means, for example, that if a stone falls in Europe and another falls in North America, both stones fall for the same reason, and the cause of that action is universal gravitation. Also, one can guess without having seen the stone fall in America that it fell owing to the same cause as that in Europe. In short, it is unnecessary to see everything or to know everything in order to realize the causes of things. According to Newton, therefore, a higher level of certainty was not required.

Still more significant is Rule III: "The qualities of bodies, which admit neither intensification nor remission of degrees, and which are found to belong to all bodies within the reach of our experiments, are to be esteemed the universal qualities of all bodies whatsoever." The key to this rule is *experimentation* and specifically that men can experiment on natural bodies in order to understand their qualities. Furthermore, if, by way of experiment, men try to determine what the qualities of those bodies are, they can deem those qualities to be universal among all bodies of the same kind whatever. Newton built upon this idea in Rule IV:

> In experimental philosophy, we are to look upon propositions
> inferred by general induction from phenomena as accurately or

> very nearly true, notwithstanding any contrary hypotheses that may be imagined, till such time as other phenomena occur, by which they may either be made more accurate, or liable to exceptions.[16]

In other words, through experimentation, one can arrive at certain kinds of hypotheses, by means of inductive reasoning, that suggest why certain phenomena happen. These hypotheses also can be accepted as accurate, unless a contrary example is found. In that event, a hypothesis can be limited by an exception.

Consequently, the answer to the question "What can men know?" is provided partly by experiments in nature. Human beings have the capacity to impose on nature certain kinds of tests, and they do not necessarily have to have any hypothesis with which to begin. In fact, Newton argued that hypotheses actually stood in the way of this process, because they added unnecessary complications to it. "If you wish to apply yourself seriously to the study of nature," echoed Voltaire, an early convert to, and devoted disciple of, Newtonian science,

> let me inform you that necessarily the way to begin is by constructing no systems [i.e., hypotheses]. One must proceed like ... Newton. Examine, weigh, calculate, and measure, but never speculate. Mr. Newton never constructed a system; he saw and demonstrated but never substituted his imagination for the truth. What our eyes and mathematics demonstrate to us we must hold to be true. For all the rest we can only say: "I do not know."[17]

This is where Newton differed from the deductive method of René Descartes (1596–1650), whose system had predominated earlier in the seventeenth century and still commanded intellectual authority in France in the early eighteenth century. But, wrote Voltaire in 1734, Descartes' works, "practically speaking, have become out of date," though the *philosophe* also admitted that few of his contemporaries had read Newton either, "because much knowledge is necessary to understand him."[18]

The Cartesian system of deductive reasoning is based upon the notion that there exists a unity among all the sciences, and that certainty in knowledge results from the application of the pure light of reason as opposed to the evidence of the senses, which Descartes rejected because they too often deceived. Hence, he turned to abstract mathematics rather than experimentation to discover absolute truths about the world, owing to mathematics' unique ability "to arrive at any proofs, that is to say, certain and evident reasons."[19] In other words, mathematics provided self-evident truths from which logical conclusions could be drawn. To that end, Descartes applied skepticism, meaning that he rejected "anything as true that [he] did not know to be evidently so," in order to "have no occasion to place it in doubt."[20] This meant denying "not only the existence of the world and of his own body ... but even his geometrical discoveries, since anyone could make logical slips in reasoning."[21] Hence, his search for self-evident truths through deductive reasoning that linked first principles with their ultimate consequences. This led him to his famous proposition, "I think; therefore, I am," for doubting is thinking and is thus linked to his existence. In other words, Descartes could perceive that he thought "without at the same time being certain that he [was]"; consequently, whatever else he perceived with the same clarity and distinction was equally true.[22]

What Newton later did, in effect, was to correct Descartes' method by uniting empiricism with Cartesian rationalism. Newton accepted his predecessor's concept of the world as having a mathematical and mechanical order, but he insisted also on adhering to the facts—that is, the evidence of nature arrived at through experimentation.[23] His point was that there are ways in which men can know things, but knowing things did not require knowing them *absolutely*. On the contrary, there was a sufficient degree of certainty resulting from Newton's process to satisfy people. That certainty existed in the fact that in every experiment on natural phenomena using the same instruments, the same effects will result. This is the foundation of the modern scientific method.

The emphasis on concrete experience, derived from Newtonian science, thus became a keystone for Enlightenment thought, for Newton had revealed a pattern of rationality in natural, physical phenomena. Indeed, the "beautiful simplicity of a single law which appeared to explain the operation of every kind of earthly and celestial movement was a triumphant example of the possibilities of the new learning" wrought by the Scientific Revolution.[24] Human reason, backed by careful observation and experimentation, could reveal the mechanism of nature, which came to be understood as a system of intelligible forces designed by God and made accessible to human intelligence in all their complexity.[25] Hence, during the eighteenth century the ancient idea of following nature was transformed under Newton's influence into the idea of following reason, and "rising by degrees to knowledge that seemed beyond the human mind."[26] For if Newton could discover the natural law that regulated the world of nature, it followed that the laws governing human society could be discovered through reason, too. Furthermore, if nature was rational, society also could be reorganized in a rational manner, which gave hope for a better future. But such improvement would take time and exact a social price, since ignorance, prejudice, superstition, and suffering in society could not be overcome easily.

Isaac Newton's scientific achievement inspired his friend and fellow countryman, John Locke, to seek a human psychology also based on experience. If in the late seventeenth century the appeal of natural law was continual and, in a practical sense, the use of the natural world (meaning the generation of wealth by exploiting nature's resources) was sanctioned by the laws of God as exhibited in the natural world, then human beings had no choice but to deal with the natural world because it was natural law. In this significant conclusion there converged two distinct points of view. First was the rule of man over nature for his own purposes, as sanctioned in the book of Genesis. Second was the notion of the laws of nature as pertaining less to the natural physical world than to *human* nature, an idea that became increasingly compelling by 1700. For if man was going to exploit nature for his own purposes, then perhaps there was something in human nature that he might usefully pay attention to.

From the viewpoint of the eighteenth-century Enlightenment, Locke's *Essay Concerning Human Understanding* (1690) was his most significant work. It "set out to discover what one might almost regard as the law of gravity controlling the formation of human ideas."[27] He began by rejecting the doctrine inherited from the ancient Greeks and much in vogue among seventeenth-century thinkers, such as René Descartes, that human beings were born into the world with innate knowledge, innate ideas. To Locke it appeared ludicrous that a person could have ideas, in fact, without having any consciousness of them. This was a very serious problem. He argued instead that knowledge was derived from the senses. A child enters the world at birth as a *Tabula rasa* (blank slate), upon which is inscribed the knowledge gained through experience and reflection on that experience. Consequently, a personality is the product of the five senses as derived from the external world throughout a single lifetime. Simple ideas are brought to the senses, and then are transformed into complex ideas by reflection. That is, knowledge gathered from the senses interacts with human reason, meaning that the human mind is the active element in the creation of knowledge, not the environment. In this way, human free will is preserved; otherwise, human beings would be victims controlled by the external world. From this psychological perspective came the significant conclusion that human nature is changeable, and that it could be molded simply by modifying the surrounding physical and social environment.

What Locke's psychology implied, in other words, was that improvement in the human condition was possible. He rejected, in effect, the Christian view of mankind as permanently flawed by original sin and redeemable only by God's grace. On the contrary, human beings did not have to wait for divine intervention to better their lives; they could take charge of their own moral destiny. That implication had, in turn, a practical application in the formation of society, which Locke explored in his great work, *The Two Treatises of Government* (1690). Though often regarded as a justification for the Glorious Revolution of 1688 against King James II, the book was written earlier and essentially refuted contemporary theories of absolutism and patriarchal government formulated by such prominent thinkers as Sir Robert Filmer. Nor was it an attack on the political philosophy of Thomas Hobbes (1588–1679) and his great work *Leviathan* (1651). Locke's *Two Treatises* nevertheless offered a positive alternative to Hobbes' pessimistic view of the origins of human society and government (see Document 23).

Building upon views drawn from contemporary science that the physical universe was matter in motion and men were simply another material substance, Hobbes had attempted to examine human nature as it existed, "rather than as philosophers idealized it."[28] Human beings were essentially amoral creatures who acted from self-interest—chiefly the pursuit of pleasure—without reference to any higher principle. But this pursuit brought men into constant conflict with each other, creating conditions of competition, suspicion, and fear. Thus, because in the state of nature, there was only a "war of every man against every man," the character of human life was "solitary, poor, nasty, brutish, and short."[29] This view implied the formation of a certain kind of civil government, a "Leviathan" or outside power to which men surrendered their natural rights in exchange for security for themselves and their property. The social contract that resulted was "a one-sided agreement whereby subjects authorized the state to do whatever it deemed necessary to preserve order and life."[30] Significantly, Hobbes was the first prominent thinker "to give the individual priority over either society or government" in developing his philosophy, and to defend man's natural right in nature "to do what was useful for his individual existence."[31]

In the *Two Treatises*, John Locke also began with a perception of men living in a state of nature and creating society and civil government by contract. But for Locke, the state of nature was benign. It was a situation in which individuals acted separately, even privately, though not communally. Otherwise, humanity lived in peace, though it lived simply. Clearly, the "noble savage" concept had influenced Locke's philosophy. Civil government (whatever form that might take) followed from a conscious and free act of men deliberating on their natural situation and concluding that their chances for survival were far greater if they cooperated than if they continued to act alone. That was the foundation of a social contract among them. But at this point they had to determine how to establish rules of conduct in order to function as a community. This led to a second government contract.

In a remarkable passage on property, Locke sought to explain how men could control their own passions and yet exercise their individual interests. In the beginning, he mused,

> all the World was *America*, and more so than it is now; for no such thing as *Money* was any where known. Find out something that hath the *Use and Value of Money* amongst his Neighbours, you shall see the same Man will begin presently to *enlarge* his *Possessions*.[32]

In this fascinating passage, Locke connected the ideas of exchange and the concept of money with the necessity of government and the defense of property. Government was designed to serve the needs of the governed and to safeguard their inalienable rights to "Lives, Liberties and Estates, which I call by the general Name, *Property*,"[33] because in Locke's thinking, property and liberty were linked inextricably by the principle that all mankind had a right to the goods of nature. This belief was derived from God's grant to Adam of dominion over the world in Genesis, as well as from the increasingly accepted notion of natural self-preservation. Additionally, every man has property in his own person—his life—while the labor of his body and the work of his hands also belong to him.

The existence of such property could not be independent, however, of a political framework. Certainly, Locke believed that political frameworks were necessary for human beings to be properly free. At the same time, it was necessary to distinguish a proper form of government from one that was not. Or as Locke put it, "*Absolute Monarchy*, which by some Men is counted the only Government in the World, is indeed *inconsistent with Civil Society*, and so can be no Form of Civil Government at all." For the purpose of civil government, he continued,

> being to avoid, and remedy those inconveniences of the State of Nature, which necessarily follow from every Man's being Judge in his own Case, by setting up known Authority [i.e., a magistrate], to which every one of that Society may Appeal upon any Injury received … and which everyone … ought to obey; whereever any persons are, who have not such an Authority to Appeal to, for the decision of any difference between them, then those persons are still *in the State of Nature*.[34]

For Locke, the problem with absolute monarchy was that because both legislative and executive authority resided in the person of the king alone, there could be no independent judiciary "from whose decision relief and redress may be expected of any Injury or Inconveniency" in the face of royal power.[35] That problem was also identified and expanded upon by the baron de Montesquieu in his great work, *The Spirit of the Laws*, which drew heavily upon Lockeian philosophy.

It is obvious from these ideas that when the original two contracts were made, individual sovereignty was not surrendered to political authority, as Thomas Hobbes had imagined. Government ruled, instead, by consent of the people, who were required by the same contractual arrangement to agree on the means by which individuals could act to the maximum of their liberty. Primarily, what Locke meant was liberty of conscience, which he united to political liberty, for he recognized the futility of trying to enforce religious conformity:

> If any one maintain that Men ought to be compelled by Fire or Sword to profess certain Doctrines, and conform to this or that exteriour worship, without any regard had unto their Morals; if any one endeavour to convert them that are Erroneous unto the Faith, by forcing them to profess things that they do not believe, and allowing them to practise things that the Gospel doth not permit; it cannot be doubted indeed but such ... is altogether incredible.[36]

In short, Locke believed for both practical and philosophical reasons that toleration was essential. It was this kind of idea, in particular, that had such powerful appeal for the *philosophes* of the next century.

Also appealing to them was Locke's notion that if civil government resists the judgment of the people or inhibits their liberties, it is no government at all. In fact, under such circumstances rebellion becomes necessary, even inevitable, for where "there is no longer the administration of Justice, for the securing of Mens Rights, nor any remaining Power within the community to direct the Force, or provide for the Necessities of the publick, ... the *Government* visibly *ceases*, and the People become a confused Multitude, without Order or Connexion."[37] That chaotic condition effectively compels them to seek their safety and self-preservation just as they would do in the state of nature. Moreover, the old form of government can be abolished in the aftermath of rebellion and replaced by something different, something new. This argument was a powerful critique of, even a threat to, monarchical absolutism on the eve of the Enlightenment. The same argument also removed, intellectually, at least, the fear of revolution, for it meant that the contract with the government could be broken, while the original social contract—and thus social order—remains intact.

There is, however, a very significant difference between the philosophers of the seventeenth century and the *philosophes* of the eighteenth. Newton, along with the other great scientists and thinkers prior to 1700, believed that his work exalted God and explained Creation in rational terms already accepted by revelation. To Newton, in other words, God was not only alive in the universe, but also corrected irregularities of the cosmos from time to time. Hence, "the Newtonian heavens proclaimed God's glory."[38] Even Locke argued that men do not make themselves, for men being "all the Workmanship of one Omnipotent, and infinitely wise Maker," he wrote, and "All the servants of one Sovereign Master, sent into the World by his order and about his business, they are his Property, whose Workmanship they are, made to last during his, not one another's Pleasure."[39]

By contrast, some Enlightenment thinkers rejected traditional Christianity and religious orthodoxy. The bitter religious wars and intolerance of the sixteenth and early seventeenth centuries, some of which still afflicted their own time, appalled the *philosophes* (see Documents 16 through 18), who were disgusted by religious fanaticism, though in their personal lives they could be intolerant and inhumane.[40] Hence, to discredit traditional Christianity and in particular the Catholic Church—which was viewed as the agent of ignorance, submissiveness, and conformity—was to take a decisive step toward an improved, secular civilization.

Religious toleration was, however, only part of their mission, which, on a broader level, was "to carry the method of science into all areas of experience and reality; and not the natural merely, but the social, the psychological and the historical as well."[41] As men of letters who wrote voluminously and intellectual virtuosi in their own right, the *philosophes* sought practical social and political change in the world they inhabited, as well as a reform of morals along secular lines. To those ends, they combined the most stringent criticism with a persistent concern for moral and political construction. They were suspicious, therefore, of theoretical speculation for its own sake, writes Peter Gay, while they certainly rejected all anti-rationalist theories of knowledge, such as the Christian world view based upon revelation, not reason, and supernaturalism.[42] In the meantime, they taught contemporary people how to pose pointed, critical questions about the world around them. Or, as conservative English thinker Samuel Johnson (1709–1784; see Document 14) observed to his friend James Boswell from a less flattering perspective on the *philosophes*, of whose methods he disapproved:

> Of modern infidels and innovators, [Johnson] said, "Sir, these are all vain men, and will gratify themselves at any expense.

Truth will not afford sufficient food to their vanity, so they
have betaken themselves to error. Truth, Sir, is a cow which will
yield such people no more milk, and so they are gone to milk
the bull.[43]

For these reasons, the *philosophes* deeply admired the achievements of, and were attracted to, the scientific method. Indeed, the
ideas of nature and reason, as set up by Newton and Locke, were to
Enlightenment thinkers what the concepts of grace, salvation, and pre-
destination were to traditional Christianity.[44] "Nature," to the *philosophes*, meant the actual physical world in which they lived. The
problem was, however, that this world of Nature, "or at any rate *human*
nature in organized society, was *unnatural*,"[45] and included social distinctions, privilege, wide contrasts of wealth and poverty, etiquette,
etc. Nature thus became the standard against which social customs,
institutions, and values were measured. Whatever was "natural" was
considered good or "normal," and whatever was "unnatural" was viewed
as bad or "abnormal." Once this concept of nature was understood in
human affairs, then "all that remained was to regulate human life
accordingly, and there would be no more unnatural behavior."[46]

Consequently, the *philosophes* were very open to the new ideas
and ways of thinking that had developed out of the Scientific Revolution and pointed them in different directions. Although science could
not answer by itself the questions, "What can men know?" and "What
can men do?" (Newton's discoveries and Rules of Reasoning provided
a partial response to that end), science at least suggested "that the old
answers were wrong" and could be replaced by new ones founded
upon the principles of reason and nature.[47] That process began with
what one modern French historian describes as a "crisis of the
European conscience."[48]

Incited by the intellectual ferment of the period between 1680
and 1715, wrote Paul Hazard, the crisis developed from the clash of
old ideas with the new. The focus of this clash was traditional authority; namely, the notion that ideas or values were acceptable as truths
simply because they had been accepted by earlier generations who had
passed them down, "whether in doctrinal or institutional form."[49] "A
thing I consider intolerable," sneered Denis Diderot in the spirit of the
new age, "is that one should lean upon some ancient writer's authority
in questions that require only the use of reason."[50] He continued:

Now, in our age, we must trample mercilessly upon all these ancient puerilities, overturn the barriers that reason never created,
give back to the arts and sciences the liberty that is so precious
to them.... The world has long awaited a reasoning age, an age

when the rules would be sought no longer in the classical authors but in nature.[51]

The power of authority was challenged by a host of scientists, philosophers, and even theologians who, consciously or not, undermined the traditional foundations of Christian European culture through their inquiries into physical nature, human psychology, religious doctrine, and political thought. The study of ancient history was similarly regarded as irrelevant to "modern times," while the history of those modern times became increasingly a source of authority in its own right. Encounters with non-Christian, non-Western societies around the globe had also challenged traditional authority by revealing that social practices "deemed to be based on reason were ... mere matters of custom, and, inversely, certain habits which, at a distance, had appeared preposterous and absurd, took on an apparently logical aspect once they were examined in the light of their origins and local circumstances."[52] As a result, there began in the late seventeenth and early eighteenth centuries the quest for a new kind of human happiness and a different version of truth. This, in effect, was the moral and spiritual crisis that precipitated the Enlightenment—a crisis "so swift and so sudden ... that it took men completely by surprise; yet it had long been stirring in the womb of Time."[53]

"Crisis, of course, need not mean cataclysm," writes Franklin Baumer, but rather a turning point. Having evolved from the past, primarily out of the Renaissance and the Scientific Revolution, the Enlightenment "marked no cataclysmic break with that past."[54] Yet, a different mode of thought did emerge among a new generation of thinkers after 1715 who, borrowing the concepts of a mechanistic universe and universal natural law from the scientists, applied these concepts to human society. The problem was, however, that if one looks for order in society, one will find only disorder and chaos instead. There developed, consequently, the notion of "optimism," though this term was understood in different ways. To the great German scientist and contemporary of Newton, Gottfried Wilhelm Leibniz (1646–1716), it meant "whatever is, is right." Convinced of the existence of a beneficent God, Leibniz asserted that God's goodness "necessarily implied that this world was the best that could possibly have been created"; hence, it was easy to conclude that whatever was "best" in the mind of God "was also most acceptable to man, and therefore most conducive to his immediate happiness."[55] That idea would be attacked rigorously by Voltaire after the devastating Lisbon earthquake of 1755 (see Document 15).

From a broader perspective, however, the optimism of eighteenth-century intellectuals "derived from the convictions about the nature of the universe," and in particular their belief that if human reason was the key to understanding natural phenomena as governed by natural law, then the further application of reason could also make the social world "more explicable and more predictable and that men would be able to plan their lives and their societies to avoid catastrophes."[56] Consequently, though society may appear to be bad, it could be redeemed through the natural goodness of man, another common element of Enlightenment thought. Once again, reason was the means to scrape away the bad to reach the good, for behind the idea of social and moral redemption in a secular milieu lay the proposition that every person is born with an innate capacity to exercise reason upon experience and observation of the world (i.e., empiricism) *à la* John Locke and Isaac Newton. Even Adam and Eve had innate reason in the Garden of Eden, though they never used it. Hence, their ejection from the biblical paradise did not represent a Fall to the *philosophes*, but rather an improvement in man's condition, because it released human free will. In their view, knowledge was superior to ignorance, just as discussion was superior to fanaticism wrought by intolerance. If, however, human reason was impaired, it was only because men tend to exercise their free will by choosing evil over good. To Enlightenment minds, the source of that evil was not necessarily mankind, who was viewed as intrinsically good, but rather the social institutions he built, which tended to corrupt him.

Although the philosophical roots of the Enlightenment are found in England, owing principally to the thought of Newton and Locke, it shifted to the continent and first of all to France where, by the mid-eighteenth century, Paris became the home of the movement and the center from which the new ideas spread across Europe. As Franklin Baumer points out, a number of factors conjoined to give France the intellectual leadership of Europe, starting with the decadence of the Old Regime. Added to this was the growing prosperity and self-consciousness of an emergent bourgeoisie (already noted), the absence of internal political barriers "which in Germany robbed would-be reformers of a national public," and the *philosophes* themselves, who constituted a new type of intellectual able through their published works to reach "a newly awakened public opinion, against the powers that be, against the learned world of church and university."[57] But Paris was also a cosmopolitan city that, since the reign of Louis XIV, had been the arbiter of European taste and culture. Hence, the Enlightenment also acquired a cosmopolitan and international character. It could be found in Scottish, German, and Italian universities; it was promoted by the rulers of Prussia, Austria, Russia, and even Poland; it also flourished in the American colonies of the New World among

men like Benjamin Franklin and Thomas Jefferson, who were capti-
vated by the new ideas.

Hence, the Enlightenment was by no means an exclusively
French phenomenon, though the movement helped to enhance the already dominant place of French culture in Europe. And although Paris
was the recognized capital of the Enlightenment and most of its intellectual leaders were French or French-speaking, these free-thinkers
continued to idolize England as the home of liberty and the source of
the new philosophy, especially political philosophy. Voltaire, who had
spent three years in England from 1726 to 1729 during a brief exile
from France, not only became enamored of the intellectual activity and
more tolerant form of government that he encountered in the island
nation, but he also learned the English language, which he spoke "with
the heart of a Briton." "He swore bloodily," recalled James Boswell of a
private conversation with Voltaire in 1764, "as was the fashion when
he was in England. ... Then he talked of our Constitution with noble
Enthusiasm."[58] In fact, the link between the English language and freedom of English political, social, and scientific thought was made
explicitly by the *philosophe* himself. "English has begun to take on
greater favor," he wrote in 1754, and although it

> will be really difficult for that language to become one of general
> intercourse like ours ... I see that everyone, even princes, wants
> to understand it because of all languages it is the one in which
> people have thought most boldly and forcefully. In England peo-
> ple ask no one for permission to think.[59]

Voltaire once even confessed a strong desire "to be naturaliz'd in England" because of its many liberties.[60] "You have the better government,"
he observed to James Boswell, as he contrasted the political systems of
France and Great Britain:

> If it gets bad, heave it into the ocean; that's why you have the
> ocean all about you. You are the slaves of laws. The French are
> slaves of men. In France, every man is either an anvil or a ham-
> mer; he is a beater or he must be beaten.[61]

Montesquieu and other *philosophes* similarly praised Britain's constitution, to which they made almost scriptural references in their own
works.

Meanwhile, their enthusiasm struck a strong chord with their
readers who, following the *philosophes'* example, also looked to Britain
for inspiration. In 1764, the Huguenot minister Charles de
Guiffardière observed that in France "the language of the people is one

thing, that of the bourgeoisie another, that of the Court still another; whereas in England the language of the people is the language of the nation." Anticipating ideas expressed by the Abbé Sieyès in 1789, he continued:

> The reason is that with you the people is everything, but in France it hardly counts at all. That is why the English people, according to report, express themselves with much more nobility and accuracy than in any other country whatever, while in France, the language of the courtier dominates that of so-called honest folk, and even sets the tone for men of letters, who, if they did not adopt it, would be considered mere pedants.[62]

Reflecting on her education in her youth, Madame Roland of French Revolution fame recalled that in addition to the works of Voltaire, Rousseau, Montesquieu, Diderot, and other French *philosophes*, she read Locke and various books on English constitutional history, "but unfortunately only in [French] translation."[63] Even Edmund Burke commented disapprovingly on the way in which the revolutionaries of 1789 alleged that "what is doing among you is after the example of England." "I beg leave to affirm," he huffed, "that scarcely anything done with you has originated from the practice or prevalent opinions of this people, either in the act or in the spirit of the proceeding."[64]

Obviously from contemporary preoccupation with the British constitution, absolute monarchy, and the issue of authority, whether political or religious, it had become apparent by the early eighteenth century that the analysis of government based on a rational view of natural law would lead to some important conclusions. Whether these conclusions were practical or not in the political realm remained to be seen. At the same time, it also had become evident that the influence of John Locke had gone some way toward establishing a rational foundation on which to explain the limits of human knowledge. So the question was, "How far could men actually go with these ideas?" The answer was that they could go far enough to determine the proper form of government, and toleration would be vital to making it work. What made all of this so appealing was the notion of experimental science, advocated by both Locke and Newton. Indeed, the experimental advances of the seventeenth century had suggested that the extent of human knowledge was almost limitless. In 1749, the English novelist and magistrate Henry Fielding (1707–1755) expanded on the concept of experimentation in knowledge creation, using very Lockeian terms. He observed:

> However exquisitely human nature may have been described by writers, the true practical system can only be learnt in the

world. Indeed, the like happens in every other kind of knowledge. Neither physic [i.e., medicine] nor law are to be practically known from books.[65]

Likewise observed his sister, Sarah, in her novel *The Adventures of David Simple* (1744), when her hero

> began to consider seriously amongst all the Classes and Degrees of Men ... when he examined Mankind, from the highest to the lowest, he was convinced, that to Experience alone he must owe his Knowledge; for that no Circumstance of Time, Place, or Station, made a man absolutely good or bad, but the Disposition of his own Mind; and that Good-nature and Generosity were always the same, tho' the Power to exercise those Qualities are more or less, according to the Variation of outward Circumstances.[66]

The *philosophes'* advocacy of rationalism did not mean, however, the creation of grandiose systems of thought to explain all things. "Philosophers who form systems on the secret construction of the universe are like our travelers who go to Constantinople and speak of the seraglio," sneered Voltaire, "They have only seen the outside and claim to know what the sultan is doing [inside] with his favorite ladies."[67] Rousseau similarly lamented those who, despite a professed passion for reason, "nevertheless wandered from one error to another in all [their] systems, in [their] desire to make men like [themselves], instead of taking them as they are, and will continue to be."[68] Denis Diderot echoed these views more eloquently, when he compared human beings to finely tuned musical instruments, gifted with sensation and memory. "Our senses are merely keys that are struck by the natural world around us, keys that often strike themselves," he observed:

> We don't draw any conclusions at all—they are always drawn by nature itself. We do nothing but describe the connections among phenomena, connections that are either necessary or contingent. These phenomena are known through experience. In mathematics and physics the connections are necessary; in morality and politics they are contingent or probable, as they are in other branches of speculative knowledge.[69]

Clearly, the *philosophes'* appeal to rationalism was an appeal at the same time to scientific method; that is, an appeal to facts (empirical evidence), experience (experimentation), and reasonableness (common sense). Nor were these free-thinkers simplistic in their approach to reason; some balanced it with the power of the passions, especially sexual passion. Diderot and Rousseau were leading advocates of this equilibrium. Asked the latter:

> From how many errors would the reason be preserved, how many vices would be strangled at their birth, if mankind knew how to compel the animal economy to support the moral order, which it so frequently disturbs! Different climates, seasons, sounds, colors, darkness, light, the elements, food, noise, silence, movement, repose—all affect the bodily machine, and consequently the mind; all afford us a thousand opportunities which will almost infallibly enable us to govern those feelings in their first beginning, by which we allow ourselves to be dominated.[70]

Added Diderot:

> People impute to the passions all of man's pains and forget that they are also the source of all his pleasures: It is an element of man's constitution of which we can say neither too many favorable, nor too many unfavorable things. ... It is only the passions, and the great passions, that can raise the soul to great things.[71]

To stifle human sexuality as Christianity, or more accurately as the Christian Church, sought to do was, therefore, to smother a crucial part of human nature.

At the same time, the appeal of the *philosophes* for freedom of expression as an individual right is a reminder that they lived, wrote, debated, and thought in an atmosphere of state censorship, at least on the continent. As Voltaire once quipped, "the *philosophes* must make the truth public but hide themselves."[72] To circumvent this problem, some published under pseudonyms, anonymously, or abroad, especially in Amsterdam. Books were often printed secretly or circulated in manuscript form to avoid the royal censors. To preserve their anonymity, and thus freedom from incarceration, many denied the authorship of their own works. Voltaire, for example, at first disavowed having composed *Candide* (see Document 15) and the *Philosophical Dictionary* (1764), partially from fear of official reprisal. Yet the announcement that a book had been banned by religious or royal authority generally ensured its commercial success. Indeed, the eighteenth century has been described as an age of best-sellers. Even so, some *philosophes*, above all Voltaire, defended freedom of expression directly and rigorously. "I know many books which fatigue," he once observed, "but I know of none which have done real evil."[73] As for the liberty to publish one's thoughts, he wrote in 1762, once again evoking the British example, it is the natural right of a citizen. He may use his pen as he uses his voice; he must no more be prohibited from writing than from speaking; and the offences committed with the pen should be punished like the offences committed with the word: such is the law of England, a monarchical country [like France], but where men are freer than they are elsewhere, because they are more enlightened.[74]

Diderot was equally distressed by official censorship. "One might think it's a deliberate plan to exterminate literature" in France, he complained, "to ruin the book trade, and reduce us to beggary and stupidity."[75]

Ultimately, the *philosophes'* advocacy of rationalism, the scientific method, and liberty of expression was an appeal for the democratization of knowledge. This trend can best be seen in the work of Jean-le-Rond d'Alembert (1717–1783), a major Enlightenment thinker; a friend of Diderot, Rousseau, and Voltaire; and after 1750 one of the editors of the great *Encyclopedia* (see Document 3). In a crucial way, d'Alembert demonstrated where the steady democratization of knowledge would ultimately lead. "One may create as many different systems of human knowledge," he observed, "as there are world maps having different projections."[76] In other words, several persons can look at exactly the same data, and that data can then be represented or interpreted by those same persons in many different ways, all of them perfectly rational.

Empiricism, which Locke and Newton had promoted in the late seventeenth century, thus had clearly prevailed after 1700. In the process, the old notion that men were born with innate ideas faded away and was replaced by an entirely new epistemology by which the investigation of nature through experimental technique would provide the facts. That method would allow, in turn, human reason to reach decisions that could discern the truth of one thing and the failure of another. Or as Diderot expressed it in more lyrical terms, the development of ideas functioned like the notes produced by the strings on a musical instrument and harmonics:

> The string vibrates and makes a sound for a long time after it is plucked. It is a vibration of this sort, it is this kind of necessary resonance, that keeps an object present to our minds while our understandings deal with whichever of its qualities we please to study. Besides, these vibrating strings have still another property—they can make other strings hum—so that in this way one idea can call forth another, the sound can call forth a third, and so on. Hence no one can set a limit to the ideas that will occur to a philosopher, for his ideas arise out of their own necessary connections while he meditates in darkness and in silence.[77]

The appeal for an empirical approach was begun by Voltaire in the 1730s and would be continued by his fellow *philosophes* through the end of the century.

Notes

1. Caponigri, 271.

2. Gay, *Party of Humanity*, x–xi.

3. Caponigri, 272.

4. Rousseau, *Confessions*, 251.

5. Diderot, *Rameau's Nephew*, 288.

6. Evelyn Schuckburgh, trans. and ed., *The Memoirs of Madame Roland* (Mount Kisco, NY: Moyer Bell Limited, 1989), 172.

7. Voltaire to the marquis d'Argence, January 20, 1761, Voltaire, *Selected Letters*, 217.

8. Caponigri, 272.

9. Voltaire to Joseph-Michel-Antoine Servan, April 13, 1766, Voltaire, *Selected Letters*, 261–2.

10. Diderot, 287.

11. Baumer, *Main Currents of Western Thought*, 365.

12. Alexander Pope, *Selected Poetry and Prose*, William K. Winsott, ed., 2nd ed. (New York: Holt, Rinehart and Winston, Inc., 1972), 202.

13. Baumer, *Main Currents of Western Thought*, 366.

14. Ibid., 365–6.

15. For the Rules, see Sir Isaac Newton, *Principia, or Mathematical Principles of Natural Philosophy and His System of the World*, vol. II, *The System of the World*, Andrew Motte, trans. (1729), Florian Cajori, ed. (Berkeley: University of California Press, 1934), 398–400.

16. Ibid., 400.

17. Voltaire to Claude-Nicolas Le Cat, April 15, 1741, Voltaire, *Selected Letters*, 87–8.

18. Voltaire, *Letters on England*, Leonard Tancock, trans. (London: Penguin Books, 1980), 71.

19. Descartes, *Discourse on Method*, 41–2.

20. Ibid., 41.

21. Moote, 336.

22. Descartes, *Discourse on Method*, 18–9.

23. Moote, 337.

24. Hampson, 37.

25. Ibid., 37–8.

26. Voltaire, *Letters on England*, 77.

27. Hampson, 39.

28. Moote, 379.

29. Thomas Hobbes, *Leviathan*, C.B. MacPherson, ed. (London: Penguin Books, 1968), 185, 186.

30. Moote, 380.

31. Ibid.

32. John Locke, *Two Treatises of Government*, Peter Laslett, ed. (Cambridge: Cambridge University Press, 1960), 301. (Emphasis Locke's.)

33. Ibid., 350. (Emphasis Locke's.)

34. Ibid., 326. (Emphasis Locke's.)

35. Ibid.

36. John Locke, *A Letter Concerning Toleration*, James H. Tully, ed. (Indianapolis: 1983), 25.

37. Locke, *Two Treatises*, 411. (Emphasis Locke's.)

38. Gay, *Party of Humanity*, 123.

39. Locke, *Two Treatises*, 271.

40. Gay, *Party of Humanity*, 115.

41. Caponigri, 273.

42. For the characteristics of the *philosophes*, see Gay, *Party of Humanity*, 114–19.

43. Boswell, *Grand Tour: Italy, Corsica, France*, 182.

44. Brinton, 289.

45. Ibid., 290.

46. Ibid.

47. Gay, *Party of Humanity*, 124.

48. Paul Hazard, *The European Mind, 1680–1715*, J. Lewis May, trans. (Harmondsworth, Middlesex: Penguin Books, 1964).

49. Caponigri, 272.

50. Diderot, *Rameau's Nephew*, 294.

51. Ibid, 298.

52. Caponigri, 26.

53. Ibid., 498, 502.

54. Baumer, *Main Currents of Western Thought*, 363.

55. Ibid.

56. Rothrock and Jones, 346.

57. Baumer, *Main Currents of Western Thought*, 364.

58. Boswell, *Grand Tour: Italy, Corsica and France*, 293.

59. Voltaire to Pierre-Joseph Thoulier d'Olivet, March 26, 1754, Voltaire, *Selected Letters*, 172.

60. Voltaire to Martin Ffolkes, 25 November 1743, Voltaire, *Selected Letters*, 108.

61. Boswell, *Grand Tour: Germany and Switzerland*, 45.

62. Ibid., 239–40.

63. Schuckburgh, *Memoirs of Madame Roland*, 186.

64. Burke, 100.

65. Henry Fielding, *The History of Tom Jones* (New York: The New American Library, 1963), 412.

66. Sarah Fielding, *David Simple*, 28.

67. Voltaire to Willem Jacob 'S-Gravesande, August 1741, Voltaire, *Selected Letters*, 95.

68. Rousseau, *Confessions*, 411.

69. Diderot, *Rameau's Nephew*, 105.

70. Rousseau, *Confessions*, 398.

71. Quoted in Gay, *The Enlightenment*, II, 188.

72. Voltaire to Étienne-Noël Damilaville, September 19, 1764, Voltaire, *Selected Letters*, 254.

73. Voltaire on "Liberty of the Press," excerpted in Baumer, *Main Currents of Western Thought*, 423.

74. Quoted in Gay, *Party of Humanity*, 89.

75. Quoted in Gay, *The Enlightenment*, II, 76.

76. d'Alembert, "Discours préliminaire" from the *Encyclopedia*, quoted in Franklin L. Baumer, *Modern European Thought: Continuity and Change in Ideas, 1600–1950* (New York: MacMillan, 1977), 145.

77. Diderot, *Rameau's Nephew*, 100.

CHAPTER 3

THE *PHILOSOPHES*, THE CHURCH, AND CHRISTIANITY

Écrasez l'infâme! (Destroy the infamous thing!)
—Voltaire, 1762

In the mid-eighteenth century, as the Enlightenment was steadily taking root in France, from where the new ideas would disseminate across the continent, Europe was experiencing both fundamental and drastic change. Industrialism was beginning in Great Britain, along with the emergence of more modern forms of politics and political theory. There were, or at least soon would be, the origins of what modern historian Robert Palmer called the Age of the Democratic Revolution, as aristocratic regimes increasingly encountered democratic forms of revolt.[1] Even the Christian church, whether Catholic or non-Catholic, was involved in turmoil resulting from such developments as the suppression of the Jesuit Order between 1750 and 1773, the rise of religious dissent in various forms (e.g., Pietism in northern Germany and Methodism in Britain), and the consequent resurgence of religious persecution. In the meantime, the nation-state was taking clearer shape, while warfare in the name of national interest was waged on a global scale in Asia and the Americas thanks to the integration of the world's sea routes, as the maritime powers of Europe fought against each other for territorial acquisition, colonial defense, commercial advantage, or strategic need.

It was on the cusp of these changing times that the Enlightenment moved geographically from its philosophical birthplace in Britain to the continent, settling first of all in France. Once there, the relationship that developed was not a simple matter of assimilation, writes Robert Caponigri. For although the problems and positions that had characterized English thought were transported to France, "the French Enlightenment is marked by a tone or accent proper to itself in clear contrast to those in England."[2] Initially, the French *philosophes* were popularizers of the new ideas, making them available to educated men and women on the peripheries of the growing movement. Over time, however, the *philosophes* "grew more radical, more combative, more convinced than ever that they were the prophets of a new age that would rise on the ruins of the old."[3] "The world is losing its innocence at a furious rate," proclaimed Voltaire in 1766, "A great intellectual revolution is everywhere in the offing."[4] Thus to iconoclasm, the *philosophes* added enthusiasm, which "became the reverse sides of the same coin, reason."[5] It was also these French free-thinkers who transmitted Enlightenment ideas across the length and breadth of Europe, "even into the growing outposts of Western society all over the world."[6]

First and foremost among the prophets of the new movement was Voltaire, a brilliant polemicist, a man possessed of fabulous talent, and an author of more than ninety volumes, who enunciated almost all of the ideas associated with the beginnings of the Enlightenment, and who became the leading advocate of Locke and Newton in France. In the event, he and others of his temper and outlook "turned the whole of France into one vast area of culture in which the most learned and abstruse questions were debated in a journalistic atmosphere, as it were, before the bar of public opinion."[7] Born in Paris in 1694 just ten years before the death of John Locke, Voltaire soon entered an intellectual atmosphere energized not only by Locke's *Essay on Human Understanding*, but also by Isaac Newton's mathematical principles of natural philosophy published in *Principia*.

Bourgeois in background, educated by Jesuits, and destined by his parents for a career in law, young François-Marie Arouet turned to letters instead. Nor was it long before he had established himself in literary circles. Then, with the success of his play *Oedipus* in 1718, which earned him wide acclaim, he adopted the pseudonym Voltaire (an anagram from "Arouet (l)e (j)eune"—Arouet the young), by which he has been known ever after. But the young man also had a tendency to antagonize important people in power, for as Rousseau once observed of his rival, "It is very well to argue against men's opinions; but to show contempt, and to say, 'You are idiots to believe this,' is to be personally offensive."[8] And offend he did. Already Voltaire had spent a year in the Bastille in 1717 for having ridiculed the French regent, the duke of Orléans. He repeated the experience a few years later when, having insulted the well-connected chevalier de Rohan, Voltaire was beaten by the aristocrat's henchmen as he left a private dinner party. Or as the future *philosophe* described the incident with his customary wit and sarcasm, "I was thrashed by the good chevalier de Rohan with the help of six ruffians behind whom he was boldly stationed."[9] After his second release from the Bastille because of this event, having been imprisoned probably more for his own protection than for any other reason, Voltaire embarked immediately for England in May 1726. There he remained for the next three years.

The interests he developed during this early period in his life reveal Voltaire's concern for toleration, whether political or religious, his doubts about Christianity, and his fascination with natural science. All of these elements came together in his book *Philosophical Letters* (sometimes also called *Letters on England*), published in 1734 after his return to France. The subject matter was derived from his experience as an exile, and reveals just how profoundly influenced he was by the empirical tradition in English philosophy, the apparent rationality of English society, and the liberality of English government, as exemplified by the degree of religious toleration in Great Britain and the relative lack of official censorship. He was certainly conscious of these factors when preparing the *Philosophical Letters* for publication. Because of the restrictions in his native land, he was compelled to soften some of his remarks and alter others so as not to attract official displeasure. After all, he confessed, because he wanted to live in France, he could not be "as philosophical as an Englishman." "In Paris I must veil what I can say only too strongly in London," he lamented, "This unfortunate but necessary precaution makes me eliminate more than one rather amusing passage.... My heart is sick over it."[10] But the precautions he took were in vain. No sooner did the *Philosophical Letters* appear in print than the book was condemned to be burned by the public hangman as subversive and irreligious, forcing Voltaire to flee for safety's sake to Champagne near the frontiers of Lorraine, which was not yet part of the French state. Indeed, notes a modern commentator, for most of the rest of his life, the *philosophe* "lived very near some frontier over which he could skip into safety at the first sign of trouble."[11]

As a result of his exile in England, Voltaire became such an admirer of English things that he was frequently accused throughout his life of being an Anglo-maniac. The copious notes he took on his encounters, meanwhile, revealed his debt to Locke and Newton in opposition to Cartesian thinking. In Letter 14 of the *Philosophical Letters*, for example, Voltaire compared the systems of Descartes and Newton directly. "A Frenchman arriving in London finds things very different, in natural science as in everything else," he wrote:

> He has left the world full, he finds it empty. In Paris they see the universe as composed of vortices of subtle matter, in London

they see nothing of the kind. For us it is the pressure of the moon that causes the tides of the sea; for the English it is the sea that gravitates toward the moon.... Furthermore, you will note that the sun, which in France doesn't come into the picture at all, here plays its fair share. For your Cartesians everything is moved by impulsion you don't really understand, for Mr. Newton it is by gravitation.... For a Cartesian light exists in the air, for a Newtonian it comes from the sun in six and a half minutes.... The very essence of things has totally changed.[12]

For Voltaire, Descartes was a "dreamer" whose natural science was "a sketch," while Newton was a "sage," whose system was "a masterpiece."[13]

As for Newton's universal law of gravitation specifically, the *philosophe* criticized his fellow countrymen for their slowness to accept the new science. He wrote in 1735:

This property of matter, discovered and demonstrated by Sir Isaac Newton, is as true as it is astonishing, and half of the [French] Academy of Sciences, i.e., those who thought it not unworthy of their reason to learn what they are ignorant of, has started to recognize this truth which is beginning to be taught in all of England, the country of philosophers. As for our university, it is still unaware of who Newton was.[14]

Infused with the spirit of an intellectual missionary, Voltaire became the leading apostle of Newtonian science. Or as he put it, reflecting on his experience with the royal censors in 1734, "I made some steps ... in the temple of philosophy toward the altar of Newton. I was even so bold as to introduce into France some of his discoveries; but I was not only a confessor to his faith, I became a martyr."[15]

Determined to preach the message of the new "Gospel," the *philosophe* was assisted in his quest by his mistress, Gabrielle-Émilie Le Tonnelier de Breteuil, marquise du Châtelet (1706–1749), who was an accomplished intellectual in her own right, the author of several important works, and Voltaire's companion in semi-exile after 1734. Under her tutelage in mathematics and natural philosophy, Voltaire became more familiar with the natural sciences and more concerted in his efforts *à la* John Locke to apply scientific rationality to the human condition. In return, he taught her English.[16] Together, they produced in 1738 an exposition of Newtonian science under the title *The Elements of Newtonian Philosophy*, which introduced the English thinker's theories in *Principia* to a wider French audience in simplified form. This very successful book, combined with the *Philosophical Letters*, drew contrasts between the Cartesian epistemology of first principles rooted in the formulation of hypotheses by means of deductive reasoning without reference to empiricism, and the Newtonian epistemology of principles rooted in the empirical examination of nature from which hypotheses were then formed. The two books became very influential popularizations of Newton on the continent.

Voltaire's appreciation of Lockeian philosophy, and especially Locke's belief in the human capacity to reason, was equally profound. He even went so far as to praise the English philosopher for having single-handedly consolidated "the authority of science to strengthen it."[17] Voltaire was influenced in particular by Locke's *Essay on Human Understanding*, asserting at one point about the book that "if what this wise and moderate philosopher has said is not satisfactory, nothing will be."[18] Certainly, he recognized in Lockeian thought a reformist philosophy that offered the optimistic view that human beings were capable of improving their own moral and material condition through reason. Indeed, he wrote, "the more I read Mr. Locke, the more I wish those gentlemen [who 'are strangely mad in their desire that we be absolutely miserable'] would study him."[19] Nor did he miss the English philosopher's emphasis on toleration as a necessary part of any political framework among the European nations.

Locke's views on toleration (see Document 16) were not merely intellectual, however, but also experiential, for he had been forced into exile in the United Provinces in the mid-1680s, having engaged in an unsuccessful campaign for toleration against the Stuart king Charles II from 1679 to 1683. In 1685 during that exile, the philosopher wrote his *Letter Concerning Toleration*, first published anonymously and even without the author's knowledge in Amsterdam in 1689. This work accomplished two ends: (1) it clearly summarized the issue of toleration in the seventeenth century, and (2) it set up a kind of program to resolve the problem that many of the early Enlightenment thinkers adopted very quickly, starting with Voltaire.

In brief, the *Letter* advocated the union of political and religious liberty on the principle that "the business of laws is not to provide for the truth of opinions, but for the safety and security of the commonwealth, and of every particular man's goods and person."[20] In his opening paragraph, Locke criticized religious fanatics and would-be persecutors for insisting on "the establishment of opinions, which for the most part are about nice and intricate matters that exceed the capacity of ordinary understanding."[21] In other words, matters of faith were by definition neither provable nor disprovable in view of the limitations of human reason; either people believed or did not believe according to their private conscience. Consequently, no man had a right to impose his beliefs upon another. Indeed, wrote Locke, "that any man should think fit to cause another man—whose salvation he heartily desires—to expire in torments, and that even in an unconverted state, would, I confess, seem very strange to me." Nor would anyone ever believe "that such a carriage can proceed from charity, love, or good will."[22]

Locke was a student of history, which had taught him that however fanatical the religious martyrs of earlier periods might have been, and however erroneous their beliefs had appeared, such people nevertheless held on to their convictions even with their dying breath. The results of trying to change such deeply held convictions by compulsion were civil strife and bloody war. That very salutary lesson had demonstrated the absolute futility of trying to enforce confessional uniformity in the religious community. For as Locke asserted, "It is not the diversity of opinions (which cannot be avoided), but the refusal of toleration to those that are of different opinions (which might have been granted), that has produced all the bustles and wars that have been in the Christian world upon account of religion."[23]

This did not mean that religious conformity was a matter of indifference. It meant, rather, that people fundamentally "know" that their own beliefs are true regardless of the personal cost, while the interference of the state in those beliefs is fundamentally unjustifiable, because the political and social costs are too high to pay. Or as Locke put it, the "whole jurisdiction of the magistrate reaches only to ... civil concernments ... it neither can nor ought in any manner to be extended to the salvation of souls," just as no individual, group, or church had "any just title to invade the civil rights and worldly goods of each other upon pretense of religion."[24] The history of religious violence and sectarian strife in the sixteenth and early seventeenth centuries had proved these points beyond any reasonable doubt. For both sound practical and philosophical reasons, therefore, toleration was an absolute necessity and the only sensible solution.

Locke did not believe, however, that the government should simply step aside on the issue, for according to his social contract theory it retained the authority and obligation to maintain public order and the public good. Because the "public good is the rule and measure of all law making," the government's role is "to take care that the commonwealth receive no prejudice, and that there be no injury done to any man, either in life or estate."[25] Hence, governments were obliged, when necessary, to prohibit religious opinions and activities when they undermined public peace and security. According to Locke, consequently, a religious zealot who refused to accept the judgment of government had no choice but to submit to political authority by way of "passive obedience," an idea first expressed in the sixteenth century by the religious reformers Martin Luther and John Calvin, who regarded overt civil disobedience against a divinely ordained monarch as rebellion against God. For Locke, the thrust of his argument was more secular. The individual believer need not change his personal confession of faith, but he must not express his convictions in a manner that caused trouble. Private conscience was thus not at stake here; at stake was public order.

That Voltaire was influenced deeply by Locke's thinking on this subject, just as he was by the English philosopher's ideas about the human capacity for reason, is clear in Letter 6 of the *Philosophical Letters*. Here, one sees Voltaire's views on toleration (see Document 17) taking definitive shape along Lockeian lines. He observed:

> Go into the London Stock Exchange, a more respectable place than many a court, and you will see representatives from all nations gathered together for the utility of men. Here Jew, Mohammedan, and Christian deal with each other as though they were all of the same faith, and only apply the word infidel to people who go bankrupt. Here the Presbyterian trusts the Anabaptist and the Anglican accepts a promise from the Quaker. On leaving these peaceful and free assemblies some go to the Synagogue and others for a drink, this one goes to be baptized in a great bath in the name of Father, Son, and Holy Ghost, that one has his son's foreskin cut and has some Hebrew words he doesn't understand mumbled over the child, others go to their church and await the inspiration of God with their hats on, and everybody is happy. If there were only one religion in England there would be danger of despotism, if there were two they would cut each other's throats, but there are thirty, and they live in peace and happiness.[26]

Although Voltaire's tone in this passage is rather sarcastic, he was right nevertheless: the only solution to differences in religion was toleration, exactly as Locke had argued. Or as Voltaire later put it, "Dissention is the great evil of mankind, and toleration is its only remedy."[27] In his view, the fact that the English largely disregarded religious differences in daily life was a compelling reason why English society worked and French society did not.

In Letter 5, Voltaire returned once more to the religious issue, this time revealing some of his doubts about Christianity itself, or at least the evident gulf between Christian precept and practice. "In morals the Anglican clergy are more virtuous than the French," he wrote. University educated "far from the corruption of the capital," English clerics attained high positions in the church only in later life "at an age when men have no other passion than avarice, when their ambition has little to feed on." Indeed, high positions were awarded for long service; hence, very few young men leaving college became bishops, as in France. Furthermore, the Anglican clergy were mostly married, which tempered their sexual urges, and if they sometimes got drunk in public, this was done "solemnly and with no scandal." In France, by contrast, "young men notorious for their debauches ... [are] appointed to bishoprics through the intrigues of women, make love in public, find fun in composing tender love-songs, give long and exquisite suppers every night, and then go straight to pray for the light of the Holy Ghost and brazenly call themselves the successors of the Apostles."[28] As for Catholic theologians, "the interpreters of the Divinity," wrote Voltaire in a private letter to Crown Prince Frederick, the future king of Prussia, they "are sometimes the most dangerous of all":

> That there are some who are as pernicious in society as they are obscure in their ideas, and that their souls are swelled with venom and pride in proportion to their being devoid of truth. They would disturb the world's tranquility for a sophism and lead all kings to avenge, with sword or firearms, the honor of an argument *in ferio* or *in barbara*. Any thinking person who does not agree with them is an atheist, and any king who does not favor them will be damned.[29]

In the face of such an indictment of the Catholic clergy, it is small wonder that the French censors reacted so heavy-handedly to the publication of the *Philosophical Letters*.

There was, however, a higher level to Voltaire's interest in Newtonian science and Lockeian philosophy, as well as in religion, which raised an important and very practical question about the connection between public interest in the emerging ideas of the eighteenth-century Enlightenment, on the one hand, and public access to those ideas through publication, conversation, or some other means, on the other hand. For access and interest were two halves of the same equation. From Voltaire's perspective, the new epistemology based upon Newton and Locke (or nature and reason) represented more than a scientific system; it was an intellectual movement that also promoted a social policy. Yet because political, philosophical, and scientific discussion automatically had religious consequences in the period, a political framework for toleration was essential for anyone concerned not just about the implications for religion of science and philosophy, but also for freedom of expression, just as Locke had argued. Hence Voltaire's shared interest in the study of history, which he once characterized as "the annals of the crimes of the human race."[30]

His concern to create just such a political framework for toleration had already surfaced in the *Henriade*, an epic poem written by

Voltaire in 1724 about the success of King Henry IV of France in forging a religious settlement to the late sixteenth-century civil wars that had almost torn the kingdom asunder. But the *philosophe* had serious misgivings about where to publish the epic, though he knew he could not do so in France because of the very problem that the *Henriade* was meant to address. He confessed:

> I have recommended a spirit of peace and tolerance in religious matters much too much in my poem. I have told the court of Rome [i.e., the papacy] too many home truths; I have spread too little venom against the Reformed [i.e., Huguenots] to hope that I might be permitted to print this poem, written in praise of the greatest king my country has ever had, in my homeland. It is a very strange thing that my work, which at heart is a eulogy of the Catholic religion, cannot be printed in the state of the very Christian king, of the [great, great, great] grandson of Henry IV, and that those whom we have called *heretics* allow it to be published in their country [i.e., the Calvinist United Provinces].[31]

"Of all religions the Christian is undoubtedly that which should instill the greatest toleration," Voltaire later added in 1764, "although so far the Christians have been the most intolerant of all men."[32]

For free-thinkers such as Voltaire, and for those engaged like him in the secular world around them, the notion of doctrinal religion was becoming anachronistic. Similar to the protagonist of Tobias Smollett's contemporary novel, *The Adventures of Ferdinand Count Fathom* (1753), many of these men increasingly conceived of dogmatic Christianity and the institutional churches that produced it with "the utmost detestation and abhorrence, rejecting [both] with loathing and disgust, like those choice spirits who, having been crammed with religion in their childhood, renounce it in their youth, among other absurd prejudices of education."[33] As far as Voltaire and many of his fellow *philosophes* were concerned, religious enthusiasm expressed in religious dogma was a myth in which people blindly believed. Moreover, as Locke had noted, it was that devotion to blind belief that made dogma so dangerous, mythical or not, because it incited intolerance, together with fanaticism and persecution. Hence, Voltaire's growing skepticism in Christianity evolved steadily into Deism, a mixture of science and hostility to Christian doctrine and pretense. As one contemporary asserted, "to be a philosophical skeptic is, in a man of letters, the first and most important step to being a sound, believing Christian."[34]

It follows, then, that if a spirit of rational criticism as applied to every aspect of human society and culture characterized the Enlightenment, traditional religion was certainly an object of special scrutiny

and concerted attack by the *philosophes*, including Voltaire, for its dogmatism and intolerance, as well as for its miracles and revelations. All
four features were viewed as irrational. Christian doctrine was thus
examined closely to prove its absurdity, Christian history to reveal its
cruelty, and Christian ritual to discover its derivation from pagan rites.
The purpose, ultimately, was to remove the superstition from Christianity to get at its essential foundation, which was considered to be
rational, even scientific. For if reason and empiricism could uncover
further natural laws to render explicable those phenomena in nature
that remained mysterious to human understanding, then reason and
empiricism just as surely could reveal miracles as "fanciful explanations of natural phenomena" that were not simply inaccurate, but even
offensive to human intelligence.[35]

In the process, the Christian world view was replaced steadily by
a non-Christian one based upon a concept of materialism,[36] (see Documents 19 and 21) with its intense belief in the here-and-now and its
thirst for knowledge.[37] If the universe had come to be intelligible as a
material and mechanical process governed by mechanical or immutable
natural laws, as the scientific achievements of a century or more had
demonstrated culminating with the work of Isaac Newton, then the
same natural laws were discernable by human reason. Moreover, natural law was the key in a very material sense that could open the gate to
wealth, knowledge, and power—that is, the improvement of man's condition on earth.[38] Materialism thus constituted the "natural position of
one freed from the trammels of religious belief and ... superstition."[39]

The ground work for the intense kind of scrutiny now applied by
the *philosophes* to Christianity had already been laid in the seventeenth
century by thinkers like Richard Simon and Pierre Bayle, whose critical
analyses of the scriptures had revealed many of their inconsistencies
and improbabilities. Even John Locke had entered the lists, not just
with his *Letter on Toleration*, but also with the publication in 1695 of his
book *The Reasonableness of Christianity*. His purpose in the second work
was to defend religion on the basis that it was both common-sensical
and simple to understand. "Locke seems to have been the first
Christian," wrote Scottish philosopher and religious skeptic David
Hume in c. 1761, "who ventured openly to assert that *faith* was nothing
but a species of *reason*; that religion was only a branch of philosophy;
and that a chain of arguments, similar to that which established any
truth in morals, politics, or physics, was always employed in discovering
all the principles of theology, natural and revealed."[40] A year later, John
Toland published *Christianity Not Mysterious* (1696), in which he too
claimed that nothing in Christianity was above reason, before criticizing
what he considered to be some of its more ludicrous doctrines.

Over time, however, the *philosophes* of the eighteenth-century developed a deep antipathy, and in some cases even a profound hatred, for Christianity that surpassed these early inquiries. Few of these men asserted personal atheism in religion, however, for according to their Newtonian view of the universe, "they still required a creator for their world-machine, an architect or engineer whose designs were the foundation of natural law."[41] Or as Voltaire argued, "whatever some present-day scholars may say, one can be a very good philosopher and still believe in God. Atheists have never responded to the objection that a clock proves the existence of a clockmaker."[42] Besides, the *philosophes* all, or almost all, appreciated the important role played by Christianity in preserving moral behavior at every level of society. Echoing Locke, who once observed that true religion was instituted to govern the life of men "according to the rules of virtue and piety,"[43] David Hume similarly noted that the "proper office of religion is to regulate the heart of men, humanize their conduct, infuse the spirit of temperance, order, and obedience."[44] Although generally opposed, on moral grounds, to all varieties of traditional religious belief and practice,[45] the Scottish philosopher nevertheless went so far as to acknowledge grudgingly that religion, "however corrupted, is still better than no religion at all." He mused:

> The doctrine of a future state [i.e., heaven or hell] is so strong and necessary a security to morals that we never ought to abandon or neglect it. For if finite or temporary rewards and punishments have so great effect ... how much greater must be expected from such as are infinite and eternal?[46]

Despite periodic shifts in his own viewpoints on religion, Voltaire similarly appreciated the moral value of Christianity in human society, which he consistently juxtaposed with his intense revulsion for fanaticism and atheism, especially at the level of the state. The more he opposed the "spirit of factionalism, fanaticism, and rebellion," the sources of intolerance, he once wrote, "the more I revere a religion whose morality makes a family of mankind and whose practices are based on indulgence and charity."[47] By the same token, he believed it was essential not just for peoples but for princes also to have deeply engraved in their minds "the notion of a supreme being, creator, ruler, remunerator, and avenger."[48] His reason was simple: "I want princes and their ministers to recognize a God, even one who punishes and forgives," for without moral restraints on their power and authority, they were "like ferocious animals who, indeed, will not devour me after they have had a big meal and are gently digesting it on a sofa with their mistress, but who certainly would devour me if they found me by chance beneath their claws when they were hungry," and would not even think "they had done something wrong."[49] Therein lay the kernel of Voltaire's indictment of atheism, "a monstrous evil in those who govern," as well as in learned men who "can affect those who hold office."[50] For even if not backed by fanaticism, which alone "produces more crimes,"[51] atheism "is nearly always fatal to virtue."[52]

It was one thing to acknowledge and even to defend Christianity as a moral force in human society, but the institutional church, and specifically the Catholic Church, were very different matters. To *philosophes* like Voltaire, Hume, and Diderot, the Church perpetuated a religious rather than a scientific view of physical nature and mankind, which stressed the essential depravity of human beings and the necessity of divine grace for salvation in the next world. As Crane Brinton notes, traditional Christianity lacked a theory of progress in nature on this earth, though there was a certain emotional basis to the faith that was not necessarily opposed to a belief in progress. The problem with formal Christianity was, however, that there was a state of innocence before the biblical Fall, a time when man was at his best. But when man lapsed, he could not reconstitute Eden on earth, nor could he better himself through any process, except through the "transcendental miracle" of salvation.[53] Heaven, in other words, could never be achieved on earth. Enlightenment thinkers, by contrast, could account for the rational steps or "ten stages" by which men "had lifted themselves from primitive savagery to the brink of perfection on earth," owing to the spread of reason and the "increasing enlightenment that enabled men to control their environment better."[54] Man is born good, the *philosophes* argued; he is only made bad by society and the social environment in which evil was an historical development "embodied in customs, laws, institutions—that is to say ... in what man had made of man."[55] Hence, although the new movement was in many respects a child of Christianity, the Enlightenment idea that improvement in human nature on earth was possible and the Christian doctrine of original sin were diametrically opposed. "Let us admit," sneered Voltaire with scorching sarcasm, "that [early Church father] Saint Augustine was the first to authorize this strange idea, worthy of the fiery and romantic head of a debauched and repentant African, Manichaen, and Christian, indulgent and persecuted, who spent his life contradicting himself."[56]

Moreover, Christianity taught people to turn away from this world, this "vale of tears," in order to concentrate on the heavenly world to come. Because "each man feels, in a manner, the truth of religion within his own breast," remarked David Hume, "from a consciousness of his imbecility or misery rather than from any reasoning, [he] is led to seek protection from that Being on whom he and all nature is dependent."[57] For this reason in particular, the *philosophes* objected to the Church's role in education, which was regarded as the key to an enlightened view of the future. Life to Enlightenment thinkers was reality and no longer a mere preparation for an afterlife of salvation or damnation. On the contrary, the world was a place "where fulfillment or frustration had to be found"; a place also where "happiness in itself might be a valid goal in life."[58] Above all, however, the *philosophes* opposed the bitter disputes over obscure doctrines among the various Christian sects that led to bigotry and the politics of intolerance, the causes of so much human bloodshed, suffering, and warfare in the past. It is thus no accident that the protagonist of Voltaire's eponymous novel *Candide* ended his wanderings in the Islamic Ottoman Empire. There he could live in peace regardless of his beliefs, having discovered that toleration existed nowhere in Europe, neither in Catholic nor in Protestant lands.

To assault the established churches of Europe in this way automatically raised important questions about life and society under the Old Regime, however. Both politically and socially, the institutional church formed an integral part of the European power structure and an essential element in the social fabric. The people were also deeply imbued with Christian belief, including most of the *philosophes*, who never could escape it. The established church constituted, as well, a privileged and powerful corporate body in every European state, but especially in Catholic states such as France. A major problem was, however, that the many internal weaknesses of the eighteenth-century Church had rendered it vulnerable to external attack. For although thousands of priests faithfully fulfilled their religious offices, "at a time when natural philosophy was offering alternative explanations of the origins of man, the nature of evil, and the purpose of life, the church needed a firmness of character, adroitness, and above all a unity that it could not muster."[59]

Rejecting accepted belief in religion by revelation as promoted by the established Church and the Christian clergy, the *philosophes* asserted that religion should be reasonable and lead to moral behavior. If, they argued along Newtonian lines, nature was rational, then God who had created nature must also be rational. It followed, therefore, that the religion by which God was worshiped should be rational, too. Furthermore, Lockeian psychology, which limited human knowledge to experience, raised serious doubts as to whether such a thing as knowledge gained through divine revelation—the foundation of Christian belief and doctrine—was even possible. After all, observed David Hume, if there could be no certainty of matter or mind on rational or empirical grounds, then the revealed truths of Christianity were similarly baseless. In his historical analysis of the origins of religion, therefore, Hume ultimately concluded that religion grew out of hope or fear. Because "men never have recourse to devotion so readily as when dejected with grief or depressed with sickness," the twin passions of fear and hope "enter into religion," since at different times they "agitate the human mind," while "each of them forms a species of divinity suitable to itself." By contrast, when a man "is in a cheerful disposition, he ... thinks not of religion."[60] Hence, the origins of religion were emotional, not rational as John Locke had argued, and they were rooted in terror—the "primary principle of religion" and its "predominant passion," which only "admits of short intervals of pleasure."[61] To Hume, therefore, human reason served only as a tool to concoct the means of satisfying "irrational impulses and desires that varied among individuals and societies"; a view that also undercut by extension the whole concept of rational, natural religion and inadvertently challenged "the very basis of Enlightenment rationalism and its derivative structure of universal morality and self-evident truths."[62]

Borrowing further from the materialistic views of Newtonian science, the *philosophes* believed that nature conformed to its own material laws in a mechanistic universe that operated without divine intervention. "Look round the world," wrote Hume with this point specifically in mind, "contemplate the whole and every part of it: you will find it to be nothing but one great machine, subdivided into an infinite number of lesser machines, which again admit of subdivisions to a degree beyond what human senses and faculties can trace and explain."[63] In such a universe, the interference of a supernatural being in physical nature fundamentally contradicted natural law and the view of the world as a great mechanism. Ironically, the same kind of divine intervention contradicted Christian belief in a perfect, omniscient, and omnipotent God as confirmed by doctrine, a problem Voltaire identified with evident glee. "A miracle is the violation of the divine, immutable, eternal laws of mathematics," he asserted:

> By this very definition a miracle is a contradiction in terms. A law cannot be at once immutable and violated. But ... cannot God suspend a law established by himself.... Why would God perform a miracle? ... It would be a confession of his weakness, and not of his power. It would seem to be the most inconceivable contradiction in him.... [I]t is to say to him: "You are a weak and inconstant being." It is therefore absurd to believe in miracles. It is as it were to dishonor the divinity.[64]

What, then, was the proper role of religion in society, and did the idea that men could exercise reason to discover the physical laws of nature necessarily eliminate the Christian notion that man himself was the product of a beneficent God, or at least of God's providence in a mechanistic world? Furthermore, did the exercise of human reason necessarily mean that the concept of divine action in the material world on a day-to-day basis could be dismissed? These were questions of intense debate among the *philosophes*. Even those strict materialists among them who denied God, religion, and theology, and who reduced all knowledge to the simple function of sensation and materialism, had difficulty denying that the human pursuit of pleasure and avoidance of pain might represent part of the divine order of things.

Hence, God was not eliminated by the trend toward materialism. Even Voltaire, as critical as he often was in religious matters, asserted that men possessed a natural benevolence absent in beasts, meaning that man was born with an inherent moral faculty which gave him the capacity to do good. Voltaire's contemporary, English writer Henry Fielding, actually linked the Christian concept of charity to natural law as reverse sides of the same coin in his novel *Tom Jones* (1749). In a discussion with another character, who denied that the word "charity" meant beneficence or generosity in scripture, Squire Alworthy disagreed on the principle that charity was "an indispensable duty, enjoined by Christian law and the law of nature itself":

> "To confess the truth," said [Alworthy], "there is one degree of generosity (of charity, I would have called it) which seems to have some show of merit, and that is where, from a principle of benevolence and Christian love, we bestow on another what we really want ourselves; where, in order to lessen the distress of another, we condescend to share some part of them by giving what even our necessities cannot spare."[65]

Thus it is obvious that even those who were inclined to view the direct intervention of God in the world with skepticism, saw in mankind an inherent capacity to do good things and to make moral judgments.

The irony of this view is, however, that as more direct, biological connections were discovered in the early eighteenth century between men and beasts, it appeared less and less that men were disposed by nature to bestial behavior. Sir Isaac Newton certainly believed that man's capacity to reason and nature's acting in harmony with natural law were proofs not just of God's presence, but of his benevolence toward men. For Newton, the universal law of gravitation, together with his notions of space and time, demonstrated that God had created a structure beneficial to man if only man was alert enough to try to discover that structure. Indeed, notes Norman Hampson, the "whole philosophy of Newton leads of necessity to the knowledge of a Supreme

Being, who created everything, arranged all things of his own free will."[66] This view was, to some extent, Voltaire's view as well, especially considering the remarkable coincidence that whenever the *philosophe* "thought of God, [he] tended to think of Newton at the same time."[67] But although the Enlightenment began with assuming that the structure of the world and its universal physical laws implied not just the benevolence of God, but also his existence, the characteristics or attributes of God remained a mystery despite a multitude of books written on the subject early in the century.

The proper place of religion thus became an element in social thought, whatever its spiritual implications. To be sure, the argument for toleration produced by Locke and subsequently adopted by *philosophes* such as Voltaire and Hume was a partial answer, insofar as it provided a political formula for stability through freedom of conscience, though even that formula required extraordinary effort to maintain. Cautioned Hume along these lines:

> [If a monarch] admits only one religion among his subjects, he must sacrifice, to an uncertain prospect of tranquility, every consideration of public liberty, science, reason, industry, and even his own independence. If he gives indulgence to several sects, which is the wiser maxim, he must preserve a very philosophical indifference to all of them and carefully restrain the pretensions of the prevailing sect, otherwise he can expect nothing but endless disputes, quarrels, factions, persecutions, and civil commotions.[68]

By the mid-eighteenth century, however, the political response proposed by Locke to the problem of religion had given way to an intellectual answer, according to which the role of religion was still viewed as a stabilizing social influence, but an influence derived from the first principles of natural justice and moral duty toward one's fellow men.

All of these considerations, from the problems with dogmatic religion and the institutional church to notions of a mechanistic universe, the benevolence (even existence) of God, the role of religion, and the place of Christian morality in regulating the behavior of men in society, gave rise to a movement for enlightened religion, known as Deism. Characterized as "natural" religion, there were two major principles in the new creed. First was a belief in the existence of a God, usually impersonal, who had created the universe—attributes that could be deduced from the contemplation of nature, of the physical world. Furthermore, because nature provided evidence of a rational God, a view obviously based upon the notion of a mechanistic structure that operated according to immutable natural law, then God also must favor natural morality, conceived of as a universal set of ideals that he had engraved on the hearts of all mankind. Deism asserted, in short, "that the heavens declared the glory of God."[69] The second major principle in Deism was a belief in life after death, when rewards and punishments would be administered according to the kind of virtuous life the individual had led on earth.

At its core, Deism was empirical, tolerant, and reasonable; it encouraged ethical living; and it was essentially pagan, meaning that it was non-Christian in terms of doctrine. Deism was, wrote Voltaire, "the most ancient [religion] and the most widespread, for the simple worship of one god preceded all the world's systems."[70] Consequently, the new creed was a true religion (as opposed to dogmatic faith), as old as creation itself, and extolled a few simple maxims about the fatherhood of God, the regularity of nature, and the brotherhood of man. "To do good" was its cult; "to submit to good" was its doctrine.[71] Deism thus also advocated peace and kindness, while it repudiated empty ritual, sectarianism, and intolerance. Perhaps the best description of Deism, and the clearest expression of its spirit, came from the pen of Thomas Paine (1737–1809). "There is a happiness in Deism, when rightly understood," he observed, "that is not to be found in any other system of religion":

> All other systems have something in them that either shock our reason, or are repugnant to it, and man, if he thinks at all, must stifle his reason in order to force himself to believe them. But in Deism our reason and our belief become happily united. The wonderful structure of the universe, and everything we behold in the system of the creation, prove to us, far better than books can do, the existence of a God, and at the same time proclaim His attributes. It is by the exercise of our reason that we are enabled to contemplate God in His works, and imitate Him in His ways. When we see His care and goodness extended over all His creatures, it teaches us our duty toward each other, while it calls forth our gratitude to Him. It is by forgetting God in His works, and running after the books of pretended revelation, that man has wandered from the straight path of duty and happiness, and become by turns the victim of doubt and the dupe of delusion.[72]

A Deist, consequently, was a man "firmly convinced of the existence of a supreme being," wrote Voltaire, "as good as he is powerful, who has created all extended, vegetating, sentient, and thinking beings, who perpetuates their species, who punishes crimes without cruelty, and benevolently rewards virtuous behavior."[73] His guiding principle was what one historian has termed rather inelegantly "uniformitarianism"; that is, the conviction that whatever is uniform, whatever is believed everywhere, is right.[74] This conviction, reinforced by contemporary travel literature, confirmed the Deists' belief, in turn, that there existed a natural religion as common to the Asians and native peoples of the New World as to Europeans. That natural religion, reduced to its most basic elements, was a simple matter of ethics.[75] Since, on that understanding, the Deist "has brothers from Peking to Cayenne, counting all wise men as his brothers,"[76] the Chinese literati, the Persian sages, the Roman stoics, and Jesus in his capacity as a teacher of ethics were all regarded as Deists, too, because they all promoted the same universal message regardless of creed or culture.

As the major, positive religious component of the Enlightenment, Deism was, in brief, a kind of halfway house between traditional Christianity and atheism, for it rejected religious superstition, yet retained the ethics. God remained, notes Franklin Baumer, but hardly as the kind of personal deity to whom one could pray.[77] This concept, united with the deistic attack on the structures and doctrine of traditional religion, explains perhaps the objection to it by Samuel Johnson, whom James Boswell once characterized as "one who employs his powers to uphold the wisdom of the centuries."[78] No honest man could be a Deist, grumbled Johnson, "for no man could be so after a fair examination of the proofs."[79] The notion of an impersonal *deus absonditus* (absent God) was certainly enunciated by Voltaire, who once declared:

> The great name of Deist, which is not sufficiently revered, is the only name one ought to take. The only gospel one ought to read is the great book of Nature, written by the hand of God and sealed with his seal. The only religion that ought to be professed is the religion of worshiping God and being a good man.[80]

If such a profession of "faith" became accepted widely, the Deists argued, religious fanaticism would cease, along with persecution and sectarian violence as wrought by zealotry, superstition, and prejudice. By the same token, there would be little or no need any longer for a priestly caste, which was largely blamed for perpetuating sectarian hatred and religious bigotry as the unavoidable results of dogmatism.

The *philosophes* thus attacked organized religion, the established churches, and the clergy vehemently as they formulated their rational religious alternative to Christianity. Indeed, notes Crane Brinton, the eighteenth century was the great period of anti-clericalism, "the century when all kinds of hostilities and grievances against Catholic and Protestant Christianity could come out in the open, thanks to the 'spirit of the age' of the Enlightenment."[81] For the first time, he adds, "Christianity felt itself under heavy attack within its own culture."[82] Throughout his life, for example, Voltaire consistently questioned the truthfulness of priests and the morality, not just the accuracy, of the

Bible itself. In his *Philosophical Dictionary*, in particular, he pointed out inconsistencies in the biblical narratives and the immoral acts of biblical heroes, using humor and sarcasm by turns, though he was just as critical of atheists, whom he characterized as "bold and misguided scholars who reason badly and who, unable to understand the creation, the origin of evil, and other difficulties, have recourse to the hypothesis of the eternity of things of necessity."[83]

Nor did Voltaire relent in his life-long struggle against religious bigotry, persecution, and intolerance. This is most evident from his involvement in the Calas Affair of 1762, when the Catholic political authorities in the French city of Toulouse executed a Huguenot merchant named Jean Calas on false charges of having murdered his own son to prevent him from converting to the Roman Catholic faith. Despite the circumstantial nature of the evidence, Calas was brutally tortured and publicly strangled without ever confessing his guilt. Though Voltaire had learned of the case only after the fact, his reaction was vehement. "I may be mistaken," he wrote, "but it seems clear as day to me that the rage of factionalism and the peculiarity of fate have coincided to cause the most innocent and unfortunate of men to be legally murdered on the rack, to disperse his family and reduce it to beggary."[84]

Adopting the cause as his own on the principle that "by raising one's voice, one manages to be heard by the most hard of hearing, and sometimes even the outcries of the unfortunate reach the court,"[85] the aging *philosophe* published a *Treatise on Tolerance* (1763), protested widely for a new investigation of the case, and even undertook to pay some of the Calas family's legal expenses from his own pocket. Finally, in 1765 the judicial decision against the dead man was reversed to Voltaire's great satisfaction. "It is a very rare thing in France," he commented in anticipation of this outcome, "for private individuals to be successful in getting the decree of a *parlement* [i.e., law court] quashed, and it is almost unbelievable that a Protestant family without influence or money, whose patriarch was broken on the rack in a far-off corner of the kingdom, has been successful in obtaining justice."[86]

It is thus small wonder that in the *Philosophical Dictionary* published at this time Voltaire wrote of fanaticism that it "is to superstition what delirium is to fever, and what fury is to anger." The only remedy for "this epidemic illness," he urged, was the "spirit of free thought, which, spreading little by little, finally softens men's customs, and prevents the renewal of the disease."[87] In general, however, the dictionary was what some historians have called a "Newtonian polemic" that presented the world of nature and of man in deistic terms. It was a world of immutable natural laws created by a God who disdained miracles as shabby admissions that he was neither omniscient nor omnipotent. It was also a world of basic constituents such as mind and matter, whose natures may remain mysterious, but whose conformity to eternal natural law was comprehensible and admirable.

David Hume shared this materialist view of the physical world, arguing that the belief in miracles—a concept fundamental to Christianity—was not grounded in reason or any empirical evidence. "A miracle is a violation of the laws of nature," he declared, "and as a firm and unalterable experience has established these laws, the proof against a miracle, from the very nature of the fact, is as entire as any argument from experience can possibly be imagined."[88] For a fact to be a fact depended upon observation and not just repeated, but also demonstrable, patterns of behavior. That a man, apparently in good health, should die suddenly, reasoned Hume, was no miracle but rather an event in the common course of nature, for such deaths were frequently observed to happen. On the contrary, it was considered a miracle that a dead man should come to life, yet the occurrence "has never been observed in any age or country" outside of scripture. "There must, therefore, be a uniform experience against every miraculous event," concluded Hume, "otherwise the event would not merit that appellation."[89] Hence the Scottish philosopher's famous quip that the greatest miracle was to believe in miracles.

A few *philosophes* went still further along materialist lines than either Voltaire or Hume. Denis Diderot, Paul-Henri Thiry, baron d'Holbach (1723–1789), Claude-Adrien Helvétius (1715–1771), and Julien Offray de La Mettrie (1708–1751), for example, enunciated perspectives that were essentially atheistic, though that view represented a minority position among Enlightenment thinkers, most of whom did not seek the abolition of religion, but only its reform. Born into a very pious family "richly endowed with priests,"[90] Diderot—like Voltaire—had been educated by Jesuits and, at one point, had contemplated joining the Catholic priesthood. For a while, he supported himself by writing sermons for bishops,[91] but as time passed the *philosophe* underwent a steady evolution "from Catholicism to theism, from theism to deism, from deism to skepticism, and from skepticism to atheism."[92] His perspective was mixed, however, for although he accepted atheism as true, he found its "cold determinism" repugnant in contrast to the rich ceremonial quality of formal Catholicism, which attracted him even though he believed it to be false.[93] It is, however, in his approach to the great *Encyclopedia* on which he labored for a quarter century, that Diderot's materialism is evident. At the heart of this project, which is regarded widely by historians as the greatest monument of the Enlightenment, was Diderot's conviction that knowledge was rational, ordered, and in accordance, therefore, with nature's laws. Moreover, because social and political institutions ought to submit to rational standards, everything was equally subject to criticism.[94] Mankind was thus elevated to the center of human inquiry, and in that sense the *Encyclopedia* represented a bold attempt to systematize and classify all knowledge that had been generated by human hands.[95]

Described variously as an arch-materialist whose fierce hostility to Christianity was "patent," a radical, and a pessimist about human nature, which he considered to be vicious, the baron d'Holbach's chief work, *La Système de la Nature* (*The System of Nature*, 1770) offered a "rigid, dogmatic, and all-inclusive materialism."[96] He argued that the structure of the universe was simple and uniform, consisting only of matter in motion and of the various combinations into which matter enters or is formed. Because matter is constant, asserted Holbach, it could neither be created nor destroyed; only motion fluctuates. It is produced, increases, and undergoes acceleration "without the intervention of external force or agency."[97] All natural beings thus result from the combination of matter and motion, the two basic constituents of the universe. According to this construction of nature and natural processes, therefore, man can claim "no real position of privilege"; his spiritual activities, like his sensations, are "but particular transformations and modifications of the motion common to all [matter]."[98]

La Système de la Nature thus belongs to a "prolific family of antireligious diatribes designed to unmask Christianity" and to trace the "sacred contagion" to its origins,[99] namely fear and "the shapeless fruit of ignorance, of an alarmed imagination, of enthusiasm, of melancholy."[100] Holbach advocated an extreme, even aggressive form of atheism, in short, "as the mark of a truly enlightened mind," while he also rejected Deism and any notion of religion's role in supporting or guiding morality.[101] In the process, writes Peter Gay, the baron brutally ridiculed such key Christian figures as Jesus, Mary, and St. Paul, while contrasting the "virtues" of reason (i.e., common sense) with the "vices" of enthusiasm and superstition.[102] Religion, Holbach asserted, "in all countries, far from being favorable to morality, shakes it and annihilates it." By promoting sectarianism, disunity, and dogmatism among men, "the slightest difference in their religious notions, renders them from that moment enemies, separates their interest, and sets them into continual quarrels."[103] Holbach's ultimate goal, therefore, was to construct a natural philosophy based on the recognition of nature's eternal, immutable laws without reference to religion. That pursuit led in turn, notes Peter Gay, to his proposal of "a consistent, if somewhat simplistic, materialism that confronted a world without God."[104] For "everything must have convinced us," the baron reasoned, "that the idea of God so generally diffused over the earth, is no more than a universal error of the human species."[105]

While Holbach's book, *La Systême de la Nature*, has been described as "the last word" in materialist insight,[106] some of his ideas were foreshadowed earlier in the century by Julien de La Mettrie and Claude Helvétius, both of whom expressed advanced forms of materialism in their thought, too. In his famous *L'Homme Machine* (1748), for example, La Mettrie offered a "realist" proposition that reduced mankind to a human mechanism that responded solely to sensations (see Documents 19 and 21). There was, he argued (anticipating Holbach), but a single substance in the world that has different manifestations. Moreover, there existed in that single substance—that matter—"a large number of properties and capacities formerly assigned to [the human] mind and spirit, such as thought, sensation, and volition."[107] In such a construction of the world, not only was mankind nothing special, but there also could be no moral question of good or evil attached to human actions, because these actions resulted only from external stimuli. "Let us then conclude boldly," declared La Mettrie, "that man is a machine, and that there is in the whole universe only a single substance differently modified."[108]

What, then, could be concluded further from this materialist argument about the differences in behavior between other kinds of machines (i.e., animals) and man? Furthermore, were such differences a simple matter of degree? In response to these two questions, La Mettrie observed that when

> I do good or evil; when I am virtuous in the morning, and vicious in the evening, it is my blood that is the cause of it.... Nevertheless, I persist in believing I have made a choice; I congratulate myself on my liberty.... What fools we are! Fools all the more unhappy for that we reproach ourselves ceaselessly for having done what it was not in our power to do![109]

In other words, as bio-mechanical contrivances that respond only to external stimuli, human beings really have no choice in their actions, whether good or bad, which removes from them all moral responsibility. This overtly materialist answer to the problems of religion, ethics, and human society attracted few adherents, while it scandalized many contemporaries. It expressed, nevertheless, an extreme form of Deism.

In his work, *De l'Esprit* (*On the Spirit*, 1758), Claude Helvétius also advocated a kind of materialist determination, later developed by the baron d'Holbach, in which he envisaged life as a perpetual state of flux "rather than as evolution in any particular direction."[110] All life, he argued, is relative to its material environment;[111] consequently, man also was the product of his environment, his mind having been shaped by manners, customs, and education.[112] Furthermore, because the human mind was set in motion only by considerations of pain and pleasure, there could be no free will. On the contrary, "all our thoughts and will must be the immediate affect or the necessary consequence of impressions we have received,"[113] an idea obviously derived from John Locke. Helvétius thus drew a distinction when using the term "spirit" (*esprit*) between the spirit as a product of education—a qualitative or "attitudinal aura" identified with individual or group life—and the "soul" as a product of nature.[114] As a result, though he equated religion with social morality like other thinkers of the day, Helvétius ultimately developed a morality of material self-interest, according to which public utility was the source of all moral values in society.[115] But his views, especially his distinctions between "spirit" and "soul," were criticized by other *philosophes* as insignificant and artificial.

If, however, men were merely mechanisms that responded solely to sensation, as Helvétius, La Mettrie and Holbach proposed, then where was there room for reason, which the majority of Deists believed was desirable in dispelling superstition in religion? For reason was regarded by them as a fundamental good. It was the essential action of human reason that also reined in the human passions, which revealed the principles of natural religion, and which led men inexorably to moral behavior along Deistic lines. In short, reason's role was to control the passions, from which moderation and toleration would naturally result.

At the same time, though, it must always be remembered that however vigorously the *philosophes* attacked organized Christianity, however critically they viewed the established Church, and however effectively they opposed doctrinal religion and its consequences, the eighteenth century remained a fundamentally religious age in which the majority of people across the social spectrum conceived of the cosmos and of humanity's place in it according to the traditional Christian worldview, whatever its denominational variations. Even some *philosophes* maintained deep personal religious convictions. Jean-Jacques Rousseau is only one example, though his profession of faith shifted by turns from Calvinism to Catholicism and back again, depending on whether he was living in France or his native Geneva.

That the mainstream of Europeans, articulate or not, continued to retain their Christian beliefs and commitment to organized religion is perhaps best illustrated by James Boswell, who read widely, and who made a point of meeting Voltaire, Rousseau, and other leading Enlightenment thinkers while traveling on the continent in the mid-1760s. He referred to the eighteenth century and the new ideas in circulation, especially as they touched upon religion, in negative terms as "an age when mankind are so fond of incredulity that they seem to picque themselves in contracting their circle of belief as much as possible."[116]

In a conversation about God and immortality with an avowed French atheist named Deleyre, Boswell objected to the man's materialist view that "to think the world has been composed by a fortuitous concourse of material substances in continual motion from all eternity did not seem more improbable than to suppose a Being who created matter." "All the arguments which I could recollect," lamented Boswell, "could not make M. Deleyre believe the existence of a Creator." Nor did Boswell find it easy to reconcile his friendship for this atheist, "the most virtuous and amiable of men," with his personal repugnance for, and horror of, atheism. At length, the Scotsman attributed Deleyr's unbelief, as perhaps most of his contemporaries would have done, to "a bad education" that had given his friend "so hideous a view of God that it was his interest to think there was none." Boswell concluded on a hopeful and very Christian note:

> I am convinced that the inclination of philosophers for or against any truth makes the same arguments seem as different to them as the same colours seem to different eyes. I returned again to a calm persuasion of the existence of the glorious fountain of all mankind, and I exalted in the hope of meeting Mr. Deleyre in a better world.[117]

Ultimately, it required a revolution to undermine traditional Christianity and overthrow the established Church, and thus complete a process begun by the *philosophes* in intellectual terms, at least.

Notes

1. See Robert R. Palmer, *The Age of the Democratic Revolution: A Political History of Europe and America, 1760–1800*, 2 vols. (Princeton: Princeton University Press, 1959–1964).

2. Caponigri, 349.

3. Gay, *Party of Humanity*, 131.

4. Voltaire to Jean-le-Rond d'Alembert, April 5, 1766, Voltaire, *Selected Letters*, 260.

5. Caponigri, 278.

6. Brinton, 291.

7. Caponigri, 350.

8. Quoted by James Boswell, *Grand Tour: Germany and Switzerland*, 263.

9. Voltaire to the comte de Maurepas, April 20, 1726, Voltaire, *Selected Letters*, 22.

10. Voltaire to Jean-Baptiste Nicolas de Formont, December 6, 1732, ibid., 29.

11. Voltaire, *Letters on England*, 8.

12. "On Descartes and Newton," Letter 14, ibid., 68.

13. Ibid., 70, 72.

14. Voltaire to René-Joseph Tournemine, August 1775, Voltaire, *Selected Letters*, 48.

15. Voltaire to Martin Ffolkes, November 25, 1743, ibid., 108.

16. Voltaire to Sir Edward Fawkener, September 18, 1735, ibid., 52.

17. Voltaire to Willem Jacob 'S-Gravesande, August 1741, ibid., 94.

18. Voltaire to René-Joseph Tournemine, August 1735, ibid., 51.

19. Voltaire to Willem Jacob 'S-Gravesande, August 1741, ibid., 94.

20. John Locke, *A Letter Concerning Toleration*, 45.

21. Ibid., 15.

22. Ibid.

23. Ibid., 57.

24. Ibid., 17, 27.

25. Ibid., 36, 39.

26. "On the Presbyterians," Letter 6, Voltaire, *Letters on England*, 41.

27. "Toleration," Voltaire, *Philosophical Dictionary*, Theodore Besterman, trans. and ed. (London: Penguin Books, 1972), 391.

28. "On the Anglican Religion," Letter 5, Voltaire, *Letters on England*, 38–9.

29. Voltaire to Crown Prince Frederick of Prussia, September 1, 1736, Voltaire, *Selected Letters*, 57. *In ferio* and *in barbara* were mnemonics for classes of syllogisms.

30. Voltaire to Antiochus Cantemir, March 13, 1739, ibid., 77.

31. Voltaire to Isaac Cambiague, December 1725, ibid., 21. (Emphasis Voltaire's.) The reference to "the very Christian king" derives from the honorific title granted in medieval times to the monarchs of France as the most Christian kings of Europe and the eldest sons of the Catholic Church.

32. "Toleration," Voltaire, *Philosophical Dictionary*, 390.

33. Smollett, *Count Fathom*, 50.

34. Hume, *Dialogues Concerning Natural Religion*, Henry D. Aiken, ed. (New York: Hafner Publishing Co., 1948), 94.

35. Rothrock and Jones, 344.

36. Gay, *Party of Humanity*, 135.

37. R.W. Harris, *Absolutism and Enlightenment* (London: Blandford Press Ltd., 1964), 3.

38. Ibid.

39. Caponigri, 369.

40. Hume, *Dialogues*, 13. (Emphasis Hume's.)

41. Rothrock and Jones, 344.

42. Voltaire to Jean-François Dufour, seigneur de Villevielle, August 26, 1768, Voltaire, *Selected Letters*, 276.

43. Locke, *Letter on Toleration*, 13.

44. Hume, *Dialogues*, 88.

45. Ibid., xi.

46. Ibid., 87.

47. Voltaire to Joseph de Vaux de Giry, February 1743, Voltaire, *Selected Letters*, 100–1.

48. "Atheist," Voltaire, *Philosophical Dictionary*, 57.

49. Voltaire to the seigneur de Villevielle, August 28, 1768, Voltaire, *Selected Letters*, 278.

50. "Atheist," Voltaire, *Philosophical Dictionary*, 57.

51. Voltaire to the seigneur de Villevieille, August 28, 1768, Voltaire, *Selected Letters*, 278.

52. "Atheist," Voltaire, *Philosophical Dictionary*, 57.

53. Brinton, 295

54. Ibid., 295, 296.

55. Ibid., 301.

56. "Original Sin," Voltaire, *Philosophical Dictionary*, 332.

57. Hume, *Dialogues*, 61.

58. Rothrock and Jones, 344.

59. Gay, *Party of Humanity*, 122.

60. Hume, *Dialogues*, 92–3.

61. Ibid., 93.

62. Rothrock and Jones, 345.

63. Hume, *Dialogues*, 17.

64. "Miracles," Voltaire, *Philosophical Dictionary*, 311–3.

65. Fielding, *Tom Jones*, 79.

66. Hampson, 79.

67. Ibid.

68. Hume, *Dialogues*, 90–1.

69. Hampson, 85.

70. "Theist," Voltaire, *Philosophical Dictionary*, 386.

71. Ibid.

72. Modern History Sourcebook: "Thomas Paine: Of the Religion of Deism compared with the Christian Religion," http://www.fordham.edu/halsall/mod/paine-deism.html.

73. "Theist," Voltaire, *Philosophical Dictionary*, 386.

74. Baumer, *Modern Currents of Western Thought*, 370.

75. Ibid.

76. "Theist," Voltaire, *Philosophical Dictionary*, 370.

77. Baumer, *Modern Currents of Western Thought*, 370.

78. Boswell, *Grand Tour: Italy, Corsica, France*, 261.

79. Ibid., 281–2.

80. Quoted in J.H. Randall, *The Making of the Modern Mind*, rev. ed. (New York: Houghton Mifflin, 1940), 292.

81. Brinton, 300.

82. Ibid.

83. "Atheist," Voltaire, *Philosophical Dictionary*, 56.

84. Voltaire to Dominique Audibert, July 9, 1762, Voltaire, *Selected Letters*, 232.

85. Ibid.

86. Voltaire to the Duchess of Saxe-Gotha, March 7, 1763, ibid., 235.

87. "Fanaticism," Voltaire, *Philosophical Letters*, 201–3.

88. Modern History Source book: "David Hume: On Miracles," http://www.fordham.edu/halsall/mod/hume-miracles.html.

89. Ibid.

90. Gay, *Party of Humanity*, 125.

91. Merriman, 408.

92. Gay, *Party of Humanity*, 125.

93. Ibid.

94. Merriman, 409.

95. Ibid., 410.

96. Caponigri, 370.

97. Ibid.

98. Ibid., 370–1.

99. Gay, *The Enlightenment*, I, 398.

100. Holbach, *La Systême de la Nature*, excerpted in Baumer, *Modern Currents of Western Thought*, 402.

101. Caponigri, 371.

102. Gay, *The Enlightenment*, I, 398–400; see also *Party of Humanity*, 114, 176, 272.

103. Quoted in Baumer, *Main Currents of Western Thought*, 403.

104. Gay, *The Enlightenment*, I, 400.

105. Holbach, *La Systême de la Nature*, excerpted in Baumer, *Modern Currents of Western Thought*, 402.

106. Caponigri, 370.

107. Ibid.

108. Quoted in Baumer, *Modern European Thought*, 167.

109. Quoted in ibid.

110. Hampson, 150.

111. Ibid., 126.

112. Harris, 29.

113. Quoted in Hampson, 126.

114. Caponigri, 372.

115. Ibid., 373; Hampson, 126.

116. Boswell, *Grand Tour: Italy, Corsica and France*, 184.

117. Ibid., 112–3.

CHAPTER 4

The *Philosophes*, Political Thought, and Enlightened Despotism

> What is the true End of Monarchy? Not to deprive People of their natural Liberty; but to correct their Actions, in order to attain the *supreme Good.*
>
> —Catherine II "the Great" of Russia, 1767

In an article published in 1784 entitled "An Answer to the Question: What is Enlightenment?" German philosopher Immanuel Kant asserted that the major intellectual change wrought by the great thinkers of the eighteenth century was to be found in "mankind's exit from its self-incurred immaturity"[1] (see Document 1). Formerly inhibited in the development of his views by external controls and direction—even dictation—from the established Church, sectarian belief, time-honored custom, and social convention, man had reached the state of intellectual maturity in the eighteenth century when, guided by his reason, he could think for himself and chart his own course through life without reference specifically to revelation or religious tradition, both of which had impeded his advancement toward freedom of thought, the virtuous life, and moral action in the here and now. "Have the courage to use your *own* understanding! is thus the motto of enlightenment," Kant declared; as for enlightenment itself, "nothing more is required than *freedom* … to make *public use* of one's reason in all matters."[2]

The newfound sense of liberty extolled by the German philosopher, notes historian M.S. Anderson, was largely "the product of criticism … of the past, of custom, of received ideas of any kind which could not stand the test of reason," and there emerged from it "man's power to make sense of the world and hence to control his own destinies."[3] That newly enlightened man, explained the baron d'Holbach further, "is man in his maturity, in his perfection; who is capable of pursuing his own happiness; [precisely] because he has learned to examine, to think for himself, and not to take that for truth upon the authority of others, which experience has taught him examination will frequently prove erroneous."[4]

Moreover, because "man is the unique point to which we must refer everything," wrote Jean-le-Rond d'Alembert in the preliminary discourse to the great *Encyclopedia*, "if we wish to interest and please amongst considerations the most arid and details the most dry,"[5] then human reason—which exalted the intellectual achievements of the age—when applied to society and social institutions could not only discover natural laws in human relationships parallel to those that governed physical nature, but also act as a solvent on existing structures (see Document 3). For if, observes historian R. W. Harris, whatever seemed contrary to man's reason in religious matters could no longer be regarded as true by the *philosophes*, or by any other rational human being of the day for that matter, by the same token those social and political institutions "which did not accord with reason" were similarly unjustifiable.[6] Hence, argue most modern scholars, it was not in their assault on the Church and organized religion that the *philosophes'* appreciation of the problems and complexities of contemporary society is most clearly apparent. That appreciation is to be found most highly developed in their political thought and criticism of contemporary social structures and mores, especially hereditary privilege, in which the Church and organized religion played their role. Consequently, nowhere was the effect of Enlightenment thought more far-reaching than in the development of such concepts as the theory of natural rights or the idea of personal liberty (building upon the philosophy of John Locke), the principle of equal access to just laws, or the notion above all that government existed solely for the happiness of its citizens, since no other explanation seemed plausible to the *philosophes*.

Under the prevailing social and political conditions of eighteenth-century life, the *Ancien Régime*—the primary symbol of "unenlightenment," with its strong corporate bodies, caste structures, legacy of feudal privilege, and divine-right monarchy—alone blocked man's path to his ultimate goals. For that reason, the *philosophes* "trained their big guns on this living relic of the past, blasting first its religion, and then its politics and economics."[7] But although, observes Franklin Baumer, Enlightenment thinkers lived at the right moment in history when confidence in scientific reasoning was at full stride (or almost), and when reason had an excellent chance "of overcoming barbarism and superstition and of solving the great political and economic problems" of the day,[8] the eighteenth century still remained a fundamentally conservative age in which the intellectual agents of change and those who read their works, listened to their ideas, and shared their views were a distinct social and intellectual minority. Certainly, these agents did not succeed in altering the essential rules by which the vast majority of contemporary people actually lived or by which their society continued to function.[9]

In his book, *Kings and Philosophers, 1689–1789* (1970), author Leonard Krieger neatly outlines the prevailing conservatism of the eighteenth century. From the middle years of the period onward, he writes, the tone of European life altered, to be sure, as the rules of international politics were "insensibly amended" and domestic institutions were compelled into "an alternation of defensiveness and accommodation as the social pressures for change grew in intensity, crystalized into definite forces, and began to occupy the center of the European stage."[10] Notwithstanding, the vast majority of the population not only continued to live under the same corporate structures, institutions and social hierarchy so familiar to their ancestors, but also saw no alternative to the established modes of life and behavior. For the overwhelming majority of contemporary men and women, "this pattern of stability held for all regions from the Urals to County Kerry" in Ireland.[11] Bound by tradition, "addicted" to ritual, and organized on the basis of privilege at every level within the social context, life was lived in accordance with ancient custom, time-tested routines, and enduring associations. Whether for the preservation of their entitlements in law and social custom or for guidance in their personal and social life, people adhered strongly to their status within the established hierarchy of social orders, as well as to the direction given by local authorities (e.g., the parish priest and the lord of the manor), urban oligarchies, corporate bodies such as guilds and the Church, and the monarchy. Indeed, these traditional centers of power "still regulated the great events of personal life, sponsored social entertainments, and articulated public conscience," precisely because of the traditions they administered and upheld.[12]

To be sure, notes Krieger, there was frequently friction in the established order of things that disturbed the stability of these customary arrangements and relations. Friction tended to arise where corporate jurisdictions at the local level in particular appeared to overlap each other or to intrude. Meanwhile, the centralizing tendencies of royal governments had been encroaching for centuries on the customary autonomy of those same local authorities, which resisted external encroachment at every turn. Increasingly, numbers of people also sought to throw off the yoke of such corporations as the guilds in order to improve their personal lot in life by escaping traditional authorities and their regulations. But, warns Krieger, however much the second half of the eighteenth century experienced social, political, and economic change, and to whatever degree, that change "can only be understood if one keeps in mind the integrated structure and static ideal of the society which continued the activities and retained the allegiance of most Europeans until the end of the Old Regime."[13] The vast majority of the population was untouched, in other words, by the Enlightenment and continued to live, "as it were, in an earlier century" that still believed in witches, magic, home remedies spurned by "modern" medicine and customary authority. These people "lived and died happily ignorant of the battle between Cartesians and Newtonians" in the rarified atmosphere of contemporary intellectual and scientific circles.[14]

By the same token, one must always bear in mind that for the Enlightenment *philosophe*, practical reform, not overthrow of existing structures, informed his attitude on the European world and remained his principle goal. For the *philosophe* was in his own way as conservative in his outlook as other contemporaries, and however critical of the political, social, and economic aspects of his age he increasingly became, he was no revolutionary.[15] There is, for example, far more concurrence between the thought of Voltaire, generally viewed as the father of Enlightened liberalism, and that of Edmund Burke, generally viewed as the father of arch-conservatism. The only real difference between the two was timing; for where Voltaire lived and wrote prior to the French Revolution, Burke's most famous book was composed in reaction to it. Otherwise, the two men shared many similar perspectives on society and politics. It would be interesting, indeed, to speculate about how differently Voltaire might be regarded today had he lived to witness and respond to the violence and political turmoil that engulfed his native France after 1789.

At the same time, most *philosophes* enjoyed their proximity to the traditional centers of power, whether in aristocratic circles or more particularly at royal courts, "partly because [such proximity] soothed their vanity, partly because it provided them with audiences and customers [for their books], partly because it protected them from the harassment of censors."[16] Besides, many of them feared, or at least scorned, the uneducated mass of people and hoped to achieve the reforms they sought without any serious dislocation of the existing framework of government or even of society itself.[17] As Voltaire once quipped, the truth was "that men are very seldom worthy to govern themselves."[18] So despite their concerted attack against aristocratic privilege based upon the principle of heredity as opposed to personal merit, not all *philosophes* would have agreed that reason or nature's laws contradicted a hereditary nobility, no more than they universally condemned all distinctions of caste or class.[19]

As humanitarians united by their common admiration of "sociability and social action," Enlightenment thinkers were committed to the practical goal of rendering the world here and now a better and more congenial place to live, by securing religious toleration, political justice, educational reform, and humane treatment of people, even of criminals, under equitable laws.[20] Above all, notes Franklin Baumer, their liberalism consisted primarily "in securing the individual from what Adam Smith called 'profusion of government.'"[21] Achieving that objective was highly problematic, however, because of the ambiguous relationship that existed between society and government, on the one hand, and the traditional character of monarchy, on the other hand.

As Leonard Krieger notes, the authoritarian regimes that prevailed in eighteenth-century Europe did not simply reflect the dominant social group or tendency, but based their stability instead on the resources "they could mobilize from the whole of society to meet the ever-present threat of war abroad and on the pressure they could exert among the groups of society to meet the still-present threat of disorder within." Because, consequently, royal governments required "social mobility to generate force and social hierarchy to control it," they shifted from one side of the social spectrum—which they sought to straddle—to the other side in response to "the changing pressures of external security, internal order, and domestic lobbyists." For that reason, the political views of individual groups in society also swayed, because these views depended more often than not upon the direction taken by government policy at any given moment, than upon any consistency in outlook toward politics as dictated by enduring social interests.[22]

At the same time, observes historian Alfred Cobban, however centralized, bureaucratic, and mechanical government had become by the turn of the eighteenth century, it was still conceived of mainly in terms of individual monarchs, even though a government mechanism existed through which personal royal authority was exercised. With few exceptions across the continent, such as the republican United Provinces, or corporate bodies like the *parlements* and provincial estates in France, the whole governmental system "was embodied in the person of the king; he was the state," and the concept of divine right "was more than a phrase."[23] The European monarchs, in short, still embodied all political authority, all sovereignty, and remained in Shakespeare's phrase "the makers of manners,"[24] as those who set the social pace and formed the standards of contemporary judgment. After all, the law, the armed forces, and justice were all "royal"; court rulings could be overridden by the Crown; even the structure of society and social tastes depended upon vertical associations that culminated in the person of the monarch at the apex. Monarchical authority was not that, therefore, "of the titular head of an administrative regime, it was the personal exercise of his individual *bien plaisir* [good pleasure]."[25] For good or ill, the success with which that authority was wielded depended in turn upon the personal qualities and capacities of the man or woman who wore the crown.

Thus, at the pinnacle of the political, social, and institutional structures of most European states in the eighteenth century stood the monarch as sovereign lord, divinely ordained, in whose person justice, political authority, and social order resided. It was upon the monarch, consequently, that the hopes of man in society traditionally depended; for he was above all else a law-giver and, "provided his laws were good laws, he deserved to be venerated and obeyed."[26] From this perspective on monarchy developed the eighteenth-century ideal of the Enlightened Despot and Enlightened Despotism advocated by many, though not all, *philosophes* as the solution to society's two great enemies: feudal privilege and religious intolerance. Under prevailing political and social conditions, only the monarch was seen to have sufficient authority to assert effective power over the aristocracy, the Church, and other established interests, in order to bring about significant reform by rationalizing the economic and political structures of the state, while also securing individual liberty and intellectual freedom. If, therefore, the Enlightenment was in its essentials a "doctrine of action" (writes R. W. Harris), then it looked to the Enlightened Despot—characterized usually as a philosopher-king—as an agent of positive change, who could reform the state, rule by just laws, and bring to his subjects "light and happiness."[27] Such a monarch was, in other words, one who not only embraced the ideas of the *philosophes*, but also put them into practice (see Documents 33 through 38).

Although there is no precise definition of Enlightened Despotism, historians generally agree that it was a form of monarchical government committed to strengthening central authority at the expense of lesser centers of political power (e.g., corporate bodies, autonomous institutions, and vested interest) by curbing aristocratic liberties, restricting the Church, developing commerce, standardizing coinage, weights, and measures, secularizing education, encouraging the arts and letters through royal patronage, humanizing law, and generally seeing to the welfare of the subjects.[28] Because the governance of such a prince responded to the real needs of contemporary society, wrote French Physiocrat Mercier de la Rivière in 1767, he had just claim to being "the true beneficiary of his people."[29]

But, cautions Peter Gay, the *philosophes* did not hope to achieve perfection in society as they imagined it through Enlightened Despotism alone.[30] As a general rule, these free-thinkers disliked the *idea* of despotism in any form; but in the actual realm of politics, many of them promoted it as a viable force—however reluctantly—because they feared the alternative still more. That alternative, continues Gay, was traditional government by a powerful aristocracy. In a world in which men "are condemned to be anvil or hammer," wrote Voltaire,[31] those princes who, "through sound philosophy ... cultivate a soul born to command ... by educating themselves, by coming to know men, by loving truth, and by detesting persecution and superstition," were enlightened monarchs and the very definition of philosopher kings "who will make men happy."[32]

Yet Voltaire was hardly consistent in promoting the virtues of Enlightened Despotism. On the contrary, his political ideas were rather vague, or shifted at least from one perspective to another, depending upon the issue or debate at hand. For example, he, like many *philosophes*, was deeply impressed by the English system of government as a constitutional monarchy, and in particular by its division of powers between the Crown and parliament, its more equitable taxation, and its social order based upon the rule of law. England's constitution having thus reached a "point of excellence," wrote Voltaire,

> every man is restored to those natural rights, which, in nearly all monarchies, they are deprived of. These rights are, entire liberty of person and property; freedom of the press; the right of being tried in all criminal cases by a jury of independent men; the right of being tried only according to the strict letter of the law; and the right of every man to profess, unmolested, what religion he chooses.... These privileges attach to everyone who sets his foot on English ground.[33]

Voltaire was far too sensible, far too realistic, and far too aware of the historical processes at work in state- or nation-building ever to believe, however, that the British constitution could or even should be superimposed upon, or emulated by, his native France.

At the same time, though his superb histories of the reigns of Kings Louis XIV, Louis XV, and Charles XII of Sweden revealed just how much he admired the power and accomplishments of great monarchs,[34] while also advocating undivided sovereignty and secular supremacy over all public and ecclesiastical matters,[35] Voltaire offered a vigorous defense of republican ideas on more than one occasion. He once wrote:

> There cannot be a state on earth which was not first governed as a republic, it is the normal course of human nature.... When we discovered America we found all the [native] tribes divided into republics.... So it was in the ancient world. All was republican in Europe before the petty kings of Etruria and Rome.... Eight republics without monarchs [alone] remain in Europe.[36]

As for the subsequent triumph of despotism over republicanism, Voltaire scolded in his *Idées républicains* (1765), it was "the punishment for men's bad conduct."[37] Moreover, he moralized further, if "a community of [free] men is subdued by an individual or by a few, that is obviously because it has neither the courage nor the ability to govern itself."[38] Yet just a year before he expressed these views, the great *philosophe* had contrasted the despotism or tyranny of one man favorably with the tyranny of many men—an allusion to republicanism, if not democracy, which (he asserted) "invades the rights of other [social] bodies, and which exercises despotism thanks to laws it has perverted." "Under which tyranny would you like to live," Voltaire asked scornfully:

> If I had to choose I should detest less the tyranny of one than the tyranny of several. A despot always has some good moments, an assembly of despots never has any.... When it is not unjust, it is at least harsh, and it never distributes favors.[39]

The obvious inconsistency, even general ambiguity, in Voltaire's political views, let alone his particular perspective on Enlightened Despotism, the nature of government, and the proper abode of sovereignty, reveals two characteristics common to the *philosophes* and their political thought. One is their distrust of, and shared disdain for, philosophical systems-building and dogmas in all fields of inquiry, not just in politics or religion. The other is what Crane Brinton identifies as a great "bifurcation" in intellectual circles between those *philosophes* who took an authoritarian position which advocated (in theory, at least) "that a few wise and gifted men in authority could manipulate the environment so that everybody could be happy," and those who urged, from a more republican stance, the active destruction of the bad political and social structures that still held society in thrall, after which all men "would cooperate spontaneously in creating the perfect environment." For ordinary people, this latter group contended, were sound and sensible enough to make their own political choices.[40]

Although many Enlightenment thinkers would have agreed with Jean-le-Rond d'Alembert that philosophy "is the dominant taste of our century,"[41] few were systematic philosophers in their own right. Among the exceptions were Rousseau and Hume (whom Voltaire regarded as "a true philosopher"),[42] and perhaps also Charles Louis de Secondat, baron de la Brède et de Montesquieu and Kant. Moreover, "abstract, *a priori* thought was almost universally condemned" by them.[43] This rejection was due partly to the purely speculative nature of such thought, partly to its taste for constructing artificial systems without reference to reality, and partly to the intellectual inadequacies of those who were identified as professional philosophers (as opposed to *philosophes*) in eighteenth-century Europe. "While thinking to please," observed d'Alembert, contemporary philosophy appeared "not to have forgotten that it is principally made to teach; this is the reason why the taste for systems, more proper to flattering the imagination than to enlightening the reason, is today almost entirely banished from good works."[44] Rousseau lamented further that "there is nothing but error and folly in the doctrine of our philosophers," which seemed only to justify the "misery and oppression in our social arrangements."[45]

As for the philosophers themselves, "what could be more ridiculous," asked Abbé Étienne Bonnot de Condillac (1714–1780) in his book *Traité des Systèmes* (*A Treatise on Systems*, 1749), "than awakening from a profound sleep, and finding themselves in the middle of a Labyrinth, they should lay down general principles for discovering a way out?"[46] Yet such action divorced from all reality, sneered Condillac, was the general conduct of contemporary philosophers who, added Voltaire, "are too lukewarm":

> They are content with laughing at the errors of men instead of crushing them. Missionaries run about the earth and over the seas; philosophers must at least run about the streets. They must go and sow the good seed from house to house.[47]

Rousseau was still more critical of the philosophers of his day for adopting "false principles of wisdom brought to perfection."[48] The same scorn for contemporary philosophy and those who generated it led Denis Diderot to advise in a more moderate tone, "Let the last century furnish examples of genius; it is for our own age to prescribe the rules,"[49] which (added the Marquis de Condorcet) would allow for a human race "emancipated from its shackles, released from the power of fate and from that of the enemies of its progress," as humanity advanced "with a firm and sure step along the path of truth, virtue, and happiness."[50]

Among the dogmatic philosophical systems that the *philosophes* opposed in particular was, of course, doctrinal Christianity that lay at the core of organized religion. For not only did it render nature and man—supposedly God's special creation, formed in His image and likeness, and endowed with certain god-like qualities—helpless before the dictates of a universal yet unknowable divine plan for Creation and the mysterious workings of Providence; it also degraded humanity as essentially evil, sinful in nature, and forever incapable of moral self-improvement through human reason or action. The same dogmatic Christianity was held responsible for the sectarianism and intolerance that had caused so much human misery in European history, as well as the perpetuation into the eighteenth century of ignorance, complacency with things as they were, and traditional authority, which obstructed man's progress toward a more enlightened, secular future. The Baron d'Holbach made that point specifically with respect to man's political life when he asserted that

> the citizen, or the man in society, is not less depraved by religion, which is always in contradiction with sound politics. Nature says to men, *thou art free, no power on earth can legitimately deprive thee of they rights*: religion cries out to him, that he is a slave, condemned by his God to groan all his life under the iron rod of his representations.[51]

Doctrinal Christianity as a dogmatic, universalist system was equally antithetical to Enlightenment belief in man's intrinsic goodness and capacity for moral improvement and social reform by his own devices, without the need for divine intercession. "Man is not born wicked," declared Voltaire, "he becomes wicked, as he falls ill":

> Collect all the children of the universe, and you will see in them only innocence, gentleness, and fear. If they were born wicked, evil-doing, cruel, they would show some sign of it, just as small serpents try to bite and little tigers to claw. But nature, not having given more offensive arms to men than to pigeons and rabbits, could not give them an instinct of destruction. So man is not born evil.[52]

Another philosophical system of the day that Voltaire, among others, found just as objectionable, and which he satirized brilliantly in his famous novel *Candide*, was the doctrine of Optimism proposed by the great German mathematician, philosopher, historian. and diplomat, Gottfried Wilhelm Leibniz.[53] In his highly complex thought Leibniz wrestled with the problem of creation, the origin of good and evil, and the difficulty, in particular, of reconciling human suffering in the world with the existence of an omnipotent, omniscient, omni-just, and omni-good Supreme Being. Stated simply, if not simplistically, Leibnitz proposed a theory of creation based upon two related philosophical concepts that he connected to traditional Christian view of Providence. The first was the "principle of sufficient reason," a variation of empiricism by which "truths of fact" about the world as it actually exists could be deduced from careful examination of existence itself and history. The second concept was "pre-established harmony," whereby God, as the universal cause of all things, had constructed the laws that govern nature in such a way that although every particle (or "monad") of which the world was composed operated independently, it operated in harmony with every other particle, too.

Upon these speculative foundations, Leibniz contended that the world took the form it did because God deliberately chose to create it so. That form was intelligible and reasonable because God always acts for a reason and, consequently, there must be a reason for everything to exist. Furthermore, God might have constructed the world in any form that He desired, but He chose this world over all other possibilities, because the totality of its structures allowed for the greatest possible harmony and degree of perfection, despite the fact that its enormous diversity included events that often indicated otherwise. This was, in short, the best of all possible worlds, and the goodness of God was "sufficient reason" for its creation.

In order to avoid any implication, however, that human behavior was also predetermined by this divinely ordained harmony, Leibniz argued that evil was a necessary and unavoidable consequence of God's having chosen to create the best of all possible worlds. Although He derived no pleasure from the existence of evil as the source of human suffering and did not will it, not even God could remove moral wrong in the world unless He also destroyed the power of man's free will, and hence the very basis of morality. For the human soul is tested in the freedom to choose good or evil, and is perfected by suffering. So however bad things may appear to human eyes, to wish that they were different is not reasonable, because things would be much worse in any other world God could have created. Happiness is to be found, therefore, in acknowledging the perfection of God, the divine creator, and the perfection of all things that He has created. That happiness is the source of human hope and thus also of optimism.

Although from personal experience of suffering and his own study of history Voltaire had already begun to doubt the existence of any such force as Providence in the world, the immediate catalyst for his merciless attack on Leibniz's doctrine of Optimism (see Document 15), or more accurately its popular perversions in circulation at the time, was the great Lisbon earthquake of 1755 that leveled much of the city and took 50,000 lives. Nor was it an isolated event, for just nine years earlier the colonial city of Lima, Peru was devastated by a similar natural disaster. In the face of such deadly occurrences, it became clear to Voltaire that the doctrine of Optimism was, in fact, a doctrine of Pessimism that offered only a counsel of despair and hopelessness "to all but those who profited by the sufferings of their fellow-creatures," but had never experienced suffering themselves.[54] "This was indeed a cruel sort of physics," Voltaire lamented about the Lisbon quake, "People will really find it difficult to divine how the laws of nature bring about such frightful disasters in the 'best of possible worlds'."[55] For even though Leibniz had done mankind "the service of explaining that we ought to be satisfied," he continued with a touch of sarcasm, "and that God could do no more for us, that he had necessarily chosen, among all the possibilities, which was undeniably the best one," this system of "All is Good" represented the divine author of nature

> only as a powerful and malevolent king who does not care, so long as he carries out his plan, that it costs four or five hundred thousand men their lives, and that the others drag out their days in want and tears. So far from the notion of the best possible world being consoling ... the problem of good and evil remains an inexplicable chaos for those who seek in good faith. It is an intellectual exercise for those who argue.[56]

Incensed by such philosophical callousness, which seemed only to add insult without offering hope to the miseries that man must endure,[57] Voltaire wrote a *Poem on the Lisbon Disaster* (1756), in which he condemned the "Eternal sermon of useless sufferings," while summoning those "deluded philosophers who say, 'All is well'," to "Hasten, contemplate these frightful ruins/This wreck, these shreds, these wretched ashes of the dead/These women and children heaped on one another/These scattered members under broken marble."[58] This poem was followed three years later by the publication of *Candide*, a masterful and unrelenting satire on Optimism, in which the character of Dr. Pangloss represents the disciples of Leibniz, "repeating the master's terms but perverting his philosophy."[59] As Candide, Pangloss, and their companions in the novel proceed from one disastrous situation to another, they remain faithful to the doctrine of Optimism "as absurdly sure as ever that [they are] living in the best of all possible worlds."[60] Only at the end of their combined misadventures is the veil lifted and they see the world as it really is. Yet throughout the story, Candide, at least, is consistently sustained in his trials and tribulations by hope for future happiness. Therein lay the resilience of human nature, which Voltaire emphasized in response to the "Optimists'" counsel of despair.[61]

But perhaps the best criticism of philosophical systems-building in the eighteenth century was expressed by an intellectual layman, not a *philosophe*. In a diary entry for September 2, 1765, James Boswell mused about why so many people had been mistaken in their search for happiness, and believed that he had discovered the reason. The philosophers and systems-builders of his day, he asserted in clearly Enlightenment terms, "have wished to establish the same general system of living for everyone without realizing that men differ as much in inclination as in appearance." It was hardly surprising, therefore,

> that men who have devoted themselves to thought and who are honored with the great name of philosopher ... [through] pride and ambition should make them wish that they could lay down the law to all their fellows and thus be almost kings of mankind. And it is not less surprising that the majority of men have submitted to this intellectual domination, since a great part of mankind are timid and lazy when it comes to thinking for themselves. As for me, who have found myself in every frame of mind and have experienced life in great variety, I think that the general rules are very badly connived and hold men in tiresome dependence, with no other advantage than to aggrandize certain famous names which have almost become oracles. It is true that a society cannot exist without general rules.... Let us therefore have laws, and let those laws be the general laws ... which are really necessary for public happiness.... [Otherwise], I wish everyone to live naturally, as he himself pleases, and then possibly we might not hear so many people complaining of this evil world.[62]

The full significance of Boswell's words lies not just in his rejection of intellectual dogmatism and philosophical systems-building, but also in his very utilitarian appeal for a set of general rules that could ensure individual liberty to all men. What he invoked, in short, was the developing concept of natural rights that permeated Enlightenment political thought. This concept was based partly upon principles of natural law, partly upon older theories of man in the state of nature and the social contract proposed by such philosophers as Thomas Hobbes and John Locke, and partly upon empiricism united to the study of history, which demonstrated that security of life, liberty, and property was essential for social stability and the full realization of the human potential. The doctrine of natural rights thus came to provide "a standard against which to measure the performance of governments."[63] Indeed, it was precisely that standard to which Voltaire appealed when extolling the excellence of Great Britain's constitution and the privileges that, he noted, "attach to everyone who sets his foot on English ground."

To the extent, therefore, that political authority—however constituted—contributed to the greater security of life, liberty, and property (the three most basic human rights enumerated by John Locke), then it fulfilled its proper function with respect to the individual citizen or subject. After all, wrote Locke in his *Two Treatises of Government* (see Document 23), "the Reason why Men enter into Society, is the preservation of their Property; and the end why they chuse and authorize a Legislative [power], is, that there may be Laws made, and Rules set as Guards and Fences to the Properties of all the Members of the Society, to limit the Power, and moderate the Dominion of every Part and Member of the Society."[64] When, however, that same security of life, liberty, and property was abrogated by some corrupting influence, such as dynastic ambition or arbitrary rule without reference to law and the responsibilities of the government to the governed, then political authority not only failed in its primary purpose, but exposed itself to popular rebellion, too, just as Locke had also warned in his philosophy. In fact, according to the English thinker, revolution was not merely the inevitable outcome of political oppression, it was the right of the oppressed to rebel and erect a new government in place of the old. He admonished:

> [For] whomsoever therefore the *Legislative* shall transgress this fundamental rule of society, and either by Ambition, Fear, Folly, or Corruption, *endeavour to grasp* themselves, *or put into the hands of any other an Absolute Power* over the Lives, Liberties, and Estates of the People; by this breach of Trust they *forfeit the Power*, the People had put into their hands [by contract], for quite contrary ends, and it devolves to the People, who have a Right to resume their original Liberty, and, by the Establishment of a new Legislative (such as they shall think fit) provide for their own Safety and Security, which is the end for which they are in Society.[65]

The Enlightenment appeal to fundamental human rights was based not just on Locke's ideas, however, but also upon a number of broad assumptions. It is almost ironic, indeed, that although the *philosophes* tended to abstain from engaging in flights of "naked reason" and repudiated such notions as innate ideas (found in Cartesian thought) and final "systems of knowledge" common to the formal philosophy of their day, they were not "averse from generalizing about the universe and man."[66] They assumed, for example, the existence of a universal law and order in physical nature *à la* Newton, as well as the capacity of human reason to discover and comprehend that law and order *à la*

Locke; they assumed the "apriority" of universal laws, of "natural laws," and thus also of "natural rights" in human society; they assumed certain general principles that underlay the variety of those related forms of law; and they assumed "a uniform human nature throughout the world."[67] Above all, the *philosophes* assumed the possibility of a new structure for society established upon individual men and women who were born free and equal, in contrast to the old order of society founded upon family units "enmeshed in a web of divinely ordained social inequality and obligations to Church and king"[68]—that is, a society in which group or corporate identities, privileges, and legal entitlements prevailed over any appeal to individual rights or the idea of individualism.

For the Enlightenment *philosophes*, therefore, the twin concepts of *liberty* (meaning the individual's freedom to choose his own destiny) and *equality* (meaning not just equitable treatment under law, but also that all individuals begin life as a *tabula rasa* on which experience writes) were the universal remedies for the social, political, and economic ills of contemporary human society. As for the state, Locke, Hobbes, and other philosophers had amply demonstrated that it was merely an artificial structure created by men for their mutual advantage.[69] It followed, therefore, that politics and economics should be discussed not from the perspective of the state, but from the perspective of the individual. As a result of this train of thought, writes Franklin Baumer, the individualism of the Enlightenment, combined with the concept of natural rights to life, liberty, and property, became the great leveler in contemporary views of society and social reform. For if human nature was the same everywhere, as the *philosophes* assumed, then individualism equalized all men, and in the process destroyed the foundations of special privilege, social hierarchy based upon hereditary status, sectarianism, and even divine right, irrespective of national or cultural differences in the world.[70]

The Enlightenment thinkers always accepted, of course, that the concept of equality had more to do with legal principles than with the intrinsic nature of men, whatever the implications for human psychology. After all, even in Locke's philosophy on human understanding, qualitative differences, quite apart from the natural effects of genetics, could produce evident inequalities among people. This certainly was the argument offered by the conservative Samuel Johnson, who scoffed at the whole notion of equality among men, whether social or intellectual. "So far is it from being true that men are naturally equal," he once sniffed, "that no two people can be left an hour together but the one shall acquire an evident superiority over the other."[71] By the same token, the *philosophes* were not narrowly class-conscious in any socialist or Marxist sense. What they opposed was the institutionalization of inequality in law, the prevailing problem of the Old Regime whose structures were based upon that very principle. That principle was, in turn, the source of special privilege accorded to specific constituencies within society on the basis of hereditary status or corporate identity, regardless of merit. It must always be remembered that in a fundamental sense, however conservative the eighteenth century remained in organization, attitudes, and social relations for the great majority of men and women, it was also a period of increasing social mobility, or at least of social aspiration, among certain segments of the population, starting with an ever wealthier, numerous, and politically ambitious bourgeoisie that wanted a greater stake in contemporary society on its own terms.

Hence, in their assault upon the *Ancien Régime* and its institutions, the *philosophes* necessarily championed the social groups that had matured during the seventeenth and early eighteenth centuries.[72] The bourgeoisie certainly had begun to evolve an identity of its own, an identity that grew more pronounced as the eighteenth century wore on. To be sure, there were still many among this rising middle class who sought access to noble ranks in the customary ways, by aping aristocratic manners, purchasing aristocratic titles though venality of office, or marrying their children into aristocratic families. At the same time, however, larger numbers of professionals (e.g., lawyers and medical doctors) within the bourgeoisie believed that they deserved greater recognition through participation in the decision-making processes of the state commensurate with their wealth, talent, and increasing prominence. These men grew ever more resentful, therefore, of an aristocratic social order that blocked their way to full political engagement or social advancement.

The emergence of a distinctly bourgeois identity and matching resentment toward aristocratic pretensions was increasingly evident in eighteenth-century literature, theater, and personal memoir. In Sir Richard Steele's play, *The Conscious Lovers* (1722), for example, Mr. Sealand, a tradesman, gently defended the social value of the middle class to Sir John Bevil, a baronet:

> Give me leave to say that we merchants are a species of gentry that have grown into the world this last century, and are as honourable, and almost as useful, as your landed folks have always thought yourselves so much above us.[73]

In his novel, *The Adventures of Ferdinand Count Fathom*, Tobias Smollett similarly praised the achievements of four real-life commoners who, despite their low birth, had risen to prominence in England by sheer merit. His fictional character Monimia identified

> several persons of note, who basked in the sun-shine of power and fortune, without having enjoyed the least hereditary assistance from their fore-fathers. One, she said, sprung from the loins of an obscure attorney, another was the grandson of a valet de chambre, a third was the issue of an accomptant, and a fourth the off-spring of a woolen-draper: all these were the children of their own good works, and had raised themselves upon their personal virtues and address; a foundation certainly more solid and honourable than a vague inheritance derived from ancestors, in whose deserts they could not be supposed to have the least share.[74]

Smollett's undisguised contempt for aristocratic status and privilege earned only through accident of birth also underlay the opposition of Pierre du Pont de Nemours' father, a Parisian watchmaker, to his son's academic education, because he "did not want his children to rise above his station." "He had noticed my mother's very profound desire for such a promotion," recalled Du Pont de Nemours in later life, "and the more acute this desire appeared to him, the more a natural sentiment of [bourgeois] dignity opposed to his wife's dreams of nobility inspired in him a repugnance for everything that would lead me to such a result."[75]

The highest expression of bourgeois self-worth in overt challenge to what many contemporaries had begun to view as the social injustice of aristocratic privilege is found, however, in the play *the Marriage of Figaro*, by Pierre de Beaumarchais. He presented the French aristocracy (his real target, despite the play's Spanish setting) as self-indulgent from motive, dissolute from boredom, and jealous from vanity.[76] "Nobility, fortune, rank, position!" shouts the main character, Figaro, in criticism of his noble employer, the count of Almaviva:

> How proud they make a man feel! What have *you* done to deserve such advantages? Put yourself to the trouble of being born—nothing more! For the rest, a very ordinary man! Whereas I, lost among the obscure crowd, have had to deploy more knowledge, more calculation and skill merely to survive than has sufficed to rule all the provinces of Spain for a century![77]

In the face of such a powerful indictment of aristocratic society of privilege and pretension, it is small wonder that the royal authorities across Europe banned the play from further performance following its première in 1784. They were well aware of, and feared, its politically charged content and the reaction it produced among the common-born members of the audience who, wrote a contemporary, "applauded not only scenes of pure comedy but also the courageous man [Beaumarchais] who dared to comment on and to ridicule the libertinage of great nobles, the ignorance of magistrates, the venality of officials, and the false pleadings of lawyers."[78] It was in direct reference also to the growing resentment of such commoners that the abbé Sieyès wrote in 1789: "What is the Third Estate? *Everything*. What has it been until now in the political order? *Nothing*. What does it want to be? *Something*."[79]

In a very real sense, therefore, the American Declaration of Independence (1776) offers a cogent recapitulation of the social and political thought of the Enlightenment, natural rights, and even Locke's social contract theory, together with its "right of revolution." "We hold these truths to be self-evident," states the document,

> that all men are created equal, that they are endowed by their Creator with certain unalienable Rights, that among these are Life, Liberty, and the pursuit of Happiness.—That to secure these rights, Governments are instituted among Men, deriving their just powers from the consent of the governed.—That whenever any form of Government becomes destructive of these ends, it is the Right of the People to alter or abolish it, and to institute new Government, laying its foundation on such principles and organizing its powers in such form, as to them shall seem most likely to effect their Security and Happiness.[80]

Historians have offered various reasons, both economic and ideological, to explain the substitution of "pursuit of Happiness" for Locke's "property." But the alternation of terms is not, in fact, that extraordinary. For the idea of the "pursuit of happiness" was embedded deeply in, and regularly enunciated by, Enlightenment philosophy. It was also an idea that reflected the Classical education of most *philosophes* and the signatories of the declaration. The pursuit of happiness, meaning a state of being in which men could achieve their fullest potential as men, rather than a fleeting state of merriment or contentment with life, was Aristotelian in origin. What the American leaders of the revolt against the British Crown envisaged, borrowing partly from ancient Greek ideals and partly from ideas circulating in their own time, was in short the establishment of a new political order in place of the old, where man's potential could best be realized.

At the same time, the Declaration of Independence underscores the bifurcation of viewpoints between those *philosophes* with an authoritarian cast of mind who looked to Enlightened Despotism as the practical solution to contemporary social and political injustices associated with the Old Regime, and those of a more liberal or populist outlook who believed that only by tearing asunder the traditional structures of society in order to rebuild could real progress be made in the human condition. What gave the authoritarian group hope for the future was the apparent impact of Enlightenment influences upon progressive rulers who both admired the *philosophes* and embraced many of their ideas. Chief among these crowned heads, the so-called Enlightened Despots, were Frederick II "the Great" of Prussia (r. 1740–1786), Catherine II "the Great" of Russia (r. 1762–1796), and Emperor Joseph II of Austria (r. 1765–1790; see Documents 33 through 38). Each of these monarchs, and others like them, undertook reforms in law, the economy, and government for the benefit of their subjects, though the same reforms more often than not helped also to extend and strengthen royal power at the expense of traditional élites and vested interests.

In any case, because of their implementation of Enlightenment principles in their acts of government, whether genuine or merely apparent, these rulers were hailed by many *philosophes* as the fulfillment of their wishes for philosopher-kings.[81] Before they quarreled bitterly in 1752–1753, for example, Voltaire frequently compared Frederick II to such great Classical figures as Caesar, Augustus, and Cicero, calling him "the Solomon of the North" and a ruler who was as well suited "for society as he is for the throne."[82] The great *philosophe* also praised the young monarch for publishing the *Anti-Machiavel* in the year of his succession, a short work in which Frederick sanctioned the ruler's obligation to govern for the welfare of his subjects, even if the Prussian king carefully ensured that any enforcement of that obligation was by the royal conscience alone, coupled with "a goodly measure of military severity and public order in the makeup of his subjects' happiness."[83]

Both Catherine II and Joseph II earned similar praise for their apparent appeal to Enlightenment ideals in governing their states, though in Catherine's case, given the circumstances by which she came to the throne, her program for reform was far more limited in extent because of her need to maintain the support of the Russian nobility. Nevertheless, she corresponded with Voltaire and Diderot among other *philosophes*, she planned to revise the Russian law code along Enlightenment lines, and she initiated a far-reaching reorganization of provincial administration (see Document 35). Of the three monarchs, however, Joseph II was the most deeply influenced by Enlightenment ideals, even declaring at one point that "he made Philosophy the legislator of his Empire."[84] (see Document 36). It was during his reign that serfdom was abolished in the Habsburg Empire and religious toleration introduced. But his well-intentioned religious, legal, and social reforms, which he implemented in a sincere wish to improve the well-being of his subjects, ultimately incited aristocratic opposition and popular rebellion across his wide-spread dominions in the last years of his reign, because he moved too quickly and appeared to threaten the vested privileges of various groups in society.

Although their efforts to reform were motivated sometimes from political opportunism, sometimes from dynastic ambition, and sometimes from economic necessity, all three monarchs nevertheless took their responsibilities as Enlightened Despots very seriously. Perhaps Frederick "the Great" (see Document 33) expressed these sentiments best when he wrote:

> Rulers should always remind themselves that they are men like the least of their subjects. The sovereign is the foremost judge, general, financier, and minister of his country, not merely for the sake of his prestige. Therefore, he should perform with care the duties connected with these offices. He is merely the principal servant of the State. Hence, he must act with honesty, wisdom, and complete disinterestedness in such a way that he can render an account of his stewardship to the citizens at any moment. Consequently, he is guilty if he wastes the money of the people, the taxes which they have paid, in luxury, pomp, and debauchery. He who shall improve the morals of the people, be the guardian of the law, and improve their education should not pervert them by his bad example.[85]

Catherine II echoed these principles of Enlightened Despotism in the guidelines she wrote for the compilation of a new code of Russian law in 1767, even though nothing concrete ever materialized from this effort, which amounted to little more than an endless series of committee meetings. If the true end of monarchy was to attain the "supreme Good" for all subjects, she observed, then the form of government "which best attains this End, and at the same Time sets less [sic] Bounds than others to natural Liberty, is that which coincides with the Views and Purposes of rational Creatures." Likewise, if the "Intention and the End of Monarchy, is the Glory of the Citizens, of the State, and of the Sovereign," then from that glory "a Sense of Liberty arises in a People governed by a Monarch; which may produce in these States as much Energy in transacting the most important Affairs, and may contribute as much to the Happiness of the Subjects, as even Liberty itself."[86] Significantly, the czarina's sentiments were borrowed almost word for word from Montesquieu's *Spirit of the Laws*.[87]

But in spite of these expressions of Enlightenment principles, Frederick II, Catherine II, and Joseph II were yet monarchs who faced the practical realities of day-to-day politics, administration, and international affairs, which too often conflicted with the ideals enunciated by all three rulers. The result was disappointment, if not disillusionment, among many of those who initially praised their good intentions. Discouraged, for example, by Frederick II's utter duplicity in seizing Silesia from Austria in 1740, which precipitated European war, Voltaire complained of "my good friend the king of Prussia, who wrote so well against Machiavelli, and acted immediately like the heroes of Machiavelli."[88] After their dispute in 1752, the *philosophe* expressed even deeper disgust with his former benefactor, though he still appreciated Frederick's good taste in conversation, freedom of thought, and philosophical nature.[89] Rousseau similarly criticized the Prussian monarch "who, in his principles and conduct, appeared … to trample underfoot all respect for natural law and human obligations." "He thinks as a philosopher," snarled Rousseau, "and acts like a king," though the *philosophe* was still grateful for the protection that Frederick II extended to free-thinkers like himself throughout his reign.[90] Comparable sentiments were expressed by Sir William Temple, who warned James Boswell in 1764:

> When you see Frederick the Great (for I must own he deserves that name), instead of being struck with the majesty of his presence and the splendor of his actions, you should have recollected with abhorrence his ruinous ambition, his perfidy and want of principles; you shall have seen not a hero who conquers but to bless, but the tyrant of his people and the enemy of mankind.[91]

Joseph II and Catherine II attracted equal censure for certain actions taken by them during their respective reigns. The Russian empress was criticized in particular for her ruthless repression of the violent and widespread Pugachev Rebellion of 1773, which so threatened the stability of her throne that she was forced into ever-closer alliance with the Russian nobility, to whom she granted privileges in 1785 comparable to, if not greater than, those enjoyed by their western European counterparts.

The lesson, in short, was that the realities of politics and power were too often incompatible with the ideals of Enlightened Despotism, and however concerted their efforts to reform law, education, religion, and government to serve the well-being of their subjects, the Enlightened Despots of Europe were kings nonetheless in whom all sovereignty resided and who had to employ methods of government, administration, and diplomacy that were frequently offensive to the *philosophes*. For a major preoccupation among all of them was to centralize authority in their own hands, while also ensuring that their respective kingdoms continued to play a significant diplomatic and military role on the continent. "Hence it is," wrote the Baron de

Montesquieu, "that many of the princes of Europe, whose aim has been leveled at arbitrary power, have constantly set out with uniting in their own persons all the branches of magistracy, and all the great offices of state."[92] With these views in mind, international treaties too easily became mere "scraps of paper" and domestic programs for reform too conveniently became means of asserting ever-greater royal authority, all in the interests of state. This political reality led Denis Diderot to assert that although it

> has sometimes been said that the happiest government was that of a just and enlightened despot, it is a very reckless assertion. It would easily happen that the will of this absolute master was in contradiction to the will of his subjects. Then, despite all his justice and all his enlightenment, he would be wrong to deprive them of their rights even in their own interests.[93]

Thus, concluded Diderot, by definition "the arbitrary government [even] of a just and enlightened prince is always bad."[94]

Notes

1. Immanuel Kant, "An Answer to the Question: What is Enlightenment?" in Goodman and Wellman, eds., *The Enlightenment*, 20.
2. Ibid., 20, 21. (Emphasis Kant's.)
3. Anderson, 412.
4. Baron d'Holbach, "A Materialist View of Nature," excerpted in Baumer, *Main Currents of Western Thought*, 408.
5. Jean-le-Rond d'Alembert, "Encyclopedia," excerpted in Baumer, *Main Currents of Western Thought*, 380.
6. Harris, 3.
7. Baumer, *Main Currents of Western Thought*, 368.
8. Ibid.
9. Leonard Krieger, *Kings and Philosophers, 1689–1789* (New York: W.W. Norton & Company, 1970), 118.
10. Ibid., 116.
11. Ibid.
12. Ibid., 116–7.
13. Ibid., 117–8.
14. Gay, *Party of Humanity*, 120.
15. Baumer, *Main Currents of Western Thought*, 370.
16. Bay, *Party of Humanity*, 275.
17. Baumer, *Main Currents of Western Thought*, 370.
18. Voltaire, "Fatherland," in *Philosophical Dictionary*, 329.

19. Brinton, 303.

20. Baumer, *Main Currents of Western Thought*, 365.

21. Ibid., 370.

22. Krieger, 131.

23. Alfred Cobban, *A History of Modern France*, 3 vols. (Harmmonds-worth, Middlesex: Penguin Books, 1965) vol. I, 29.

24. William Shakespeare, *Henry V,* Act V, scene 2, in *The Complete Works* (London: Abbey Library, 1977), 493.

25. Cobban, vol. I, 30.

26. Harris, 3.

27. Ibid., 34.

28. Ibid., 4–5.

29. Quoted in ibid., 3–4.

30. Gay, *Party of Humanity*, 274.

31. Voltaire, "Tyranny," in the *Philosophical Dictionary*, 398.

32. Voltaire to Frederick, Crown Prince of Prussia, September 1, 1736, in Voltaire, *Selected Letters*, 56.

33. Voltaire, "Government," excerpted in Baumer, *Main Currents of Western Thought*, 421.

34. Harris, 26.

35. Gay, *Party of Humanity*, 60.

36. Voltaire, "Fatherland," in *Philosophical Dictionary*, 328.

37. Quoted in Gay, *Party of Humanity*, 56, 87.

38. Quoted in ibid., 87.

39. Voltaire, "Tyranny," in *Philosophical Dictionary*, 398.

40. Brinton, 303.

41. d'Alembert, "Preliminary Discourse" to the *Grande Enclyclopédie*, excerpted in Baumer, *Main Currents of Western Thought*, 377.

42. Boswell, *Grand Tour: Germany and Switzerland*, 280.

43. Cobban, vol. I, 102.

44. d'Alembert, "Preliminary Discourse" to the *Grande Enclyclopédie*, excerpted in Baumer, *Main Currents of Western Thought*, 378.

45. Rousseau, *Confessions*, 405.

46. Quoted in Cobban, vol. I, 102.

47. Voltaire to d'Alembert, June 26, 1766, in Voltaire, *Selected Letters*, 263.

48. Rousseau, *Confessions*, 411.

49. Diderot, *Rameau's Nephew*, 288.

50. Quoted in Cobban, vol. I, 102.

51. Baron d'Holbach, "On Theology and Morality," excerpted in Baumer, *Main Currents of Western Thought*, 404. (Emphasis his.)

52. Voltaire, "Wickedness," in the *Philosophical Dictionary*, 299–300.

53. The following discussion of Leibniz's philosophy is derived from: Ellen J. Wilson, *Encyclopedia of the Enlightenment* (New York: Facts on File, 1996) 244–5; Edward Craig, ed., *Routledge Encyclopedia of Philosophy*

(London: Routledge, 1998) vol. V, 545–6; Donald M. Bourchert, ed., *Encyclopedia of Philosophy*, 2nd ed. (Farmington Hills, MI: Thomas Gale, 2006) vol. V, 263–5.

54. Voltaire, *Candide or Optimism*, John Butt, trans. (London: Penguin Books, 1947), 9.

55. Voltaire to Jean-Robert Tronchin, November 24, 1755, *Selected Letters*, 181.

56. Voltaire, "All is Good," in the *Philosophical Dictionary*, 68, 74. Ibid. (Emphasis ours.)

57. Voltaire, *Candide*, 9–10.

58. *Poem on the Lisbon Disaster, or: An Examination of that Axiom "All is Well"*, 1, http://geophysics.tau.ac.il/personal/shmulik/LisbonEq-letters.htm.

59. Voltaire, *Candide*, 10.

60. Ibid.

61. Ibid., 11.

62. Boswell, *Grand Tour: Italy, Corsica and France*, 119–20.

63. Rothrock and Jones, 346.

64. Locke, *Two Treatises of Government*, 412.

65. Ibid., *412–13*. (Emphasis Locke's.)

66. Baumer, *Main Currents of Western Thought*, 366.

67. Ibid., 366–7.

68. Rothrock and Jones, 346.

69. Baumer, *Main Currents of Western Thought*, 371.

70. Ibid.

71. Quoted by James Boswell, *Grand Tour: Italy, Corsica and France*, 286.

72. Baumer, *Main Currents of Western Thought*, 365.

73. Quoted in ibid.

74. Smollett, *Count Fathom*, 299–300. The four men referred to are respectively Philip Yorke, first Earl of Hardwicke (1690–1764); Henry Fox, first Baron Holland (1704–1774); John Aislabie (1700–1742), a statesman and politician; and Sir Horace Mann (1709–1782), a British diplomat.

75. Elizabeth Fox-Genovese, trans. and ed., *The Autobiography of Du Pont de Nemours* (Delaware: Scholarly Resources Inc., 1984), 123.

76. Pierre-Augustin Caron de Beaumarchais, *The Barber of Seville and the Marriage of Figaro*, John Wood, trans. (London: Penguin Books, 1964), 29, 112.

77. Ibid., 199.

78. Quoted in ibid., 30.

79. Abbé Emmanuel Joseph Sieyès, *What is the Third Estate?* M. Blondel and S.E. Finer, trans. and eds. (London: Pall Mall Press, 1963) 51–2. (Emphasis Sieyès'.)

80. See http://www.ushistory.org/declaration/document/index.htm.

81. Gay, *The Enlightenment*, vol. II, 483.

82. Voltaire to Marie-Louise Denis, December 18, 1762; to Jean-Baptiste de Boyer, marquis d'Argens, October 2, 1740; and to Charles-Jean-François Hénault, October 31, 1740, *Selected Letters*, 84, 85, 167.

83. Krieger, 251.

84. Quoted in Harris, 4.

85. From J. Ellis Barker, trans., *The Foundations of Germany* (New York: E.P. Dutton, 1916), 22–3, excerpted in the Modern History Sourcebook: "Frederick II: Essay on Forms of Government," http://www.fordham.edu/halsall/mod/18fred2.html.

86. From Catherine II, "Proposals for a New Law Code," excerpted in the Modern History Sourcebook, 2, http://www.fordham.edu/halsall/mod/18catherine.html.

87. The only aim of contemporary monarchy in Europe, wrote Montesquieu, was "the glory of the subject, of the state, and of the sovereign. But hence there results a spirit of liberty, which in these states is capable of achieving as great things, and of contributing as much, perhaps, to happiness, as liberty itself" (*Spirit of the Laws*, 162).

88. Voltaire to Sir Everard Fawkener, June 1742, *Selected Letters*, 98.

89. Voltaire to Marie-Louise Denis, December 18, 1752, ibid., 167.

90. Rousseau, *Confessions*, 580–1.

91. Boswell, *Grand Tour: Germany and Switzerland*, 276.

92. Montesquieu, *Spirit of the Laws*, 152.

93. Quoted in Harris, 28–9.

94. Quoted in Gay, *Party of Humanity*, 275.

CHAPTER 5

THE ALTERNATIVE VISION OF MONTESQUIEU AND ROUSSEAU

The government that governs best governs least.

—Montesquieu

The alternative to enlightened despotism was a more liberal form of government, therefore, in which the will of the people superceded the will of the monarch (assuming there was a monarch), just as Diderot implied. That liberal form of government ranged in Enlightenment thought from a political system of checks and balances, as outlined by the Baron de Montesquieu, to popular sovereignty proposed by Rousseau and embraced by the authors of the American Constitution (1787), to "philosophical anarchism," which held that because any form of government was bad, all government should be abolished. An extremist point of view, "philosophical anarchism" reached its culmination in the thought of English radical William Godwin (1756–1836). In his book *Political Justice* (1793), he maintained that men only did wrong because they endeavored to obey, and make others obey, established laws. If, however, all people were at liberty to do what they wanted at any given moment, they would all act rationally, for "no reasonable man would injure another, amass more goods than he could use, or be jealous of anyone who did something he could not do."[1] It is perhaps no coincidence that Godwin's book appeared the same year as the French Revolution entered its most radical phase with the Reign of Terror, and two years after conservative thinker Edmund Burke had defended aspects of the Old Regime in his widely read *Reflections on the Revolution in France*. But philosophical anarchism was a position held only by a small minority of European thinkers.

More appealing was the system of checks and balances advocated by Montesquieu in his seminal work, *De l'esprit des lois* (*The Spirit of the Laws*, 1748; see Document 31). But this book needs to be read with caution, for the baron's thought can be interpreted in two widely divergent ways. The conventional interpretation focuses on his empirical approach to the study of government, and his belief (using illustrative examples from Europe, Asia, antiquity, and so on) that no single set of political laws could apply to all societies in the world at all times. The best form of government, however constituted, depended ultimately upon the combination of various elements, ranging from a country's size and population to its religious and social customs, its economic structure, and even its climate and soil. The primary purpose of that government was to preserve the liberty of the subject through the application of just laws, for in societies directed by laws, wrote Montesquieu,

> liberty can consist only in the power of doing what one ought to will, and in not being constrained to do what we ought not to will.... Liberty is a right [therefore] of doing whatever the laws permit, and if a citizen could do what they forbid, he would no longer be possessed of liberty, because his fellow-citizens would have the same power.[2]

Because for Montesquieu justice was the supreme criterion of the laws, he devoted his six final chapters in *The Spirit of the Laws* to an analysis of the various types of laws. Montesquieu remained first and foremost a lawyer and was concerned about the application and formation of law. His influence on his contemporaries was considerable. Voltaire greatly admired him as did the jurist Beccaria who regarded Montesquieu's influence as seminal in his own work, which has been and still is regarded as the most important treatise on law ever written (see Document 32). Even later political theorists such as Alexis de Tocqueville frequently cited him. Still many regard Montesquieu's work on the various types of government, republic, monarchy, and despotism, and his stress on the balance and separation of the powers of government in order to secure individual liberty as more influential. Those who drafted the American constitution cited Montesquieu more than any other writer.[3] For Montesquieu, power must check power; the elimination of intermediary powers opened the way for a "descent into despotism."[4]

With reference specifically to his native France, Montesquieu implied a monarchical form of government in which royal power was constrained by various intermediary institutions, such as the aristocracy, towns, and other corporate bodies, all of which enjoyed certain privileges or liberties by law that the monarch could not override. "The executive power," he argued, "ought to be in the hands of a monarch, because this branch of government, having need of dispatch, is better administered by one than by many: on the other hand, whatever depends on the legislative power is often times better regulated by many than by a single person."[5] For he was well aware from historical precedent that "every man invested with power is apt to abuse it, and to carry his authority as far as it will go." To prevent this abuse, "it is necessary from the very nature of things that power should be a check to power."[6]

To that end, Montesquieu proposed a division of political authority among three branches of government, an idea he borrowed from Great Britain's constitution, which he had encountered firsthand during his visit to the island nation in 1729 through 1731. According to this model, the king would wield executive power, the parliament or Estates would wield legislative power, and the law courts would wield judicial power, thus providing a system of checks and balances to prevent any single branch of government from asserting absolute authority over the others and to preserve popular liberty. Or as the baron explained it:

> When the legislative and executive power are united in the same person, or in the same body of magistrates, there can be no liberty; because apprehensions may arise, lest the same monarch or senate should enact tyrannical laws, to execute them in a tyrannical manner. Again, there is no liberty if the judiciary power be not separated from the legislative and executive. Were it joined with the legislative, the life and liberty of the subject would be exposed to arbitrary control; for the judge would be then the legislator. Were it joined to the executive power, the judge might behave with violence and oppression. There would be an end to everything, were the same man or the same body, whether of the nobles [oligarchy] or of the people [democracy], to exercise those three powers, that of enacting laws, that of executing the public resolutions, and that of trying the causes of individuals.[7]

"Here, then, is the fundamental constitution of the government we are talking of," concluded Montesquieu, "The legislative being composed of two parts, they check one another by the mutual privilege of rejecting." Both parts are further constrained by the executive power, meanwhile, "as the executive is by the legislative."[8] The baron defined this government of checks and balances as "moderate."

Montesquieu's perception of Great Britain's constitution was flawed, however. He was unaware of the way in which patronage and electoral corruption (e.g., the so-called "rotten boroughs") permitted a core of powerful peers to dominate the government. He was equally unaware of the cabinet system, which was only just emerging in the 1730s and 1740s as the real executive power within parliament's control. What he envisaged, nevertheless, was a constitutional form of monarchy that set strict limits on royal authority and placed the executive, legislative, and judicial powers in separate branches of government. For that reason, he also defended the political role and social privileges of the French aristocracy, "which ought to be hereditary," as a particular check on executive power.[9] Yet he developed his ideas at a time when, following the death of Louis XIV in 1715, there was a resurgence in France of the Second Estate, which sought actively to reclaim its traditional position in relation to the Crown, including its claims to a monopoly on state offices, military ranks, and social preeminence, in a concerted effort to weaken royal authority.

This coincidence points to a second possible interpretation of Montesquieu's thought. As a nobleman and a former *parlementaire*, the baron belonged to the very caste whose privileges he defended against royal interference, and the very institution—dominated by aristocrats—that was vested with a powerful judicial check on royal power. Was his sole purpose, therefore, to promote constitutional monarchy as the best form of government, or was part of his goal to strengthen the aristocracy as the major power-broker in France? His fellow *philosophe* Claude-Adrien Helvétius certainly suspected that this was the real motive. Similarly, despite his admiration for Montesquieu's great work, Voltaire never would have accepted an expanded role in government for the French aristocracy, especially in view of his opposition to the vested interests of a judiciary that consistently protected feudal privilege against royal prerogative. Hence his enthusiastic support of Louis XV, for example, when the usually lethargic monarch banished the disobedient judges of the *parlement* of Paris in 1771 for having opposed general reform measures designed to put the kingdom's poor finances permanently on a solid foundation. Louis' action prompted one of the *philosophe*'s more memorable quips, that it was better to be ruled by one lion of stout heart than 200 rats of his own kind.

But where Voltaire and many other exponents of the Enlightenment put their trust in princes because they lacked sufficient faith in the common man in order to advocate popular sovereignty, whatever lip service they might otherwise have paid to its ideals or at least to those of republicanism, Jean-Jacques Rousseau was the eighteenth century's leading apostle of democracy. "Only he is mad enough," Voltaire once wrote, "to say that all men are equal and that a state can survive without a hierarchy."[10] For Rousseau envisaged a whole new political structure that would make it possible for all people to enjoy freedom and full membership in civil society, without necessarily surrendering their personal sovereignty to government in exchange for those ends. Liberty and virtue were the two major underlying themes of Rousseau's political philosophy, and they were first developed in the prize-winning entry he wrote for an essay competition sponsored in 1750 by the Academy of Dijon. All submissions were to respond to the query, "Has the revival of the arts and sciences done more to corrupt or purify morals?"

Rousseau's answer to "one of the greatest and finest questions ever debated," as he put it,[11] was that far from serving humanity, science was bringing on ruin, and that human happiness—which belonged properly to man's life in a state of nature—had in no manner been improved by the onward march of civilization (see Document 25). On the contrary, progress was an illusion, and "what appeared to be advancement was in reality retrogression," for the attainment of virtue was impossible in modern sophisticated society by which "man was corrupted, and the greater the sophistication the greater the corruption."[12] Hence, Rousseau concluded, while

> Government and Laws provide for the safety and well-being of assembled men, the Sciences, Letters, and Arts, less despotic and perhaps more powerful, spread garlands of flowers over the iron chains with which men are burdened, stifle in them the sentiment of that original liberty for which they seemed to have been born, make them love their slavery, and turn them into what is called civilized peoples.[13]

Those civilized peoples cultivate, in turn, "the semblance of all the virtues without possessing them."[14]

Rousseau's position was both unorthodox and the object of scorn by various critics. In fact, he later recalled, "no sooner had my Essay appeared, than the defenders of literature fell upon me as if by common consent."[15] Among those "defenders" was Poland's King Stanislaus II Poniatowski (r. 1764–1795), one of Europe's Enlightened Despots, who affirmed the orthodox view that the arts and sciences "serve to make known the true, the good, and the useful of all kinds, a precious knowledge which, by enlightening minds, ought naturally to contribute to purifying morals."[16] The embattled *philosophe* defended his ideas nevertheless and in such a manner, he wrote, that his critics "no longer had the laugh on their side." This staunch republican was especially proud of his response to Stanislaus Poniatowski, for in it he "seized the opportunity of showing the public how a private individual could defend the cause of truth, even against a sovereign."[17]

Clearly undaunted by his critics, Rousseau returned to his theme in an essay he submitted for a second competition sponsored by the same Dijon Academy in 1754. This time, the entries were to respond to the question, "What is the origin of inequality among men, and is it authorized by natural law?" In his *Confessions*, the *philosophe* described in fascinating detail the thought processes by which he arrived at his answer. Residing near Saint-Germaine at the time, he took long walks in the surrounding forest, where he "sought and found the picture of those primitive times" in which men had lived originally, and of which he sketched out the history. In the process, boasted Rousseau,

> I demolished the pitiful lies of mankind; I dared to expose their nature in all its nakedness, to follow the progress of time and of the things which have disfigured this nature; and, comparing the man, as man has made him, with the natural man, and I showed him, in his pretended perfection, the true source of his misery....
> [And], seeing my fellow creatures following blindly the path of their prejudices, their errors, their misfortunes, and their crimes, I cried aloud to them with a feeble voice which they could not hear, "Fools, who continually complain of Nature, learn that you bring all your misfortunes upon yourselves.[18]

Concentrating on the first half of the competition's question, Rousseau began his new essay by developing the idea of man, living in an original state of nature (see Document 25), whose only genuinely human characteristics are his ability to feel pity or compassion, his freedom, and his capacity for moral self-improvement. Otherwise, this "natural" man lacked other qualities generally associated with humanity, such as language, reason, or the need for the society of other men. This depiction of "natural" man was entirely artificial, but it served as a useful foundation upon which Rousseau constructed his theory.[19] Society, argued the *philosophe*, came to be through an act of human will. Men living in the state of nature lived freely, but in isolation. They first associated, therefore, for mutual benefit and protection against the natural elements. But as society developed, and their original sense of consideration and obligation to others was eroded by the acquisition of property, men became wicked and corrupt.

Thus property, represented by the initial fencing-off of a bit of land for the sake of cultivation, was the real villain in the Rousseauian drama of the establishment of civil society.[20] Property was the source of human degradation, human inequality, and humanity's social ills. Or as Rousseau described it:

> The first man, who after enclosing a piece of ground, took it into his head to say, *this is mine*, and found people simple enough to believe him, was the real founder of civil society. How many crimes, how many wars, how many murders, how

many misfortunes and horrors, would that man have saved the human species, who pulling up the stakes or filling up the ditches should have cried to his fellows: Beware of listening to this imposter; you are lost, if you forget that the fruits of the earth belong equally to us all, and the earth itself to nobody![21]

With the acquisition of property there necessarily followed the inequality of fortunes, as the different talents and skills among men led some to prosper more than others. That prosperity, or accumulation of wealth, in turn enabled some men to enslave others, while also exciting such passions as envy and jealousy, and engendering conflict. Because society breeds strife, a system of laws was required to impose stability and good order. But the demand for laws that underlay the contractual agreement among men to live in civil society was heard loudest among the rich, whose right to life in common with everyone else was threatened equally with their alleged right to property. Hence, the unavoidable result of civil society's onward development was the institutionalization, perpetuation, and expansion of inequality (see Document 13). Rousseau concluded:

Such was, or must have been the origin of society and of law, which gave new fetters to the weak and new power to the rich; irretrievably destroyed natural liberty, fixed for ever the laws of property and inequality; changed an artful usurpation into an irrevocable right; and for the benefit of a few ambitious individuals subjected the rest of mankind to perpetual labor, servitude, and misery.[22]

Once more, Rousseau's essay, which failed to win the competition on this occasion, was the object of debate. Chief among his critics this time, however, was his intellectual rival, Voltaire, who wrote in his famous letter to the *philosophe* (dated August 30, 1755), "I have received your new book against the human race, [and] I thank you for it." "You will please mankind," continued Voltaire, "of whom you tell a few home truths, but you will not correct it," for "you depict with very true colors the horrors of human society, which out of ignorance and weakness sets its hopes on so many comforts." At this point, the elder man adopted a caustic tone as he sneered:

Never has so much wit been used in an attempt to make us like animals. The desire to walk on all fours seizes one when one reads your work. However, as I lost that habit more than sixty years ago, I unfortunately sense the impossibility of going back to it, and I abandon that natural gait to those who are worthier of it than you and I.[23]

With that snub, Voltaire dismissed Rousseau's work. This time, the latter had to admit that he was no match for one "who was arrogant, wealthy, supported by the credit of the great, brilliantly eloquent, and already the idol of the women and young men."[24]

The eight years between the composition of Rousseau's *Discourse on Inequality* and the publication in 1762 of his seminal work, *The Social Contract*, formed the most creative period of his life.[25] During this time he wrote a number of important works, including his *Letter to Voltaire on Providence* (a defense of religious faith in response to his rival's *Poem on the Lisbon Disaster*), his novel *La Nouvelle Héloïse*, and *Émile*, among others. Thus, by the time he finished *The Social Contract*, his political philosophy had matured fully. In this deeply republican book, Rousseau returned to his two major themes of liberty and virtue, to which he added the problem of political obedience. His purpose, as he explained in the work's introduction, was "to consider if, in political society, there can be any legitimate and sure principle of government, taking men as they are and laws as they might be."[26] In other words, Rousseau hypothesized about abstract problems that appeared to him "to emerge from philosophical reflection on the actual nature of man and the possible order of laws and government."[27]

The Social Contract opens with the famous declaration, "Man was born free, and he is everywhere in chains."[28] The rest of the book is devoted to explaining that transformation, and legitimizing the authority of a properly organized society over its citizens. Why is man enchained? Because he has had to exchange the state of nature for the state of civilization. In nature, men obeyed only their own whims and desires; they enjoyed absolute freedom of action. But in civilization, men must obey commands that, they know, do not come from within themselves.[29] Nevertheless, Rousseau argued, society is more important than its individual members, and through their relationship with the larger community they become moral beings capable of significant action—unlike independent human beings living alone in the state of nature, who are concerned only with themselves. The major question that arises from that relationship is, therefore, what kind of political or civil society best enables people to behave morally?

Rousseau envisaged an egalitarian republic, modeled after the ancient Greek polis or small cities in his native Switzerland, where direct participation in democratic decision-making would bind the individual to the community. In such a society, men would consent to be governed and would remain obedient to the law, because both the government and the law were created in accordance with the "General Will"—that is, "a higher will of some sort of which men's individual wills are a part."[30] The General Will itself is created by the social contract, into which men enter after reaching a point "where the obstacles to their preservation in a state of nature prove greater than the strength that each man has to preserve himself in that state."[31] Furthermore, the General Will "alone can direct the forces of the state in accordance with that end which the state has been established to achieve—the common good."[32]

Unlike earlier social contract theories, however, in Rousseau's philosophy individual members of political society do not surrender their sovereignty to an absolute monarch à la Thomas Hobbes; rather, the citizens treat the governing authorities as mere agents that are dismissible whenever the General Will thinks such dismissal is appropriate or necessary. By the same token, and "in order that the social pact shall not be an empty formula,"[33] the citizen who rejects the authority of the General Will becomes a rebel, which renders the democracy unstable.[34] Consequently, he "shall be constrained to [obey] by the whole body, which means nothing other than that he shall be forced to be free," for

> this is the necessary condition which, by giving each citizen to the nation, secures him against all personal dependence. It is the condition which shapes both the design and the working of the political machine, and which alone bestows justice on civil contracts—without it, such contracts would be absurd, tyrannical, and liable to the grossest abuse.[35]

The concept of the General Will is rather ambiguous, however, with the result that The Social Contract has been the subject of dispute for many years between those who view it essentially as a defense of individual liberty combined with a remarkable vision of direct democracy, and those who interpret it as an argument for "authoritarian collectivism" and an antecedent of modern totalitarianism, because the General Will "seems to sacrifice the individual too completely to the state."[36] That Rousseau should have pressed his analysis of human society to the point where he made the General Will sovereign and unimpeachable, observes historian Crane Brinton, "is an interesting example of where the human mind can go along the track of abstract thought." Rousseau as a person, continued Brinton,

> was an eccentric, an individualist, a man whose basic emotional objection to the pressure of any kind on the individual reminds one of [nineteenth-century American essayist Henry David] Thoreau's; and yet here he is ... one of the prophets [also] of modern collectivist society.[37]

Ultimately, for Rousseau and the philosophes in general, the question of forms of government involved also the question of the masses: "Should ordinary men, usually illiterate and almost definitely unfit for self-government, be allowed a share in political life? Should they be told the truth about religion and be trusted to exercise moral self-restraint? Or should they be kept in check by political lies?"[38] These were issues of evident concern for Voltaire, Montesquieu, d'Holbach, Hume, Rousseau, and others who attacked the problem of man's capacity to achieve liberty and virtue in civil society. Each tried to find a solution, whether by appealing to the principle of authority from above as exercised through Enlightened Despotism, popular sovereignty as expressed through republican or democratic ideals, or (in the case of William Godwin) philosophical anarchism. Nevertheless, the balance of opinion among these thinkers, writes Peter Gay, favored telling the truth as opposed to offering "organize[d] deceit."[39] "It is not a matter of indifference that the minds of people be enlightened," asserted Montesquieu in the introduction to *The Spirit of the Laws*:

> Could I but succeed so as to afford new reasons to every man to love his prince, his country, his laws; new reasons to render him more sensible in every nation and government of the blessings he enjoys, I should think myself the most happy of mortals.... [For] it is endeavoring to instruct mankind that we are best able to practice that general virtue which comprehends the love of all.[40]

Rousseau echoed the baron's outlook, adding in his own turn that as the citizen of a free state and a member of its sovereign body, "the very right to vote imposes on me the duty to instruct myself in public affairs, however little influence my voice may have in them."[41] Therein lay the key to human liberty in civil society and virtue, which Voltaire defined as "a commerce of beneficence." "No account should be taken of any man," he asserted, "who had no part in this commerce."[42] On that principle, at least, Voltaire and Rousseau could agree.

Notes

1. Brinton, 306.
2. Montesquieu, *Spirit of the Laws*, 150.
3. Paul Rahe, *Twilight of Liberty, Democracy's Drift to Soft Despotism* (New Haven, Ct: Yale University Press, 2008), 14.
4. Ibid., 425.
5. Ibid., 156.
6. Ibid., 150.
7. Ibid., 151–2.

8. Ibid., 160.

9. Ibid., 156.

10. Voltaire to the duc de Richelieu, June 22, 1762, Voltaire, *Selected Letters*, 231.

11. Jean-Jacques Rousseau, *Discourse on the Sciences and Arts, and Polemics*, Roger D. Masters, Christopher Kelley, and Judith R. Bush, trans. and eds. (Hanover, NH: University Press of New England, 1992), 3.

12. Jean-Jacques Rousseau, *The Social Contract*, Maurice Cranston, trans. (London: Penguin Books, 1968), 16.

13. Rousseau, *Discourse on Sciences and Arts*, 5.

14. Ibid.

15. Rousseau, *Confessions*, 354.

16. Stanislaus Poniatowski, "Reply to the Discourse which was awarded the prize of the Academy of Dijon," Rousseau, *Discourse on Sciences and Arts*, 29.

17. Rousseau, *Confessions*, 355.

18. Ibid., 378.

19. Jean-Jacques Rousseau, *The Social Contract and Discourse on the Origin of Inequality*, Lester G. Crocker, trans. and ed. (New York: Pocket Books, 1967), x–xi.

20. Ibid., x.

21. Rousseau, *Discourse on the Origins of Inequality*, Ibid., 211–12. (Emphasis Rousseau's.) Significantly, Voltaire had arrived at a parallel conclusion when exploring the origins of evil. Why are some men afflicted by "this plague of wickedness?" he asked. "It is because their leaders, being infected by the disease, communicate it to the rest of mankind.... The first ambitious man corrupted the earth." ("Evil," in Voltaire, *Philosophical Dictionary*, 300.)

22. Rousseau, *Discourse on the Origins of Inequality*, 228.

23. Voltaire to Rousseau, August 30, 1755, in Voltaire, *Selected Letters*, 179.

24. Rousseau, *Confessions*, 386.

25. Rousseau, *Social Contract*, 24.

26. Ibid., 49.

27. Ibid., 27.

28. Ibid., 49.

29. Brinton, 307.

30. Ibid.

31. Rousseau, *Social Contract*, 59.

32. Ibid., 69.

33. Ibid., 64.

34. Brinton, 309.

35. Rousseau, *Social Contract*, 64.

36. Brinton, 309.

37. Ibid.
38. Gay, *Party of Humanity*, 277.
39. Ibid.
40. Montesquieu, *Spirit of the Laws*, xii–xiii.
41. Rousseau, *Social Contract*, 49.
42. "Virtue," in Voltaire, *Philosophical Dictionary*, 398.

Denis Diderot, 1713–1784. Courtesy of Library of Congress.

Marie Jeanne (Philpon), Roland de la Platière, 1754–1793. Courtesy of Library of Congress.

Sir Isaac Newton, 1642–1727. Courtesy of Library of Congress.

John Locke, 1632–1704. Courtesy of Library of Congress.

Jean-le-Rond d'Alembert, 1717–1783. Courtesy of Library of Congress.

François-Marie Arouet (1694–1778), better known as Voltaire. Courtesy of Library of Congress.

Gabrielle-Émilie Le Tonnelier de Breteuil, marquise du Châtelet (1706–1749), Enlightenment writer and commentator. Courtesy of Library of Congress.

Messieurs Delaunay Flexelles Berthier Foulon et les deux Gardes du Corps qui ont été Decolés par le Peuple, voudraient passer jusquaux Champs Elisées en depit de Caron qui ne recoit dans sa barque que le S.r Remy François Boulanger Victime innocente de la Fureur Aristocratique: L'infortuné Calas et autres viennent le recevoir a l'autre bord.

Charon accepting the baker Sr. Remy, mistakenly beheaded, into his boat while rejecting several government officials and guardsmen, all who carry their severed heads atop pikes; on the opposite shore, the Elysian Fields, the unfortunate Jean Calas and others have come to welcome the baker. Courtesy of Library of Congress.

David Hume, 1711–1776. Courtesy of Library of Congress.

ENCYCLOPÉDIE,

OU

DICTIONNAIRE RAISONNÉ

DES SCIENCES,

DES ARTS ET DES MÉTIERS,

PAR UNE SOCIÉTÉ DE GENS DE LETTRES.

Mis en ordre & publié par M. *DIDEROT*, de l'Académie Royale des Sciences & des Belles-Lettres de Pruſſe ; & quant à la PARTIE MATHÉMATIQUE, par M. *D'ALEMBERT*, de l'Académie Royale des Sciences de Paris, de celle de Pruſſe, & de la Société Royale de Londres.

Tantùm ſeries junɛturaque pollet,
Tantùm de medio ſumptis accedit honoris! HORAT.

TOME PREMIER.

A PARIS,

Chez
BRIASSON, *rue Saint Jacques, à la Science.*
DAVID l'aîné, *rue Saint Jacques, à la Plume d'or.*
LE BRETON, Imprimeur ordinaire du Roy, *rue de la Harpe.*
DURAND, *rue Saint Jacques, à Saint Landry, & au Griffon.*

M. DCC. LI.

AVEC APPROBATION ET PRIVILEGE DU ROY.

Title page of Diderot's *Encyclopedie*, vol. 1, with angel amidst books, globes, measuring tools, and other instruments. Courtesy of Library of Congress.

James Boswell, 1740–1795. Courtesy of Library of Congress.

Immanuel Kant, 1724–1804. Courtesy of Library of Congress.

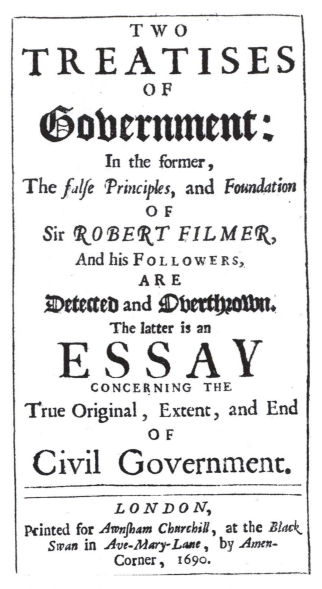

TWO
TREATISES
OF
Government:
In the former,
The *false Principles*, and *Foundation*
OF
Sir *ROBERT FILMER*,
And his FOLLOWERS,
ARE
Detected and Overthrown.
The latter is an
ESSAY
CONCERNING THE
True Original, Extent, and End
OF
Civil Government.

LONDON,
Printed for *Awnsham Churchill*, at the *Black*
Swan in *Ave-Mary-Lane*, by *Amen-*
Corner, 1690.

Title page of John Locke's *Two Treatises of Government* (London, 1690). Courtesy of Library of Congress.

Catherine II "the Great" of Russia, 1729/1762–1796. Courtesy of Library of Congress.

Joseph II, 1741/1765–1790. Courtesy of Library of Congress.

Charles-Louis de Secondat, baron de Brède et de Montesquieu, 1689–1755. Courtesy of the Library of Congress.

Jean-Jacques Rousseau, 1712–1778. Courtesy of Library of Congress.

BIOGRAPHIES

François-Marie Arouet (1694–1778)

Better known as Voltaire, François-Marie Arouet was born the son of a notary and minor government official in the city of Paris where, as a youngster, he quickly came under the influence of his free-thinking godfather, the abbé de Châteauneuf, who launched the boy's introduction to the progressive thinking of the day. Educated next by the Jesuits at the Collège Louis-le-Grand, where he earned a degree in philosophy in 1711, the young Arouet abandoned his original plan to pursue a career in law for one in literature, instead. He also began to participate in the early salon culture of the French capital, though his need to support himself led him to accept briefly the position of secretary at the embassy in the Dutch city of The Hague.

In 1713, Arouet returned to Paris, where his early forays into the literary world began to make his reputation and important enemies. As a result, for example, of a series of poems he wrote to satirize the licentious behavior of the French regent, the duc d'Orléans, Arouet was incarcerated briefly in the Bastille in 1717 and sent into temporary exile outside of Paris. At his return, however, he won popular acclaim in 1718 for his play *Oedipus*, which launched his literary fame. After this triumph, he adopted his famous pen name Voltaire. He also enjoyed the patronage of the French Queen (though her royal husband, Louis XV, was an ardent opponent), circulated in the city's growing salon culture, and began to learn English to read the philosophical works of John Locke. Although he admired the language, which was "rendered more agreeable by good English authors," its "coarseness and barbarism" did not yet "allow one to compare it [favorably] with Italian which is so pure and naturally elegant."[2] At the same time, he complained that "the frivolous authors of our Académie Française have weakened our language."[3] But

Voltaire's brilliant and caustic wit, already evident, soon put him in trouble once again. His criticism of a well-connected courtier, the chevalier de Rohan, led to a beating and a second incarceration in the Bastille (1726). Following his release, he sought refuge in England, where he remained until 1729.

Voltaire's introduction to the island kingdom was crucial in the subsequent development of his thought, perspectives, and direction of his literary career—for he was brought face to face with English structures of government, social institutions, religious toleration, freedom of expression and the press, political plurality, liberalism, empiricism, and commerce. The experience left an indelible impression on his mind, reinforced by his wide reading in the works of Locke and Sir Isaac Newton. He also encountered such prominent figures as the poet Alexander Pope and writer Jonathan Swift; he witnessed Newton's funeral procession in 1727 and engaged actively in many aspects of English life. In short, his exile in England led him to regard the kingdom's thought and institutions as the high point in human development.

Returning to France in 1729, Voltaire soon published his famous *Letters on England* with the view of introducing English ways, structures, and empiricism to the French reading public. The book, which he wrote "in that spirit of freedom which will perhaps bring persecution upon me in France,"[4] was condemned and burned by the royal authorities, and later regarded as "the first bomb thrown at the ancient regime."[5] The publication also forced Voltaire to flee Paris for the provinces in the company of his mistress, the marquise du Châtelet. Undaunted by the official opposition to his work, and likely because of it, the next fifteen years of Voltaire's life were highly productive. He wrote widely on various themes and collaborated with Mme. du Châtelet to introduce French and continental readers to Newtonian Science. Through careful speculation in French money markets, the *philosophe* built a personal fortune which allowed him the leisure to concentrate on his writing. As a result of his literary output, some of which was actually flattering to the French monarchy, Voltaire became the royal historiographer, a gentleman of the king's bed chamber, and a member of the prestigious French Academy. But Louis XV's enmity continued and, coupled with opposition from the devout party at the Bourbon court, compelled Voltaire and Mme. du Châtelet to once more abandon Paris in 1742 to avoid persecution. The next nine years were for Voltaire highly productive, however, though they ended in personal loss with the death in 1749 of his beloved mistress.

At this point, the grieving *philosophe* accepted an invitation from King Frederick II of Prussia to move to Berlin, an invitation the monarch had proffered several times. From 1750 to 1752, Voltaire lived at the Prussian court as a guest of his royal benefactor, one of the so-called Enlightened Despots of contemporary Europe, until the *philosophe's* tendency to dispute the ideas of others and to embroil himself in various tawdry scandals caused conflict and resulted in a rupture with the king (Hence Jean-Jacques Rousseau's expressed distaste "for brutal quarrels, *à la Voltaire*).[6] Compelled to leave Prussia, therefore, but prohibited from returning to his native country, the French free-thinker lived for a time in Geneva. But quarrels with the civic authorities over a critical article on Geneva published in the seventh volume of the great *Encyclopedia*, authored by Jean-le-Rond d'Alembert though inspired by Voltaire, forced the *philosophe* to move yet again. This time, he settled on his recently purchased château de Ferny, just inside the Swiss border, while also acquiring the estate of Tourney, just inside the French border, so that he always had a safe refuge whenever threatened with official censure in either country.

Over the next twenty years, Voltaire received a torrent of visitors, including the Scotsman James Boswell and the Venetian Giacomo Casanova; he carried on a voluminous correspondence with friends, acquaintances, and contacts across Europe, and he continued to write. One product of this period was perhaps his most famous book among modern readers, *Candide*. In this novel, he satirized the doctrine of Optimism which he derided as an acceptance of the status quo and one which had been proposed by the German philosopher Gottfried Wilhelm Leibniz, "whose only contribution," Voltaire once wrote, "was to put science into confusion."[7] These years also witnessed the great *philosophe's* outrage over the judicial murders of Jean Calas (1762) and the chevalier de la Barre (1766), both of whom had fallen victim to religious prejudice and persecution. Throughout his life he was concerned with the question of toleration. His call to "crush the infamous thing" has been widely regarded as an attack on religious intolerance.

Twenty-eight years after leaving Paris, Voltaire returned to his place of birth in spring 1778, to oversee the production of his new play, *Irène*. So great was his fame and so warm his reception that on the day of his first open house, he received over 300 callers. Yet he was prevented from enjoying the acclaim for very long. On May 18 he developed a kidney disease that killed him twelve days later. He was buried at the Abbey of Scellières according to Catholic ritual, but during the subsequent French Revolution his remains were reinterred in the Pantheon at Paris, a monument reserved for France's most highly honored literary figures.

Voltaire was among the greatest personalities of the French Enlightenment, a distinction shared by only a few others, such as Rousseau, Diderot, and Montesquieu. Throughout his life, the *philosophe* was an impassioned advocate of freedom of thought, religious toleration, scientific progress, patronage of the arts, judicial reform, and empiricism, all of which he had witnessed in practice during his three-year sojourn in England. Voltaire, together with the baron de Montesquieu, largely defined the direction taken by the first generation of Enlightenment thinkers. As a satirist of social conditions on behalf of human progress he was unequaled; as an historian he dealt not with the deeds of great men, but rather with the cultural, social, and political history of nations from a broad perspective; as the author of over ninety works; and as a polemicist his nimble wit and ability to distill difficult ideas into palatable terms comprehensible by a wider reading lay audience, he was without par. Voltaire has been described, in short, as the enduring model of the Enlightenment *philosophe*, whose prescription for the many "follies and evils which distress the best of all worlds" was simple: "Cling to morality, scorn theology, leave the quarreling to the obscurity of schools where it is begotten by pride, persecute only those unruly minds who disrupt society over matters of words. Amen!"[8] Shortly before he died, he told one of his friends: "I die adoring God, loving my friends, not hating my enemies, and detesting persecution."[9]

Marchese di Cesare Bonesana Beccaria (1738–1794)

Criminologist and economist, Marchese di Cesare Bonesana Beccaria wrote one of the most influential treatises on the reform of the law, *Dei delitti e delle pene* (*Crimes and Punishments*) in 1764. Born to a noble family, Beccaria studied at the college of Parma and the University of Padua and was greatly influenced by the ideas of Montesquieu. He not only contributed frequently to *Il Caffè*, a journal dedicated to reform, but also held the chair of economics at the College of Milan as well as a number of public offices, including counselor of state. For Beccaria the prevention of crime was far more important than its punishment. He was one of the first to call for the abolition of inhumane laws, especially those on capital punishment. In his writings he stressed that the certainty of punishment was more important than its severity and that the penalty should be proportional to the offense. He attacked many of the savage penalties of the day and denounced the use of torture and secret judicial proceedings. For him the laws in the 18th century were "the dregs of the most barbarous of centuries."[10] His book was widely read, commented upon by many of the thinkers of the day, such as Bentham and Voltaire, quickly translated into twenty-two languages, and helped to stimulate law reform throughout Europe. His other seminal work, *Elementi di economia pubblica*, in which he analyzed the division of labor and the growth of population, was not published until after his death. Although not as influential as his earlier work, it too was important and had an impact on other thinkers, such as Thomas Malthus.

James Boswell (1740–1795)

The future lawyer, essayist, chronicler, and biographer of the great Samuel Johnson (1709-1784), James Boswell was born in Edinburgh, Scotland, where he was given a strict Calvinist upbringing, of which he complained in later life. "I shall never forget the dismal hours of apprehension," he recorded in his journal, "that I have endured in my youth from narrow notions of religion while my tender mind was lacerated with infernal horror."[11] His childhood and youth were made additionally difficult by frequent conflict with his father, Alexander Boswell, Lord Auchinleck, a judge and stern parent who often disapproved of his son's personal and later professional choices. Finally unable to tolerate his situation at home any longer, the twenty-year-old James fled to London in 1760, but, unable to elude his father's grasp, he was soon discovered and sent back to Edinburgh on Lord Auchinleck's instructions. This youthful experience of family tension and parental conflict no doubt contributed to the incidents of deep depression that James suffered throughout his life.

Before surrendering to his father's wishes by taking up a career in law, during the early 1760s James was permitted to make the Grand Tour of Europe to finish his formal education like other young men of the period. He visited France, Prussia (where he saw Frederick II "the Great"), Switzerland, and Italy, and in the course of his journey he made a particular point of meeting prominent men, most importantly Voltaire and Rousseau, many of whose respective works the reflective young Scotsman had read with intense interest and understanding. The journals he kept and the letters he wrote during this period in his life reveal a man of acute perceptions with an eye for detail and a contemplative mind, who mused about many of the great philosophical and social issues of his day. He thus reflects many of the attitudes common to articulate individuals of the period.

In 1768, after returning to England, Boswell published an account of his visit to the Mediterranean island of Corsica, which propelled him into literary circles. In fact, within five years he had become prominent enough for election into the Literary Club of London, which had been established privately by the court painter Sir Joshua Reynolds (1723–1792) in honor of writer and critic Samuel Johnson, whom Boswell had met initially in 1763 during a second visit to the British capital. The two men became very close, Johnson as Boswell's surrogate father and Boswell as Johnson's occasional traveling companion and eventual biographer. Moreover, Johnson admired his young friend deeply, writing to him in August 1775 in that unique mixture of formality and intimacy which characterized eighteenth-century letters: "Never, my dear Sir, do you take it into your head that I do not love you; you may settle yourself in full confidence both of my love and my esteem; I love you as a kind man, I value you as a worthy man, and hope in time to reverence you as a man of exemplary piety. I hold you as Hamlet has it, 'in my heart of heart'."[12] In the meantime, Boswell's journal entries and reminiscences of the journey the two men made together to Scotland and the Hebrides islands provided much of the material for Boswell's *Life of Samuel Johnson* (1791), regarded by many scholars to be the finest biography in the English language. Boswell is noted, as well, for a number of other works, but today is best known through his journals, some of which were published posthumously.

Catherine II "the Great" (1729/1762–1796)

Born Sophia Augusta Frederica of Anhalt-Zerbst, Catherine II "the Great" was the daughter of a minor German prince employed by Frederick II, king of Prussia. Intelligent, accomplished, and well educated, as an adolescent Sophie was taken by her mother to Russia for the purpose of arranging a marriage between the young princess and her second cousin, Peter, the great grandson of Peter I "the Great" (1672/1682–1725) and heir to the imperial Russian throne after the death of Empress Elizabeth (1709/1741–1761). The marriage was duly contracted, and Sophie—who had taken the name Catherine, converted to Russian Orthodoxy, and began to learn the Russian language in preparation for her future life—wed Peter in 1745. The union was unhappy from the beginning, however, and both Peter and Catherine took lovers. Perhaps most notable among Catherine's many early liaisons was Stanislaus Augustus Poniatowski (1732/1764–1795), eventually the last king of Poland before the country was successively partitioned out of existence by the rulers of Prussia, Russia, and Austria-Hungary, and a so-called Enlightened Despot. Also during this period of her life, the princess continued to exercise her intellect, reading the works of the French Enlightenment and beginning a correspondence with such leading *philosophes* as Voltaire, Jean-le-Rond d'Alembert, and Denis Diderot, whom she supported financially in his later years.

Within six months of her ineffectual husband's accession to the Russian throne in December 1761 as Czar Peter III, Catherine organized a palace coup against him with the support of Russian troops and sympathetic noblemen, such as the brothers Olav. She thus usurped the crown, becoming czarina in her own right, and subsequently had her husband imprisoned and then murdered. The early part of her reign was devoted to consolidating her hold on the throne, as well as to continuing the process—begun by Peter I—of Westernizing the Russian state. To that end, Catherine convened a number of royal commissions to review policies related to church, military, and judicial matters. A series of legislative committees also provided her with data about existing conditions in her vast territories as a preliminary to reform, which aimed initially at the eradication of extreme forms of torture, the introduction of a degree of religious toleration, and the codification of Russian law, though the latter project was never achieved despite the czarina's good intentions. Nor did the deadly and widespread Pugachev rebellion of 1773 encourage Catherine toward further reform. On the contrary, the revolt so frightened her that, after its brutal suppression, her policies became more oppressive as she strengthened her relationship with the Russian nobility, to whom she granted greater privileges than those enjoyed by their Western European counterparts.

Nevertheless, Catherine is remembered as one of the eighteenth century's Enlightened Despots. In addition to reading widely among Enlightenment works, coupled with her efforts to encourage various *philosophes* such as d'Alembert and Diderot to accept appointments in Russia, she permitted a degree of freedom of the press; she reformed the Russian system of education; she sponsored the foundation of academies for specific intellectual and scientific studies; and she patronized the arts. Otherwise, many of her reform efforts in law, society, and economics proved to be superficial, a fact revealed by the so-called "Potemkin villages"—named after Catherine's chief minister—which consisted of false fronts specially erected and peopled by poor peasants disguised as prosperous farmers, that were set up for display purposes to impress the Habsburg emperor, Joseph II, and the Polish king, Stanislaus II Augustus Poniatowski, during their tour of Russia with their imperial hostess in 1787. Far closer to reality was Catherine's determination to rule her empire as an absolute monarch, to heighten Russia's profile in Western Europe. She also extended imperial territory by conquest to the Black Sea and the frontier of Eastern Poland before seizing the largest part of the Polish domain, a helpless kingdom that was thrice partitioned by she and her fellow monarchs in Prussia and Austria-Hungary.

Unlike two other notable Enlightened Despots, Frederick II and Joseph II, Catherine II lived long enough to witness not just the outbreak of revolution in France in 1789, but also its worst excesses. Like other monarchs of the day, she feared the spread of the revolutionary political message across Europe and vehemently opposed it. Consequently, the final years of her reign were marked by more repressive policies in Russia that heralded the autocracy for which the empire was noted in the nineteenth century.

Gabrielle-Émilie Le Tonnelier de Breteuil, Marquise du Châtelet (1706–1749)

The future writer and commentator on the science of Sir Isaac Newton and Gottfried Wilhelm Leibniz, Gabrielle-Émilie Le Tonnelier de Breteuil, marquise du Châtelet was the daughter of a well connected French aristocrat attached to the Bourbon court. After receiving an education in literature, science, and music, which was uncommon for young women in the period, she married Florent-Claude, marquis du Châtelet in 1725. Within a few years, however, husband and wife became estranged from each other, owing in large part to the marquis' extended absences as a soldier on campaign or as a royal governor.

Settling in Paris in 1730, Mme. du Châtelet became deeply involved in the salon culture of the day, and in 1733 she met Voltaire, who became her lover. Even after their affair had ended, they remained life-long friends and intellectual collaborators, particularly interested in promoting Newtonian science. In fact, it was she who protected Voltaire in 1734 when, faced with arrest following the publication of his *Philosophical Letters*. She gave him refuge at her country estate of Cirey. It was there that Voltaire and his mistress-benefactress began their collaboration on the *Elements of the Philosophy of Newton* (1738), which was designed to introduce the natural philosophy of the great English scientist to the French reading public in popular form.

Thereafter, Mme. du Châtelet began preparation of a separate book on physics, drawing not only upon Newtonian principles but also upon the work and ideas of Leibniz, some of whose theories she defended even over and above those of Newton on a number of subjects. Her research and writing resulted in the publication of the

Institutions of Physics (1740), which established her reputation as an intellectual in her own right. Mme. du Châtelet next embarked upon a French translation of Newton's *Principia Mathematica* in 1745, though the book was not published until 1756 and 1759, after her death. During her work on the project, which remains the only French-language translation of Newton's masterpiece to date, she met and began an affair with a young military officer named J.F. de Saint-Lambert. Soon pregnant by him, Mme. du Châtelet died of complications from childbirth in 1749 to the intense sorrow of Voltaire, who deeply regretted the loss of a woman he referred to as his one and only soul-mate. Indeed, it was for her sake that he had declined the repeated invitations of Frederick II of Prussia to go to Berlin prior to 1750, writing that "I cannot leave Madame du Châtelet to whom I have dedicated my life, not for any prince, not even for this one."[13] She was also among the very few women who participated actively in the scientific world of the Enlightenment, and whose independent contributions are important in their own right.

Marie de Vichy-Chaumond, Marquise du Deffand (1679–1780); Louise-Florence-Pétrouille de la Live, Madame d'Épinay (1726–1783); and Marie-Thérèse Rodet, Madame Geoffrin (1689–1777)

Marie de Vichy-Chaumond, Louise-Florence-Pétrouille de la Live, and Marie-Thérèse Rodet were three of the most famous hostesses to preside over the scintillating salon culture of eighteenth-century Paris. Intelligent, wealthy, and well-educated women, they vied with each other to attract the luminaries of the French Enlightenment into their homes, where they held regular gatherings that brought together the intellectual and social elites of the day. Among the *philosophes* who graced their separate salons were Voltaire, Jean-le-Rond d'Alembert, the baron de Montesquieu, Jean-Jacques Rousseau, Denis Diderot, the baron d'Holbach, and Claude-Adrien Helvétius, as well as distinguished foreign guests such as Scottish philosopher David Hume and the Polish king, Stanislaus II Augustus Poniatowski. Among the three women, however, it was the salon of Mme. Geoffrin—a *bourgeois* married to a man of commerce, unlike her two social rivals, both of whom were aristocrats—that emerged by 1730 to dominate the Parisian social scene. It was also Mme. Geoffrin who exercised the most influence through her material support of various *philosophes* in need.

Although she received her early education in a convent, the future marquise du Deffand was a spirited girl, rebellious by nature, who opposed certain conventional behavior expected of her gender and social status of the day. Her unhappy marriage to a military officer eventually resulted in separation in 1772, which left Mme. du Deffand free to pursue her own interests. Within a short time, she became the mistress of the French regent, the duc d'Orléans (1674–1723), and thus began associating with the leading political and intellectual figures of the period. While in Paris, she held a weekly salon, assisted by her niece, Mlle. Julie de Lespinasse (1732–1776), until the two quarreled and the younger woman began to attend the gatherings held by Mme. Geoffrin. Both the marquise and her niece were on intimate terms, wrote Rousseau, with such prominent *philosophes* as Voltaire and d'Alembert, "with the latter of whom Madmoiselle de Lespinasse finally lived—of course, in a most respectable manner: let no one imagine that I mean anything else."[14] Although she authored no major works in her own name, the lively correspondence that the marquise du Deffand maintained throughout her life with prominent individuals casts light on many of the social and cultural elements of the Enlightenment and eighteenth-century Paris.

At least one prominent individual wrote critically of the marquise, however, whom he pitied "on account of the loss of her eyesight" later in life. Complained Rousseau, she exercised such little power of discernment that he was discouraged "from the attentions which I was ready to pay her." He also found distasteful Mme. du Deffand's "extravagant passion for trifling displays of wit; the importance which she attached to the most contemptible rags which appeared, whether complimentary or abusive; the despotic violence of her oracular utterances; her exaggerated prepossessions in favor of or against everything, which prevented her from speaking of any subject except hysterically; her incredible prejudices, her unconquerable obstinacy, [and] her unreasoning enthusiasm to which she was carried away by the stubborness of her impassioned judgments." Although Rousseau understood "how greatly a woman of this character was to be feared," he chose rather to expose himself "to the scourge of her hatred than to that of her friendship."[15]

Her contemporary, madame d'Épinay, was also a woman of noble birth whose marriage was equally unfulfilling. To find solace, she turned to the literary and cultural world of the French capital, immersing herself in the salon culture of the age. Described by Rousseau as "amiable, witty, and talented, and certainly a very desirable acquaintance," madame d'Épinay also had "a very exacting disposition, [but] was endowed by Nature with qualities admirably adapted to regulate or counter balance its extravagances."[16] Until she established her own salon at her country seat of La Chevrette near Saint-Denis, where Rousseau lived as her guest in the mid-1750s at The Hermitage, a pavilion situated on the estate, she frequented the gatherings held by Mme. Geoffrin and the marquise du Deffand. Unlike the other two hostesses, however, madame d'Épinay was a writer of modest talent who authored several works on such topics as education—in addition to her correspondence—that, although not considered to be efforts of the first rank in terms of their quality of thought, are nonetheless worth considering.

Of the three hostesses, however, it was the bourgeois-born Mme. Geoffrin who presided over one of the most brilliant salons in contemporary Paris. Described as an intelligent, attractive, strong-willed, and practical woman, she held gatherings in her home at the Hôtel de Rambouillet twice a week, which drew the intellectual, social, and artistic elites of the day. She also liberally supported the *philosophes* with money and influence; in fact, it was owing to her financial largesse that production of the grand *Encyclopedia* was able to resume after 1759, when publication stalled owing to the lack of money and problems with official censorship. Not only Frenchmen but also foreigners were attracted to her salon, which came to dominate the Parisian social scene.

Although apart from their surviving correspondence and, in madame d'Épinay's case, a few minor written works, these three women published nothing of significance. Their real contribution was exercised through the salons over which they each presided, and demonstrates the important role of the hostess during the eighteenth century in providing venues for the exchange of Enlightenment ideas and provided support, as well as protection, for the *philosophes* who generated those ideas.

Jean-le-Rond d'Alembert (1717–1783)

The future French mathematician, writer, and co-editor (after 1750) of the great *Encyclopedia* with Denis Diderot, Jean-le-Rond d'Alembert was the illegitimate child of Mme. de Tencin and Louis Camus, chevalier Destouches-Canon. Because his mother, a salon hostess, felt no affection for her newborn son, he was abandoned on the steps of a baptistry, called the church of Saint-Jean le Rond, which was part of Nôtre Dame cathedral in Paris. Hence, in accordance with contemporary custom, the infant was given that name. Despite Mme. de Tencin's lack of interest in the welfare of her child, the chevalier

Destouches remained partially engaged in his son's life. He placed the youngster in the home of a Parisian glass maker, where the child was reared in partly bourgeois circumstances, and provided also for his education. In addition, the chevalier left the boy a modest inheritance that paid him a small annuity. It was doubtless owing to his illegitimate birth, the humble social circumstances of his upbringing, and his association with members of the artisan class in Paris that Jean-le-Rond later developed a philosophy that praised, rather than derided, such a humble background for a man of letters.

After studying under the Jesuits and taking a degree in law in 1735, Jean-le-Rond, who by this time had adopted the surname of d'Alembert, indulged his interests in mathematics and mechanics. He evidently prospered, for in 1741 he was elected to the astronomy section at the Academy of Sciences in Paris, and in 1745 he was awarded an annual pension. His publications in calculus, terrestrial and celestial mechanics, and related subjects were numerous and well received by the intellectual community. In the mid-1740s, he also joined the salon culture of Paris, in which he was a popular figure. One of his admirers was Giacomo Casanova (1725–1798), the Venetian traveler, writer, and adventurer, who encountered the *philosophe* on a visit to France at the salon of Mme. De Graffigny. "That great philosopher," lauded Casanova, "had in the highest degree the talent of never seeming learned when he was in an agreeable company of people who were not scientists. He also had the art of imparting intelligence to those who argued with him." Indeed, added Casanova, "I never knew a man more naturally modest than the famous D'Alembert."[1] The *philosophe*'s association with and participation in the salon, particularly of Mme. Geoffrin, did more than just spread his fame, however. That relationship bore additional fruit, because it was she who arranged for his appointment in 1759 to the prestigious French Academy.

In 1750, d'Alembert was approached by Denis Diderot to co-edit the great *Encyclopedia*, for which d'Alembert also wrote the preliminary discourse published with the first volume of the project the following year. Then in 1759 he was invited (but declined the invitation) by Frederick II of Prussia to preside over the Berlin Academy. He nevertheless accepted a pension from the king and paid two visits to the Prussian capital. He similarly refused an invitation from Catherine II of Russia in 1762 to become tutor to her son and successor, Paul. He preferred to remain in his native France, the intellectual center of the Enlightenment, where he was appointed the perpetual secretary of the French Academy in 1772. D'Alembert died eleven years later after a long and distinguished career, having made important contributions to eighteenth-century science.

Denis Diderot (1713–1784)

Denis Diderot came from an artisan or petty bourgeois background. Born into a deeply religious family at the French town of Langres and educated in his youth by the Jesuits, Diderot originally contemplated joining the priesthood, though his views changed over time as he became increasingly skeptical of Catholic Christianity. At the age of sixteen, he moved to Paris where, in 1732, he earned a Masters degree at the University of Paris. Having by this time abandoned his earlier idea of taking holy orders, he thought of studying law or medicine, though he soon relinquished these ideas too. Instead, he undertook independent study, supporting himself, in the meantime, as a tutor and translator of English books into French. The latter activity not only opened the door to a literary career but also brought him into contact with the printer André le Breton. Their resulting association provided the inspiration for publication of the grand *Encyclopedia*, perhaps the greatest legacy in print of the Enlightenment, a legacy apparent even to contemporaries. "I consider the enterprise of the *Encyclopédie*," wrote Voltaire in 1760, to be "the most beautiful monument that could be erected to the honor of science."[17]

Named general editor of the ambitious project in 1747, Diderot exploited his growing contacts among the leading *philosophes* of the day to assist him in the task by contributing articles for the encyclopedia, according to their individual areas of expertise. He prevailed upon Rousseau, for example, to "undertake the musical part of it," in view of the *philosophe*'s musical background and livelihood as a copiest of musical scores.[18] In 1750 he also invited Jean-le-Rond d'Alembert to serve as co-editor. For the next quarter century, Diderot devoted his time and energy to the project, progress on which was interrupted periodically by financial difficulties (for which he received generous assistance from the salon hostess, Mme. Geoffrin) and official censorship. Though he also was engaged in the intellectual circles of eighteenth-century Paris and wrote a large number of important, even radical, works, he rarely published but circulated his efforts in manuscript form, instead. His experience of imprisonment for several months in 1749 in the medieval fortress of Vincennes just outside Paris, owing to such earlier publications as his *Pensées politiques* and his *Lettre sur les Aveugles*, his editorship of the *Encyclopedia* project, and his continuous struggles with the royal censors "had made a terrible impression upon him," wrote Rousseau, and discouraged him from further publishing his own writings.[19]

But these hindrances did not prevent Diderot from associating with d'Alembert, Voltaire, Rousseau, and the other major intellectual figures of the French Enlightenment, nor did they prevent him from corresponding with such crowned heads as Empress Catherine II of Russia, who not only invited him to Russia in 1773, but also sought his advice in reforming the Russian law code, even if she ultimately rejected most of the suggestions he made. Diderot thus acquired a Europe-wide reputation, which earned him election to several learned academies across the continent. Moreover, because of his position as chief editor of the *Encyclopedia*, and in view also of his own impressive body of written work, even if it was circulated largely in manuscript to avoid censorship, Diderot was well-placed to influence significantly the development of Enlightenment ideas, and to spread them across national and international boundaries far beyond the narrow confines of the salon culture or the intellectual hub of Paris. Certainly by the time of his death in 1784, he was regarded as one of the most prominent *philosophes* in Europe and a leading figure of the Enlightenment.

Frederick II "the Great," King of Prussia (1712/1740–1786)

Frederick II "the Great" was born the son and successor of Frederick William I (1688/1713–1740), the "soldier king," with whom the young prince's relationship was stormy. An impressionable youth whose interests tended toward letters, philosophy, and music, Frederick was very different from his gruff father in temperament, values, and ideas about the exercise of royal power and the role of government. In fact, the prince, whose pastimes included playing the flute, writing verse, and reading widely in the works of the French Enlightenment, represented everything that Frederick William despised; his pastimes, by contrast to those of his son, consisted of hunting, drinking with his male friends, and drilling the troops of the Prussian army. In addition, where Prince Frederick admired French culture and, despite his German heritage, spoke and wrote French throughout his life almost exclusively, Frederick William detested anything French. The tensions between father and son only increased when the king discovered that the prince, together with his mother Sophia Dorothea of Hanover, secretly sought to ally Prussia with Great Britain, as opposed to Austria. To escape his father's wrath, Frederick attempted to flee the country, but he was captured, court-martialed, and reprimanded by the king. Following a public reconciliation between the two, however,

Prince Frederick devoted more attention to matters of government and developed his political views.

Upon his father's death in May 1740, the prince succeeded to the Prussian throne as Frederick II. Almost immediately, he opened war with Austria by seizing the province of Silesia from Empress Maria Theresa, whose succession to the Habsburg throne the same year provided the stimulus for what grew rapidly into a European war (1740–1748) over the Habsburg inheritance, which the late Emperor Charles VI had tried throughout his reign to preserve intact for his daughter. Frederick II's seizure of Silesia was thus a pure act of opportunism that revealed his double intention of elevating Prussia into a major European power and increasing the kingdom's territorial possessions even by conquest. Prussia's new international status was confirmed by the Treaty of Aix-la-Chapelle (1748), which ended the War of the Austrian Succession, but which also rendered Maria Theresa and the Habsburg Empire implacable enemies of the king.

With the restoration of peace, Frederick attended to domestic matters, and between 1746 and 1756 he launched a major program of economic, religious, legal, and political reform that not only reflected the king's liberal views, thus earning him the reputation as the epitome of the Enlightened Despot in Europe, but that served at the same time to strengthen royal authority and further centralize the Prussian state. Among his efforts, Frederick promoted manufacturing and imported talented workers from outside Prussia to that end; he undertook improvements in agriculture by draining swamps, introducing new crops, encouraging cultivation of unused land, and providing state loans to assist farmers; he instituted a high degree of religious toleration for the protection of his Catholic and Jewish subjects in the largely Lutheran kingdom; and he began the process of codifying Prussian law to streamline the existing judicial system, to make it more rational, efficient, free from external influence, and humane. Already he had relaxed state censorship of the press in 1740, the same year that he mounted the throne and published the *Anti-Machiavel*, a short work that sanctioned the ruler's obligation to govern for the benefit of his subjects. Finally, he sponsored a major building program in the Prussian capital of Berlin, which included a new opera house and government buildings, improvements to Charlottenburg Palace, and the construction of a summer residence at nearby Potsdam, which he called "Sans Souci" (Without Worry).

In 1756, Frederick again initiated continental war by invading the Electorate of Saxony. This time, however, he faced a strong coalition of enemies, including France, Austria, and Russia, while his only major ally was Great Britain. The Prussian monarch nevertheless demonstrated his genius as a soldier, just as he had proved himself to be an able administrator, though toward the end of the Seven Years' War (1756–1763) his kingdom was exhausted and at the point of defeat. But he was saved by a sudden shift in alliances brought about by the death of the Russian Empress Elizabeth and the succession of Peter III, who deeply admired the Prussian monarch. With the conclusion of peace, Frederick returned to the business of domestic government, as he rebuilt the state and reorganized the administration. As he grew older, however, the king became increasingly suspicious of his servitors, and thus instituted a system of internal surveillance over the bureaucracy. Despite this development toward the end of his life, Frederick II maintained his belief that the monarch's primary duty as first servant of the state was to govern for the welfare of his subjects, ensure military efficiency, and spend royal revenues responsibly. For these reasons, coupled with his reforms and published statements, his rule was regarded by his contemporaries as the outstanding example of Enlightened Despotism.

David Hume (1711–1776)

The future philosopher, historian, economist, and essayist, David Hume was born into the Scottish gentry and as a youth was educated at the University of Edinburgh, where he took a strong dislike to formal education because of its rigid structure. Hence, he devoted himself to an independent program of reading and study that might have contributed to his nervous breakdown in 1729, partly as a result of exhaustion. Following his recovery, he turned his hand unsuccessfully to business. When that effort failed, he moved to France in 1734 to devote his time to study and composition of his *Treatise on Human Nature*. Although the book was not warmly received after his return to England three years later, Hume nevertheless embarked upon an intellectual career. To be sure, his second effort, *Essays Moral and Political* (1741–1742) enjoyed better acclaim than his first publication; however, his writing was not enough to sustain him. Hence, he applied for an academic position at his *alma mater*, the University of Edinburgh, but was refused. Through his philosophical works, it appeared to his detractors that he was heretical in his religious views, if not openly atheistic. James Boswell shared these misgivings about his fellow-countryman's beliefs, writing that "I talked with vehemence against David Hume and other infidels who destroyed our [moral] principles and put nothing firm in their place."[20]

Between 1744 and 1763, Hume held a variety of jobs as tutor, private secretary, and librarian, among others, but during this period of his life he continued to think and to write. He published in succession *An Enquiry Concerning Human Understanding* (1748), arguably his greatest work, as well as the *Political Discourses* (1752), a *History of England* (1754–1762, which, wrote Boswell, forgetting for a moment his suspicion about Hume's religious principles, "entertains and instructs one ... elevates my mind and excites noble feelings of every kind"),[21] and the *Four Dissertations* (1757, including the Natural History of Religion, Of the Passions, Of Tragedy, and Of the Standards of Taste). Returning to France in 1763 as secretary to the British ambassador for the negotiations over the Treaty of Paris, ending the Seven Years' War (1756–1763), Hume immediately joined the salon culture of the French capital where he was warmly welcomed. On his return to Britain three years later, he was even accompanied by Jean-Jacques Rousseau, though the two men soon quarreled and parted ways. After serving for two more years in London as under-secretary of State, Hume went back to Edinburgh in 1769, where he remained until his peaceful death in 1776. As his friend and contemporary, the economist Adam Smith, wrote at the time, "thus died our most excellent, and never-to-be forgotten friend; concerning whose philosophical opinions men will no doubt judge variously, everyone approving or condemning them according as they happen to coincide, or disagree with his own; but concerning whose character and conduct there can scarce be a difference of opinion."[22]

Among the most controversial figures of the eighteenth-century Enlightenment, Hume contributed significantly to shaping the movement's ideas on epistemology (the nature and origins of human knowledge), psychology, and moral and natural philosophy. Yet, it was in the French kingdom, not Great Britain (noted Rousseau), that Hume had acquired "a great reputation ... especially amongst the Encyclopedists, through his commercial and political treatises." In fact, before they quarreled, the *philosophe* also confessed that he had "entertained as high an opinion of [Hume's] virtue as of his genius," and had actively sought to make the acquaintance "of this singular man and [gain] his friendship."[23] Voltaire echoed these sentiments, referring to his Scottish counterpart as "a true philosopher"[24]—praise, indeed, from Caesar.

Joseph II (1741/1765–1790)

Joseph II was the eldest son and heir of Holy Roman Emperor Francis Stephen of Lorraine (1708/1745–1765) and Maria Theresa

(1717/1740–1780), whose accession to the throne of the Habsburg dominions of her late father, Charles VI, provided the impetus for a European war over the Austrian succession, during which the wealthy province of Silesia was lost permanently to Frederick II of Prussia, Maria Theresa's life-long nemesis. Upon his father's death in 1765, Joseph, whom one biographer described as having a "sublime confidence in the infallibility of his own judgment," [25] became Holy Roman Emperor and ruled the Habsburg territories jointly with his hard-working mother until she died in 1780.

His brother Leopold, an astute judge of character, described his sibling as a ruler who "tolerates no contradiction and is imbued with arbitrary, brutal principles and the most severe, brutal, and violent despotism … He despises everything which is not his own idea and likes and wants around him only those men who have no talent, who obey like nothing more than mere machines, and who give him credit for everything that is done."[26] Thereafter, he ruled the empire alone, earning the reputation in the meantime as one of Europe's most committed Enlightened Despots. Even more, perhaps, than his fellow monarchs (and occasional rivals), Frederick II of Prussia and Catherine II of Russia, Joseph II was devoted to the idea that state policy should be guided by humanitarian considerations, and for this purpose he inaugurated an almost radical reform program from above, while still maintaining the fundamental policies initiated by his late mother to consolidate and strengthen the Habsburg realm and imperial power.

Dedicated to the ideals of social, or at least legal, equality, humanitarianism, religious toleration, universal education, and economic prosperity, when the pace of Joseph's reform program appeared to move too slowly for his tastes, he asserted his authority in the belief that meaningful change had to come from the ruler, in whom resided all legitimate authority to effect such change. At once idealistic and authoritarian, like his fellow monarchs in contemporary France, Prussia, and Russia, Joseph refused to share his sovereignty with lesser centers of power (e.g., the nobility, the guilds, the Catholic Church, and so on), because he believed these various intermediate groups would more likely promote their own interests rather than the common good. In the process, the emperor directly attacked traditional institutions, privileges, and corporate bodies that appeared to obstruct his reform measures, which he was impatient to implement. But his efforts served only to antagonize many constituencies within the Habsburg realm, from aristocrats to peasants, and hence the close of his reign was marked by domestic strife and revolt.

Despite this turmoil, Joseph II remained committed to Enlightenment ideals to the end of his life. As ruler of one of Europe's greatest powers, he continued the centralization of the state and political authority in the hands of the monarchy, but at the same time he limited the influence of the Catholic Church in secular affairs and confiscated some Church lands, though he saw the value of religion as a moral force in society. He also worked to secularize education and to place marriage more fully under state supervision. He even clashed with the papacy over matters of Church governance, and introduced a measure of religious toleration for his non-Catholic subjects. In addition to these ecclesiastical reforms, Joseph sought to improve economic affairs by implementing a universal land tax and placed restrictions on the fiscal privileges of certain corporate groups; he similarly relaxed official censorship of the press. But as conservative opposition grew to what was regarded as an assault on traditional entitlements and privileges, Joseph responded with a heavy hand by restricting the freedom of specific groups, outlawing others (e.g., the freemasons), and generally curtailing individual liberties under the law, all of which incited still more intense opposition from many of his subjects and contradicted, ironically, many of the very ideals he held. Joseph was not even popular with his ministers, one of whom, Kaunitz, upon hearing of the emperor's death remarked: "That was good of him."[27] As a result of the mounting domestic strife, following his death in 1790 most of the emperor's reforms were rescinded by his successor, Leopold II (1747/1790–1792), who shared many of his late brother's Enlightenment ideals but who recognized the impracticability of his reform policies.

Immanuel Kant (1724–1804)

Born in Königsberg, then part of Prussia, Immanuel Kant was the sixth of nine children to a father who was a sadler and a devout Pietist. Kant's early education did not endear him to this popular movement but rather alienated him. He later derided Pietists as those who tastelessly make the idea of religion dominant in every discourse. At the age of 10 he attended the Collegium Fredericianum where he excelled in classics but later studied math and physics. Poverty forced him to serve as a private tutor for a number of years, where he had the opportunity to read widely and was greatly influenced by David Hume and Saint-Pierre before he became professor of logic and metaphysics in 1770. A very influential and prolific author, he wrote *Critique of Pure Reason* (1781), a *Prologomena* to it (1783), *Foundations of the Metaphysic of Morals* (1785), *Critique of Judgment* (1790), *Perpetual Peace* (1795), *Metaphysic of Morals*

(1798), to name but a few. A highly disciplined individual, Kant rose every day at 5 A.M. His movements were so predictable that his contemporaries remarked that they could set their clocks by them. In 1792 the government forbade him from either lecturing on or publishing about religious matters because they believed that his ideas undermined Christianity. Depressed, Kant stopped lecturing completely in 1797. A courteous man, Kant had, however, retained his sense of humor and pointed out in his treatise on peace that "To Eternal Peace" had been a satirical notice posted by a Dutch innkeeper that indicated a graveyard. Kant was also widely regarded as gregarious, charming, and witty. In his later life he suffered from melancholy and a prolonged deterioration of both mind and body and was rarely coherent in the last two years of his life. Kant himself recognized his growing infirmity and remarked as early as 1799: "I am old and weak. Consider me as a child."[28] He died gently and quietly. His breathing simply stopped.

John Locke (1632–1704)

The future moral, political, and natural philosopher John Locke was born into an English family of Puritan background, the son of an attorney. As a youth, Locke was educated first at Westminster College in the 1640s, before attending Oxford University. There he took his Bachelor of Arts degree in 1656, lectured for a time while he studied for his Masters degree, and finally entered Oxford's medical school. Although he earned his M.D., he rarely practiced medicine. Instead, while at university he met (in 1666) Anthony Ashley Cooper, the future statesman and first earl of Shaftsbury. Not only did the two men become close friends, but Locke served Cooper successively as his personal physician and private secretary. The latter activity ushered the future philosopher into the world of English politics, because of his friend and employer's membership in the liberal Whig Party, which opposed the succession of King Charles II's Catholic brother, James Duke of York, to the English throne after the childless Stuart monarch's death. Eventually, Whig opposition culminated in the so-called Popish Plot—a conspiracy in which Cooper was involved to spread fear by means of allegations that the Catholics near to Charles' throne were planning to return the kingdom to the papal fold. When the Whig plot was discovered, Cooper, among other participants, was tried but acquitted for treason, after which he fled to safety in the United Provinces in 1682. Also suspected of complicity, though he was never arrested, Locke joined his employer in exile a year later, following a massive book-burning of "treasonable" literature at Oxford by royal command.

Between 1683 and 1688, Locke worked closely with Cooper and became involved to some extent in the events that led to the outbreak of the "Glorious Revolution" (1688), which brought about limited constitutional monarchy in Great Britain under William II of Orange and his wife Mary, the elder daughter of deposed King James II (r. 1685–1689), who accepted the crown offered to them by Parliament in return for certain concessions that restricted royal authority. In 1689, Locke returned to England, never to leave again, as part of the escort for the newly declared Queen Mary II. Thereafter, Locke continued to study and to write, while serving also as tutor to the grandson of his old friend and benefactor, Anthony Cooper, who was now earl of Shaftsbury. Locke was also appointed through political influence to the Board of Trade and Plantations, a post he retained until failing health compelled him to resign in 1700. He died four years later.

Although it was not until 1689, when he was fifty-seven years old, that Locke published any of his works, he had already begun to write. His works reveal the influence on his thought by many of the dominant ideas of the day. Not only had he spent his youth and begun his education at a time of political crisis in England during the Civil Wars of the 1640s between King Charles I and Parliament, in which his father had fought for the Puritans, Locke had the opportunity, as well, to meet some of the leading scientists and thinkers of the period while convalescing from an illness in France from 1675 to 1679. Moreover, his close association with Anthony Cooper and the Whig party exposed him to the religious tensions over the looming succession crisis, among other issues, and gave him direct insight into English politics, constitutional matters, and the question of toleration, all of which formed the subjects of his philosophy. Although his earliest printed works, including the *Letter of Toleration* (1689), the *Two Treatises of Government* (1690), and the *Reasonableness of Christianity* (1695), were published anonymously at his direction, it became widely known among contemporary readers that he was the author of each. In his *Two Treatises on Government* he argues that man in a state of nature forms a government to protect his rights. Should the government no longer protect his rights to life, liberty, and property then man has the right to rebel. This contractual theory of government then justified rebellion and has often been cited as an apologia of the Glorious Revolution. In his *Essay Concerning Human Understanding* (1690), Locke attacked Descartes' concept of innate ideas and argued that all ideas came from man's experiences, through the senses, and that man was in essence a *tabula rasa*. An original thinker, he also wrote *Some Thoughts Concerning Education* (1693). Like many of his contemporaries he believed in religious toleration, but with limitations. Toleration, for example, could not be extended to those who did not tolerate others, those who were atheists, or those who owed allegiance to foreign powers. He appreciated the ephemeral nature of life and remarked the day before he died that "after all this life is nothing but vanity."[29]

As one of the early and most prominent theorists of human psychology and the origins of knowledge, the ideals of civil liberties within constitutional monarchy, the social contract theory, the need for religious toleration, and the structure of government based upon a system of checks and balances, Locke was one of several leading seventeenth-century thinkers who laid the intellectual foundations for the Enlightenment that unfolded during the next century. Locke saw reason as "the candle of God"[30] and believed that "there is truth opposite to falsehood, that it may be found if people will it and is worth seeking, and is not only the most valuable, but the pleasantest thing in the world."[31] "Never, perhaps," eulogized Voltaire, "has a wiser, more methodical mind, a more precise logician existed than Mr. Locke."[32] His basic assumptions about the development and application of man's Reason, Natural Law, inalienable rights, religious freedom, and so on profoundly influenced such prominent *philosophes* as Diderot, Montesquieu, Rousseau, and Voltaire, and did much to shape the development and direction of Enlightenment thought.

Charles-Louis de Secondat, Baron de Brède et de Montesquieu (1689–1755)

Charles-Louis de Secondat was born into a recently ennobled family that resided near the French port city of Bordeaux. Although his great grandfather had been elevated into the aristocracy as a reward for services rendered under King Henri IV (1553/1593—1610) during France's sixteenth-century civil wars of religion, the family became part of the nobility of the robe during the subsequent generation with the purchase of offices in the *parlement* (law court) of Bordeaux. As a youth, the future *philosophe*, historian, and satirist studied in Paris and at the University of Bordeaux, where he took a degree in law. He was thus well prepared by his education to inherit his late uncle's office as *président à mortier* (presiding judge over one section of the *parlement*) in 1716, a position he held for the next eleven years.

During this professional period of his life, Montesquieu engaged in his judicial responsibilities, while also participating in the local Bordeaux Academy as director and tending to his family's vineyards. In the meantime, he entered the literary world with wide acclaim in 1721, following the publication that year of his famous work, the *Persian Letters*, which was a penetrating satire of French society and government during the regency (1715–1723) of the duc d'Orléans. Inspired by the book's success and warm reception, Montesquieu moved to Paris where he quickly indulged in the salon culture of the day and in 1728 was elected to the prestigious French Academy. Shortly afterward, he relinquished his position with the *parlement* of Bordeaux and sold his office in the process.

Now free from all official obligations, Montesquieu embarked on an extended tour of Europe, during which he spent two-and-a-half years in Britain, from 1729 to 1731. While there, he joined the Freemasons, listened to debates in parliament, studied the British constitution, and examined the English political system. He was also elected to the Royal Society of London, arguably a greater distinction even than his reception into the French Academy, because of the English institution's illustrious membership and international reputation. The observations he made and the information he gathered during his European tour, meanwhile, provided much of the material for his next two works. The first, entitled *Considerations on the Causes of the Greatness of the Romans and Their Decline* (1734), received only modest praise, though Voltaire contrasted it favorably with *The Persian Letters*. "Only time can fix the value of each thing," wrote the great *philosophe* to the marquis de Vauvenargues in April 1743, "the public is always dazzled at first. To begin with they went mad over the *Persian Letters* …; they disregarded the small book on *The Decline of the Romans* by the same author." "However," continued Voltaire, "I notice that all solid minds prize the great intelligence governing that good book which was at first scorned, and now set very little worth on the frivolous imagination of the *Persian Letters* whose boldness in certain passages constitute its greatest merit."[33] The second and by far more important and influential book was *The Spirit of the Laws* (1748), which Voltaire also praised highly as being "as methodical and true as it is full of wit and great maxims."[34]

Based on the baron's convictions derived from personal study, judicial experience, and observation of the British constitution in practice, that the rule of law and the preservation of political freedom were both achievable in civil society, *The Spirit of the Laws* was so widely acclaimed that within two years of its initial publication, twenty-seven editions had appeared across Europe in various translations. Though he died relatively soon after, in 1755, Montesquieu lived long enough to enjoy the accolades that his works had earned. Moreover, in view of the impact that *The Spirit of the Laws* had on European thought, even influencing the framers of the American Constitution (1787), the baron is rightly regarded as one of the most significant thinkers of the eighteenth-century Enlightenment, sharing that distinction with Voltaire, Jean-Jacques Rousseau, and Denis Diderot.

Sir Isaac Newton (1642–1727)

Isaac Newton was born into a family of yeoman farmers in England. Three years after his birth, his father died and he was reared by his widowed mother until, following her remarriage, his care was entrusted to his maternal grandmother. Newton might have followed in his late father's footsteps and taken up farming, had a teacher and an uncle not recognized his intellectual gifts early in his education and thus sent him to study at Cambridge University in 1661. He graduated in 1665 with a Bachelor of Arts degree, followed by a Masters degree in 1668 and his subsequent appointment a year later to a major professorship. It was during the years of his university training that Newton formulated the basic principles and views that framed the scientific insights which led in turn to the great discoveries in mathematics and natural philosophy for which he is famous. By 1665, for example, he had developed the general binomial theorum (and thus calculus), a distinction he shared—and quarreled over—with the German philosopher Gottfried Wilhelm Leibniz; also during this highly creative period of his life, Newton outlined the basis principles behind his hypothesis on the universal law of gravitation. Curiously, however, though he regularly presented papers on his findings at meetings of the prestigious Royal Society of London, of which he became a member in 1672, he was reluctant to publish his scientific research.

In subsequent years, Newton continued to pursue his interests at Cambridge University, where he served as an administrator as well as a faculty member, and refined his theory of gravitation in particular. The hypothesis explained the early laws of planetary motion proposed by Johann Kepler earlier in the century. Finally, at the urging of his friend, the astronomer Edmund Halley (of Halley's Comet fame), and with sponsorship from the Royal Society, Newton published his work on gravitation in *Principia Mathematica* (1687). Meanwhile, he followed-up his interests in other fields, such as the science of optics (on which he published in 1704), alchemy, and biblical commentary. In 1693, the scientist appears to have suffered a nervous breakdown owing to exhaustion, though he retained his Cambridge professorship until 1701. He also served for two terms as a Member of Parliament for Cambridge (1689–1690, 1701–1702), and in 1696 accepted a government post as Warden of the Royal Mint in London.

Now resident in the English capital, Newton continued his research, engaged fully in the proceedings of the Royal Society of which he eventually became president, used his influence to secure pensions and patronage for his fellow scientists, and earned a knighthood from Queen Anne in 1705. He remained a prominent figure in scientific circles until his death in 1727 at the age of eighty-five years: "Honored by his compatriots," wrote Voltaire, and "buried like a king who had done well by his subjects." "His great good fortune," continued the French *philosophe*, "was not only to be born in a free country, but at a time when scholastic extravagances being banished, reason alone was cultivated and society could only be his pupil and not his enemy."[35] Like his friend and older contemporary, John Locke, Sir Isaac Newton is regarded as one of the intellectual forebears of the eighteenth-century Enlightenment, without whose influence the new movement could not have developed along the lines it did. Certainly, his theory of gravitation, his explanation of Natural Law, the Rules of Reasoning, and his emphasis on empiricism over speculative thinking and philosophical systems-building without reference to experience, exercised a powerful influence on such *philosophes* as Voltaire, who devoted much of his own intellectual talent and energy to popularizing Newtonian science for contemporary readers across Europe.

Jean-Jacques Rousseau (1712–1778)

Jean-Jacques Rousseau was a native of the French-speaking Swiss republic of Geneva. One of fifteen children born into a family of artisans, he was reared by his widowed father, Isaac—a watchmaker—who also oversaw his son's early education. Even at this early date, the boy's reading and conversations with his father formed in him, Jean-Jacques later recalled, "the free and republican spirit, the proud and indomitable character unable to endure slavery or servitude, which ... tormented [him] throughout [his] life in situations the least fitted to afford it scope."[36] He also developed an early passion for music. In 1712, however, as a result of disputes with the Genevan authorities, the elder Rousseau was expelled permanently from the city. His ten-year-old son was placed in the care of an uncle, who sent him to board with a Calvinist minister at nearby Bossey. Three years later, the boy followed in his father's artisanal footsteps when he was apprenticed to an engraver, who ill-treated him, only to leave Geneva once again in 1728 when, as a result of finding the city gates locked against him at his return late one night from an excursion in the country side, Rousseau abandoned his apprenticeship to avoid punishment and turned his steps southward toward the kingdom of Savoy. After visiting the Savoyard capital of Turin for a time, where he converted to Catholicism from Calvinism, he took up residence at Annecy just across the French border. While there, he devoted his spare time to furthering his education. Not only did he read widely, but he also refined his writing as he "thought about the [French] language and style, and the elegance of the constructions."[37]

In 1742, Rousseau moved to Paris, the intellectual center of the growing Enlightenment, where he hoped to make his reputation with the Royal Academy of Sciences from a new system of musical notation he had developed. Though disappointed in this endeavor, he remained in the French capital, where he began to engage in the intellectual and social circles of the *philosophes*. With patronage from the Dupin family, Rousseau supported himself until 1751 as a tutor, secretary, and music copyist, at which he was skilled. He also began his liaison with Thérèse Lavoiseur, with whom he had several illegitimate children. All, however, were abandoned by the couple to be reared as orphans. That action morally outraged Voltaire, who exclaimed against the man "who refused to raise any of his sons and put them all in foundling homes!"[38]

The year 1750 marked the real turning point in Rousseau's life, however, when his *Discourse on the Sciences and Arts* took first prize in an essay competition sponsored by the Academy of Dijon in Burgundy. This was the first of his works to develop a theme that remained consistent in his philosophy; that is, the moral corruption of modern civilized society in contrast to the intrinsic virtue of human beings living in a pristine state of nature. He also won popular acclaim in Paris at this time with the successful staging of his opera *The Village Fortune-Teller* (1752), boasting afterward that even Louis XV was heard to sing one of its airs "with the most execrable voice in his kingdom, and utterly out of tune."[39] That public triumph was followed by another serious work, the *Discourse on the Origins of Inequality* (1755), which he submitted for a second essay contest sponsored by the Dijon Academy. This more sophisticated piece included the memorable, often quoted phrase: "Born free, the human is everywhere in chains."[40] While his new submission did not win the prize on this occasion, it was nonetheless significant for further developing the theme of his first discourse, by identifying private property as the source of political inequality and moral corruption in contemporary society—a view to which many of his fellow *philosophes* took deep exception. Among them was Voltaire, who once wrote in derision of his rival to the duc de Richelieu, "I flatter myself that you make a distinction between Parisian men of letters and this madhouse philosopher."[41]

For the remainder of the decade, Rousseau continued to expand his ideas through a variety of works, including various articles he wrote for the *Encyclopedia* on music and political economy. He also laid the philosophical foundations for the three major works on which his reputation as a leading Enlightenment thinker is based. Meanwhile, he left Paris for Geneva in 1754, where he reconverted to Calvinism, only to return to France in 1756 because of quarrels with Voltaire, who also by this time had taken up residence in the Swiss republic. Back in France, Rousseau accepted an invitation by the salon hostess, Madame d'Épinay, to live at her country estate near Paris. Soon, however, the two quarreled and the *philosophe* shifted his residence to the town of Montmorency, where he lived until 1762. Despite the unsettled circumstances of, and commotion in, his personal life, these years proved to be the most productive and creative of his literary life. In swift succession he published his popular novel, *La Nouvelle Héloïse* (1761); his treatise on education, *Émile* (1762); and his great work on the origins of civil society, *The Social Contract* (1762). Threatened, however, with arrest by the royal censors, who had condemned portions of his work, Rousseau fled from France to Geneva, only to face similar opposition from the civil authorities there. In protest, he renounced his Genevan citizenship in 1763.

Between 1767 and 1776, Rousseau was almost continually moving from residence to residence, owing to his anxiety over official censure. He even accepted an invitation from Scottish philosopher David Hume to visit England. After a year and a half, the *philosophe* returned to France where he was permitted to live without further harassment from the royal authorities. Always a sensitive man, prone to restlessness, lack of confidence, and fear of conspiracies that he saw everywhere, Rousseau had both a complex and occasionally disturbed personality. Having encountered and befriended most of the leading Enlightenment thinkers, including Voltaire, Diderot, d'Alembert, and Hume, he managed to quarrel with all of them and was criticized in turn for contributing to the disunity that persisted among the *philosophes*. That Rousseau was probably aware of these weaknesses in his character (and eager to defend himself, too) is evident from *The Confessions*, a probing and deeply self-reflective autobiography that was published posthumously in 1781. Finally growing tired of Paris in his latter years, the *philosophe* moved to the town of Ermenonville, where he died suddenly in 1778. Though buried in the local cemetery, during the French Revolution his remains were transferred to the Pantheon in Paris, the resting place of France's most illustrious thinkers.

Always underlying Rousseau's philosophy was the intellectual problem faced by every *philosophe*; namely, how to safeguard individual liberty within the structures of modern civil and political society. Building upon contemporary ideas of natural man, natural law, reason, and intrinsic human virtue, he recognized that while civilization was essential for human progress and ultimate happiness, the society and social institutions of his day, especially the concept of property, corrupted rather than improved people morally, by pitting them against each other. Education and the reconstitution of society were the solutions Rousseau proposed for this question, in the belief that individual liberty could best be preserved in a society created by social contract. Although an old idea already developed by previous thinkers such as Thomas Hobbes and John Locke, the novelty of Rousseau's approach lay in his concept of the General Will, to which individuals would submit and relinquish their individual rights for the benefit of the whole. Despite his quarrels with his fellow *philosophes* and their frequent criticism of his ideas, they nonetheless acknowledged and praised the originality of his thought and its powerful influence in shaping Enlightenment ideals. Perhaps the last word belongs to James Boswell, who wrote of this troubled yet "illustrious philosopher" in 1765 that "I should like to have him bring out a complete edition of his works, and leaving to that ungrateful corner of the earth [Europe] a body of precepts to make them happy when their minds shall have been purified of gross prejudices—I should then like him to go to the delightful East, to live the rest of his days in the secret tranquility of a paradisial retreat."[42]

Adam Smith (1723–1793)

An illustrious Scottish economist, Adam Smith was the son of a comptroller of customs at Kircaldy. Although his father died before he was born he was nonetheless able to study mathematics and natural philosophy at Glasgow and later Balliol College, Oxford. In 1750 he met and formed a life long friendship with Hume. In 1751 he became Professor of Logic and in 1752 Professor of Moral Philosophy at the University of Glasgow, where he wrote *Theory of Moral Sentiments*, a persuasive tract on moral approval and started to acquire an international reputation. In 1763 he resigned his professorship and took a much more lucrative position as a private tutor. He traveled to Paris where he met a number of *philosophes*, including d'Alembert, and some of the most influential of the Physiocrats, including Quesnay. His most influential work remains *An Inquiry into the Nature and Causes of the Wealth of Nations* (1776), in which he talked about the division of labor and argued that value arises from the labor expended. He also argued for an economy based on *laissez faire* because he believed that the self interest of each individual would ultimately benefit the entire society. Although he opposed mercantilism, monopolies, and restraint on trade, he did acknowledge that sometimes such restraint of trade, as seen in the Navigation Acts, was necessary. In his later life he was appointed commissioner of customs for Scotland (1778). He devoted a considerable part of his income to charity and died quite painfully on July 17, 1790. Shortly before his death he destroyed most of his manuscripts. His last work, *Essays on Philosophical Subjects,* appeared posthumously in 1795. His fame to this day rests largely on his *An Inquiry into the Nature and Causes of the Wealth of Nations*, which has often been viewed as the most influential work on political economy ever written.

Notes

1. Giacomo Casanova, chevalier de Seingalt, *History of My Life*, Willard R. Trask, trans. and ed., 12 vols. (New York: Harcourt, Brace & World, Inc., 1968), vol. 3, 189; vol. 5, 265.

2. Voltaire to Cardinal Domenico Passionei, January 9, 1746, Voltaire, *Selected Letters*, 119.

3. Voltaire to Jacob Vernet, September 14, 1733, ibid., 30.

4. Ibid.

5. Peter Gay, *Voltaire's Politics* (New York: Random House, 1965), 48.

6. Rousseau, *Confessions*, 594.

7. Voltaire to Jean-Jacques Dortous de Mairan, May 5, 1741, Voltaire, *Selected Letters*, 89.

8. Voltaire to Élie Bertrand, December 26, 1763, ibid., 242.

9. Gay, *Voltaire's Politics*, 32.

10. Quoted in Peter Gay, *The Enlightenment: An Interpretation, The Science of Freedom* (New York: Norton and Co., 1969), 438–9.

11. Frederick A. Pottle, ed., *Boswell's London Journal, 1762–1763* (New York: McGraw-Hill Book Company, Ind., 1950), 102.

12. Samuel Johnson to James Boswell, August 27, 1775, R.W. chapman, ed., *The Letters of Samuel Johnson*, 3 vols. (Oxford: The Clarendon Press, 1952) vol. 2, 431.

13. Voltaire to Jean-Baptiste de Boyer, marquis d'Argens, October 2, 1740, Voltaire, *Selected Letters*, 84.

14. Rousseau, *Confessions*, 543.

15. Ibid., 543–4.

16. Ibid., 333, 334.

17. Voltaire to Charles Palissot de Montenoy, June 4, 1760, Voltaire, *Selected Letters*, 213.

18. Rousseau, *Confessions*, 336.

19. Ibid., 339.

20. Pottle, *Boswell on Tour: Germany and Switzerland*, 179.

21. Pottle, *Boswell's London Journal*, 173.

22. Adam Smith to William Strahan, November 9, 1776, in *The Portable Age of Reason Reader*, Crane Brinton, ed. (New York: The Viking Press, 1956), 613.

23. Rousseau, *Confessions*, 618.

24. Pottle, *Boswell on Tour: Germany and Switzerland*, 280.

25. T.C.W. Blanning, *Joseph II and Enlightened Despotism* (New York: Harper and Row, 1970), 43.

26. Ibid.

27. T.C.W. Blanning, *Joseph II* (New York: Longman, 1994), 198.

28. Manfred Kuehn, *Kant, a Biography* (New York: Cambridge, 2001), 1.

29. Maurice Cranston, *John Locke, a Biography* (New York: Longman, 1957), 480.

30. John Dunn, *Locke* (New York: Oxford University Press, 1984), 87.

31. Ibid.

32. Voltaire, *Letters on England*, 62.

33. Voltaire to Luc de Clapiers, marquis de Vauvenargues, April 15, 1743, Voltaire, *Selected Letters*, 103.

34. Voltaire to Charles-Emmanuel de Crussol, Duc d'Uzès, September 14, 1751, ibid., 164.

35. Voltaire, *Letters on England*, 69, 70.

36. Rousseau, *Confessions*, 7.

37. Ibid., 106.

38. Voltaire to Jean-le-Rond d'Alembert, June 17, 1762, Voltaire, *Selected Letters*, 230.

39. Rousseau, *Confessions*, 370.

40. *Jean Jacques Rousseau, Discourse on the Origins of Inequality* (Indianapolis, Ind: Hackett Publishing, 1992), xvi.

41. Voltaire to the duc de Richelieu, June 22, 1762, ibid., 231.

42. Pottle, *Boswell on Tour: Italy, Corsica and France*, 321.

PRIMARY DOCUMENTS

I. The *Philosophes* Define Themselves

Document 1: What Is Enlightenment? by Immanuel Kant

In this selection (written in 1784) the great German philosopher grappled with the question of what constituted the Enlightenment. Throughout his career at Königsberg he addressed many important philosophical questions such as the possibility of peace, the metaphysic of morals, and a critique of pure reason.

> A man is enlightened when he emerges from a state of self imposed pupilage. Pupilage is the inability to use one's own understanding without the guidance of another. This state is self-imposed when the cause of it lies, not in a deficiency of understanding, but of determination and courage to use it without the guidance of another. *Sapere aude!*—to have the courage to use your *own* understanding, is therefore the motto of the enlightenment.
>
> Indolence and cowardice are the causes why so large a portion of mankind, long after nature has emancipated them from the guidance of others, (*naturaliter majorennes,*) voluntarily remain in a state of pupilage during their whole lives; and why it is easy for others to assume the character of their guardians. It is so convenient to be under guardianship. If I have a book that possesses an understanding for me, a guardian of souls that has a conscience for me, a physician that prescribes my diet, and so forth, I need take no trouble myself. So long as I can pay, I need not think; others will undertake that toilsome business for me. By far the larger half of the human race (including the whole of the fair sex) regard the step to majority not only as laborious and difficult, but also as extremely dangerous; an idea which the guardians who have so benevolently taken upon themselves the

supervision and guidance of their conduct, have assiduously inculcated....

In order to have enlightenment nothing is wanted but liberty; the safest and most innocuous that can be called by that name,—that is, liberty to make a public use of one's reason on all subjects. But I hear exclamations from every side against the use of reason. The officer says, "Don't reason, but obey orders;" the priest, "Don't reason, but believe." These are so many restrictions of freedom. It is therefore necessary to inquire, what restrictions are adverse to enlightenment; what, not only not adverse, but favorable to it. I answer, the public exercise of reason must be constantly and invariably free; this is the sole means by which mankind can be enlightened: but the private exercise of it may often be subjected to very rigorous restrictions, without much prejudice to the progress of enlightenment. It is necessary to explain, that by the *public* use which each man makes of his own reason, I understand that which every man of science, in that capacity, makes it in addressing the whole reading public. By the *private* use, I mean that which a man makes of his reason in any civil post confided to him, or as member of a political community.

If it is asked, Is the age we live in an enlightened one? The answer is, No; but it is an age of enlightenment. That, as things now stand, the mass of mankind are capable, or can be rendered capable, of using their own understandings safely and usefully, without the guidance of another, is far from being the fact. But that the road to self-culture is now opened to them, and that the obstacles to an universal enlightenment, or to emancipation from a self-imposed pupilage, are gradually becoming fewer, we have clear and abundant indications. In this sense this is an age of enlightenment ...

Source: Austin, Sarah, trans. *Fragments from German Prose Writers* (New York: D. Appleton and Company, 1841), 228–38.

Document 2: Diderot's Preface to the Last Installment of the *Encyclopedia* (1765)

Denis Diderot in many ways epitomized the enlightened spirit of the 18th century. A playwright, novelist, and satirist, he also edited the *Encyclopédie*. It was he, along with d'Alembert, who urged the most important thinkers of the time to contribute to this vast compendium of knowledge. In the following passage he describes his goals as well as some of the difficulties inherent in the project.

When we began this enterprise we looked forward only to those difficulties to which its extent and the variety of the subjects to be treated would give rise; but this proved to be a momentary illusion, and we soon beheld the multitude of material obstacles which we had foreseen reinforced by an infinite number of intellectual hindrances for which we were in no way prepared. The world grows old, but in vain, for it does not change. Perhaps the individual may become better, but the mass of our species grows neither better nor worse. The sum of noxious passions remains the same, and the enemies of every good and useful thing are innumerable, as they always have been.

Among all the various forms of persecution inflicted, in all times and among all peoples, upon those who have yielded to the dangerous temptation of endeavoring to inscribe their names on the list of benefactors of the human race, there are almost none which have not been directed against us. We have ourselves experienced every species of aspersion springing from envy, falsehood, ignorance, and bigotry of which history furnishes us any example. During twenty consecutive years we can look back to hardly a moment of rest. After days devoted to continuous and ungrateful labor, how many nights have we passed in apprehension of the evils with which malice threatened us! How often have we risen uncertain whether, yielding to the cries of slander, we should not tear ourselves away from our relatives, friends, and fellow-citizens to seek the necessary peace and protection tendered us beneath a foreign sky. But our country was dear to us and we continued to hope that prejudice would give way to justice. Such, moreover, is the character of the man intent on good, and who is fully conscious of the righteousness of his purpose, that his courage is only increased by obstacles which he meets, while his innocence hides from him or leads him to despise the dangers which menace him. One with a high purpose experiences an enthusiasm of which the evil-minded can form no conception.

We have, moreover, met in a few others the same generous sentiments which have sustained us. All our colleagues hastened to support us. When our enemies facilitated themselves upon having finally overwhelmed us, we found men of letters and men of affairs, who had previously contented themselves with encouraging or pitying us, coming to our aid and associating themselves with our work. Would that we might publish the names of all these capable and courageous allies, who will merit public recognition....

Compatriots and contemporaries, however harshly you may judge this work, remember that it was undertaken, continued, and completed by a little band of isolated men, thwarted in their designs, exhibited in the most odious light, slandered, and outraged in the most atrocious manner, without other encouragement than their devotion to the good, with the support of a very few sympathizers and the assistance which they owed to three or four men of business....

No one will deny, I believe, that our work is on the level of our century, and that is something. The most enlightened person will find ideas there that are new to him and facts of which he was ignorant. May general education advance with such rapidity during the coming twenty years that there will be in a thousand of our pages scarce a line that that will not then be known to everybody! It is the duty of the masters of the world to hasten this happy consummation.

Source: James Harvey Robinson and Charles A. Beard, *Readings in Modern European History* (New York: Ginn & Company, 1908), 185–7.

Document 3: d'Alembert Defines a Philosophe

In a 1760 article entitled "Reflections on the Present State of the Republic Letters," Jean-le-Rond d'Alembert defined and defended what it meant to be a *philosophe*. Embedded in his definition is the full program of the Enlightenment and what its proponents sought to change, in contrast to the conservative elements of contemporary society (i.e., the Catholic Church, the monarchy, the privileged groups, etc.) that opposed the appeal for reform.

Among men of letters there is one group against which the arbiters of taste, the important people, the rich people, are united: This is the pernicious, the damnable group of *philosophes*, who hold that it is possible to be a good Frenchman without courting those in power, a good citizen without flattering national prejudices, a good Christian without persecuting anybody. These *philosophes* believe it right to make more of an honest if little-known writer than of a well-known writer without enlightenment and without principles, to hold that foreigners are not inferior to us in every respect, and to prefer, for example, a government under which the people are not slaves to one under which they are. This way of thinking is for many people an unpardonable crime. What shocks them most of all, they say, is the tone the *philosophes* use, the tone of dogmatism, the tone of the master who knows. I admit that those of the *philosophes* who do indeed deserve this reproach would have done well to avoid deserving it ... [Yet] Truth can hardly be too modest, Truth indeed, just by being truth, runs always a sufficiently great risk of being rejected. But after all, this truth, so feared, so hated, so insulted, is so rare and precious, it seems to me, that those who tell it may be pardoned a little excess of fervor. The writer who wants to write more than ephemerally has got to be right.... If a dogmatic tone, one that tells the truth crudely, shocks our delicate judges, they will do well never to open geometry books; they won't find more insolent ones.

Source: Jean-le-Rond d'Alembert, "On men of letters," *The Portable Age of Reason Reader,* Crane Brinton, ed. (New York: The Viking Press, 1956), 90–1.

Document 4: Dumarsais Describes a Philosophe

The following description of the *philosophe* is attributed to Cesar Chesneau Dumarsais (1675–1756), a French grammarian and philosopher who wrote this article for Denis Diderot, to be included in the grand *Encyclopedia* as the entry for "Philosopher." While drawing attention to the temperament, methods, and general outlook of the Enlightenment thinkers, what Dumarsais emphasized significantly is the importance placed by them on being *engagé*, that is, fully involved in the society of their day, which they sought to improve.

> Reason is to the philosopher what grace is to the Christian. Grace determines the action of the Christian; reason determines that of the philosopher. Other men are carried away by their passions, without their actions being preceded by reflection: these are men who walk in the shadows; whereas the philosopher, even in his passions, acts only after reflection; he walks in the night, but he is preceded by a torch. The philosopher forms his principles on the basis of an infinite number of discrete observations. The people adopt a principle without thinking about the observations that produced it: They believe that the maxim exists, so to speak, in itself; but the philosopher follows the maxim to its source; he examines its origin; he knows its true value, and only makes the use of it that is appropriate. Truth is not for the philosopher a mistress who corrupts his imagination, and that he thinks he finds everywhere; he is satisfied to be able to bring it to light when he is able to perceive it.... The philosophic spirit is thus a spirit of observation and of precision, which relates all things to their true principles; but it is not the philosophic spirit alone which the philosopher cultivates, he carries his attention and his concerns further.... Our philosopher does not find himself in exile in this world; he does not at all believe himself to be in enemy territory; he wants to enjoy like a wise housekeeper the goods that nature offers him; he wishes to find pleasure with others ... thus he seeks to get along with those with whom he lives by chance or his own choice; and he finds at the same time those who suit him: he is an honorable man who wishes to please and to make himself useful.... [In short,] our philosopher, who knows how to divide his time between retreat and the commerce of men, is full of humanity.... Civil society is, as it were, a divinity on earth.... The temperament of the philosopher is to act according to the spirit of order or by reason; as he loves society deeply, it is more important to him than to the rest of men to make sure

that all of his actions produce only effects that conform to the idea of the honorable man.... This love of society so essential to the philosopher, makes clear how true is the remark of the emperor Marcus Aurelius: "The people will be happy when kings are philosophers, or when philosophers are kings!"

Source: Goodman, Dena, trans. "Definition of a Philosophe," generally attributed to Cesar Chesneau Dumarais. The Encyclopedia of Diderot and d'Alembert Collaborative Translation Project. http://hdl.handle.-net/2027/spo.did2222.0000.001.

Document 5: Casanova Talks about the Importance of Pen Names

The Venetian adventurer Giacomo Casanova offered an interesting comment on names, whether given or adopted as in the case of pseudonyms (e.g., Voltaire), and the kind of respect or authority that they could command if well-sounding or somehow significant, or the kind of derision they could attract if they appeared silly to the ear, weak, or bore an unintentional meaning. Names, or at least the choice of an appropriate pen name, were of special importance for the Enlightenment *philosophe*, and lent their reputations additional respect. Also interesting is the paraphrase of Leibniz in the first sentence.

> ... an ill-sounding name is degrading in this our stupid society. My opinion is that men who have an ill-sounding name, or one which presents an indecent or ridiculous idea, are right in changing it if they intend to win honour, fame, and fortune either in arts or sciences. No one can reasonably deny them that right, provided the name they assume belongs to nobody. The alphabet is general property, and everyone has the right to use it for the creation of a word forming an appellative sound. But he must truly create it. Voltaire, in spite of his genius, would not perhaps have reached posterity under his name of Arouet, especially amongst the French, who always give way so easily to their keen sense of ridicule and equivocation. How could they have imagined that a writer 'a rouet' could be a man of genius? And D'Alembert, would he have attained his high fame, his universal reputation, if he had been satisfied with his name of M. Le Rond, or Mr. Allround? ... I think that King Poniatowski ought to have abdicated the name of Augustus, which he had taken at the time of his accession to the throne, when he abdicated royalty.

Source: Arthur Machen, trans. *The Memoirs of Jacques Casanova de Seingalt, 1725–1798* (London, 1894). Available online through the University of Adelaide Library at http://ebooks.adelaide.edu.au/c/casanova/c33m/c33m.html.

II. The *Philosophes*: A House Divided.

Document 6: Voltaire Regrets the Divisions among the Philosophes

Although united in a common cause to reform society and to improve the human condition here and now, the *philosophes* were not a united group and very often fell to quarreling with each other over their differing ideas about society, government, economics, and other aspects of the eighteenth-century world. Intellectual rancor sometimes lay behind their attacks on each other's works and personalities. Particularly bitter was the quarrel between Voltaire and Rousseau, who returned each other's verbal assaults blow for blow. Voltaire clearly had no patience for Rousseau's tendency to withdraw from the community of thinkers, his petty jealousies, or his lack of moral conduct. James Boswell in fact commented on Voltaire's view of Rousseau whom he often referred to with a satirical smile as "*ce garçon*" [that boy]. (Pottle, *Boswell on Tour: Italy, Corsica and France*, 196.) Rousseau resented Voltaire's arrogance and stinging words. The fact is that Rousseau alienated himself over time from his fellow *philosophes*, owing to a difficult temperament that many contemporaries and modern historians agree was a symptom of some mental illness. Sometimes these quarrels were public and bitter, but the real damage they did was to render the disunited *philosophes* vulnerable to attack by their conservative, ecclesiastical, or political opponents, who presented a much more unified front. This problem was noted by Voltaire in a letter to Denis Diderot, dated August 14, 1776, in which he lamented the continuing disunity among his fellow men of letters and the potential damage that could result to their intellectual efforts to stimulate reform.

> Sound philosophy has been gaining ground ... but our enemies still have the heavenly dew, the fat of the earth, the bishop's mitre, wealth, the sword and the riffraff on their side. We have been limited completely to informing decent people throughout Europe that we are in the right and perhaps to making general conduct a little more pleasant and civil ... The horrible thing is that the *philosophes* are not united and the persecutors will always be.

Source: Richard A. Brooks, trans. and ed., *The Selected Letters of Voltaire* (New York: New York University Press, 1973), 307–8.

Document 7: Hume Analyzes the Effects of the Disunity among the Philosophes

Like Voltaire, Scottish philosopher David Hume complained how the philosophical debates of his day had alienated the general populace, which remained profoundly conservative and could not follow the endless disputes among intellectuals, in any case. Hence, the disunity that existed in European intellectual circles had the additional drawback that it reinforced popular belief in, and commitment to, the old ideas, doctrines, and especially religious beliefs that the *philosophes*, as an intellectual community, sought to change.

> The vulgar, indeed … who are unacquainted with science and profound inquiry, observing the endless disputes of the learned, have commonly a thorough contempt for philosophy, and rivet themselves the faster, by that means, in the great points of theology which have been taught them.

Source: David Hume. *Dialogues Concerning Natural Religion* (1779), Edited by Henry D. Aiken (New York: Hafner Publishing Co., 1948), 6.

Document 8: Voltaire to Jean-le-Rond d'Alembert, March 19, 1761 and June 17, 1762 on the Quarrels among the Philosophes

> Your Jean-Jacques is the one I'm most angry with [for causing disunity among the *philosophes*]. This stark mad man, who could have amounted to something if he had let you be his guide, has taken it into his head to go on his own. He writes against the theater after producing a bad comedy … he writes against the France that feeds him…. He abandons his friends; he writes me the most impertinent letters ever scribbled by a fanatic.
>
> Excessive pride and envy have destroyed Jean-Jacques, my illustrious philosopher. That monster dares speak of education … ! A man who refused to raise any of his … sons and put them all in foundling homes! … I do not know whether he is abhorred in Paris as he is by all the upright people of Geneva. You may be sure that whoever abandons the *philosophes* will come to an unhappy end.

Source: Richard A. Brooks, trans. and ed., *The Selected Letters of Voltaire* (New York: New York University Press, 1973), 219, 230.

Document 9: Rousseau on Voltaire's Character and the Influence of His Work

> … [Voltaire], as vilified as he is now admired, caused me to lament sincerely the misfortune by which he seemed to be pursued, and which is so often the heritage of great minds…. Voltaire seemed born never to enjoy any [happiness in life]…. Nothing that Voltaire wrote escaped us. The pleasure which these readings afforded one inspired me with the desire of

learning to write elegantly, and of attempting to imitate the beautiful coloring of this author, which enchanted me.

Source: Jean-Jacques Rousseau. *The Confessions* (1781; Ware, Hertford-shire: Woodsworth Editions Ltd., 1996), 207.

Document 10: Rousseau Explained the Source of His Split with his Fellow *Philosophes* as Their Jealousy over His Musical Talent

I believe that my friends would have forgiven me for writing books—even excellent books—because such a reputation was attainable by themselves; but they were unable to forgive me for having composed an opera, or for its brilliant success, because not one of them was capable of following the same career, or aspiring to the same honor.

Source: Jean-Jacques Rousseau. *The Confessions* (1781; Ware, Hertford-shire: Woodsworth Editions Ltd., 1996), 376.

Document 11: Reflecting on the Famous Poem That Voltaire Had Written on the Lisbon Earthquake, a Copy of Which He Had Sent Rousseau, the Latter Angrily Criticizing His Rival's Attack on Doctrinal Religion

Voltaire, while always appearing to believe in God, has never really believed in anything but the Devil, since his pretended God is nothing but a malicious being, who, according to him, finds no pleasure except in doing injury. The absurdity of this doctrine, which is obvious, is particularly revolting in a man loaded with blessings of every kind, who, from the bosom of happiness, endeavors to reduce his fellows to despair by the fearful and cruel picture of all the calamities from which he is himself exempt.

Source: Jean-Jacques Rousseau. *The Confessions* (1781; Ware, Hertford-shire: Woodsworth Editions Ltd., 1996), 417-8.

Document 12: Boswell Recorded the Comments of Other Individuals Whom He Encountered during His Tour of Western Europe, Some of Whom Disapproved Intensely of Both Voltaire and Rousseau

A conversation with Rousseau, from a journal entry on December 15, 1764

Boswell: "Monsieur de Voltaire has no liking for you. That is natural enough."

Rousseau: "Yes. One does not like those whom one has greatly injured. His talk is most enjoyable; it is even better than his books."

A conversation with the Italian antiquarian, Guiseppe Bartoli, from a journal entry on January 11, 1765

... [Bartoli expressed deep dislike for Voltaire and Rousseau], for he was a man attached to the Catholic religion. I told him Rousseau said, "I live in a world of chimeras." He [Bartoli] replied, "Then let him keep his books there, and not be sending them out into the real world."

A conversation with English writer, Horace Walpole, from a journal entry on January 22, 1766

... [Walpole] looked on Rousseau as [a] mountebank with great parts.

Source: Frank Brady and Frederick A. Pottle, eds., *Boswell on the Grand Tour: Italy, Corsica and France, 1765–1766* (New York: McGraw-Hill Book Company, Inc., 1955), 271, 280; Frederick A. Pottle, ed., *Boswell on Tour: Germany and Switzerland, 1764*, (New York: McGraw-Hill Book Company, Inc., 1953), 262.

III. The *Philosophes*: Their Views of Social Inequality and Optimism

Document 13: Rousseau Attacks the Old Regime

Rousseau's philosophy argued, in part, for sovereignty of a free people living in civil society, in which government served the needs and interests of the governed. He envisaged a society based upon legal and natural equality, and that individuals living in such a society should conduct themselves in accordance with the General Will. In Rousseau's view society had corrupted man. Rousseau's philosophy evolved not just from the social context of the eighteenth century, but also from his personal experience of the way in which those who occupied the lower strata on the social scale were often abused or discounted by those who enjoyed privilege above them, and that there was little recourse. Rousseau's lack of success in settling accounts for money owed to him by his former employer, M. de

Montaigu, the former French ambassador to Venice, led him to reflect on what he regarded as the inequities of social institutions under the Old Regime.

> The justice and uselessness of my complaints left in my mind the seeds of indignation against our foolish civil institutions, whereby the real welfare of the public and true justice are always sacrificed to an apparent order, which is in reality subversive of all order, and of which the only effect is, to bestow the sanction of public authority upon the oppression of the weak and the injustice of the strong.

Source: Jean-Jacques Rousseau. *The Confessions* (1781; Ware, Hertfordshire: Woodsworth Editions Ltd., 1996), 280.

Document 14: Johnson Defends the Old Order

Despite the criticisms of the *philosophes*, not everyone was opposed to the social status quo and society of privilege that prevailed under the Old Regime. Among them was the great English writer and literary critic Samuel Johnson, who rigorously upheld a conservative position that defended social distinctions not just as natural, but also as conducive to public order and essential to human happiness. James Boswell, Johnson's friend and biographer, recorded a discussion that the older man had with George Dempster, who held more liberal views, on this issue.

> Dempster ... argued that internal merit *ought* to make the only distinction amongst mankind. Replied Johnson: "Mankind have found from experience that this could not be. How shall we determine the proportions of internal merit? Had we no other distinction but that, we should soon fall a fighting about the degrees of it. Were all distinctions abolished, the strongest would not permit it long. And why not let people be distinguished by their bodily strength? But, Sir, as subordination is absolutely necessary for society, and contentions for it very dangerous, mankind (that is to say, all civilized nations) have settled it upon a plain invariable footing. A man is born to hereditary rank or his obtaining particular offices gives him a certain rank. Subordination tends greatly to the happiness of men. There is a reciprocation of pleasure in commanding and in obeying. Were we all upon an equality, none of us would be happy, any more than single animals who enjoyed mere animal pleasure."

Source: Frederick A. Pottle, ed., *Boswell's London Journal, 1762–1763*, (New York: McGraw-Hill Book Company, Inc., 1950), 315.

Document 15: Voltaire Attacks Optimism

In a letter to Jacob Vernes, dated March 15, 1759, Voltaire denied his authorship of the novel, *Candide*, which he had published anonymously to protect himself against the royal censors. Indeed, Voltaire denied his authorship of several works for the same reason. In the process, however, his denial gave him the opportunity to expatiate further against the Doctrine of Optimism, which his satirical novel had so bitterly attacked.

> I have finally read *Candide*. They must have lost their senses to attribute that filth to me. Thank God, I have better things to do.... I would forgive this optimism provided that those who uphold this system added that they believed God will give us in another life, according to his mercy, the good he deprives us of in this world according to his justice. It is the eternity to come that makes for optimism and not the present moment.

Source: Richard A. Brooks, ed., *The Selected Letters of Voltaire* (New York: New York University Press, 1973), 199–200.

IV. The *Philosophes*: Arguments for Religious Toleration and against Superstition

Document 16: Locke Argues for Toleration

John Locke addressed the question of toleration in *A Letter Concerning Toleration*. For him as for many others it was one of the problems of the day. Locke, also like others, advocated that toleration should be limited. The state, for example, could not tolerate those who did not tolerate others or those who had allegiance to foreign rulers.

> Since you are pleased to inquire what are my thoughts about the mutual toleration of Christians in their different professions of religion. I must needs answer you freely that I esteem toleration to be the chief characteristic mark of the true Church.... Now, I appeal to the conscience of those that persecute, torment, destroy and kill other men upon pretence of religion, whether any do it out of friendship and kindness towards them or no? ... The toleration of those that differ from others in matters of religion is so agreeable to the Gospel of Jesus Christ, and to the

genuine reason of mankind, that it seems monstrous for men to be so blind as not to perceive the necessity and advantage of it in so clear a light. I will not here tax the pride and ambition of some, the passion and uncharitable zeal of others.... The care of the salvation of men's souls cannot belong to the magistrate; because, though the rigour of laws and the force of penalties were capable to convince and change men's minds, yet would not that help at all to the salvation of their souls. For there being but one truth, one way to heaven, what hope is there that more men would be led into it if they had no rule but the religion of the court and were put under the necessity to quit the light of their own reason, and oppose the dictates of their own conscience, and blindly to reign themselves up to the will of their governors and to the religion which either ignorance, ambition, or superstition had chanced to establish in the countries where they were born? ... Let us now consider what a church is. A church, then, I take to be a voluntary society of men. joining themselves together of their own accord in order to the public worshipping of God in such a manner as they judge acceptable to Him, and effectual to the salvation of their souls....

Source: John Locke, *A Letter Concerning Toleration* (1689), trans. by William Popple. Found online at http://www.constitution.org.

Document 17: Voltaire Defends Toleration

Of all the Enlightenment thinkers, Voltaire was probably the most vocal advocate of religious toleration against doctrinal religion in his day. In the entry on "Toleration," which Voltaire wrote for his *Philosophical Dictionary*, he commented on the union between persecution, which only created martyrs and attracted new adherents to the dissenting opinion, and royal power, which was often applied in contradictory ways, depending upon the Crown's domestic and foreign interests. In any case, religious intolerance joined with absolutism was a dangerous combination, the negative effects of which had been demonstrated throughout history, a point Voltaire made with respect to the history of France. This constant theme can also be seen in his *Philosophical Dictionary* and in letters to his friends.

It is clear that every individual who persecutes a man, his brother, because he does not agree with him, is a monster. This is obvious enough. But the government, the magistrates, the princes, how should they behave to those who have a different form of worship? If they are powerful foreigners it is certain that a prince will contract an alliance with them. François I, most

Christian, joined with the Moslems against Charles V, most Catholic. François II gave money to the German Lutherans to help them in their rebellion against the [Habsburg] emperor; but he started off according to custom by burning the Lutherans in his own country. He subsidized them in Saxony for political reasons, he burned them for political reasons in Paris. But what has happened? Persecutions make proselytes: France was soon full of new Protestants.

Source: Voltaire, *Philosophical Dictionary* (1764), trans. and ed. by Theodore Besterman (London: Penguin Books, 1972), 389.

It is well known that the inquisition is an admirable and thoroughly Christian invention to make the pope and the monks more powerful and a whole kingdom hypocritical.

Who is a persecutor? It is he whose wounded pride and furious fanaticism irritate the prince and the magistrate against innocent men guilty only of the crime of holding different opinions.

Source: Voltaire, "Inquisition" and "Persecution," *Philosophical Dictionary* (1764), trans. and ed. by Theodore Besterman (London: Penguin Books, 1972), 252, 333.

Document 18: Mme. Roland Criticizes Christianity

Although not a *philosophe*, as an adolescent and young woman, Mme. Roland read widely among the works of the Enlightenment thinkers and was influenced deeply by the ideas in circulation during the eighteenth century. Among these ideas was criticism of doctrinal Catholic Christianity, which she also opposed. Reflecting on her early religious experience in later life, Mme. Roland objected in particular to religious intolerance and the expectation of unconditional belief.

The first thing I found repugnant in the religion which I was professing so seriously and so steadfastly was the eternal damnation of all who disowned it or who had never heard of it. I had, after all, studied history and when I thought of the size of the world, the succession of the centuries, the march of empires, the public virtues and errors of so many nations, I found it paltry, ridiculous, atrocious to think of a Creator who would consign to eternal torment those innumerable individuals, feeble creatures of his own hands, whom he himself had cast into this perilous world and into the darkness of ignorance. I must be mistaken about this proposition, surely. But are there others? Let us look and see! The moment a Catholic starts thinking like that, the Church may consider him a lost soul. I can understand perfectly well why the priests want blind submission and are so assiduous in preaching a religious faith which demands unquestioning acceptance of what they say. It is the only basis for their power. The moment people start reasoning, the priests lose control over them.

Source: Schuckburgh, trans. and ed., *The Memoirs of Madame Roland* (Mount Kisco, NY: Moyer Bell Limited, 1989), 167.

Document 19: La Mettrie Condemns Religious Fanaticism

In his book, *Man a Machine*, Julien Offray de La Mettrie challenged contemporary notions of natural law, and at the same time condemned religious fanaticism on materialist grounds that nothing in nature suggested the existence or non-existence of a supreme being, and that atheism was a viable approach to religion.

You see that natural law is but an intimate feeling that, like all other feelings (thought included) belongs also to imagination. Evidently, therefore, natural law does not presuppose education, revelation, nor legislator—provided one does not propose to confuse natural law with civil laws, in the ridiculous fashion of the theologians. The arms of fanaticism may destroy those who support these truths, but they will never destroy the truths themselves. I do not mean to call in question the existence of a supreme being; on the contrary it seems to me that the greatest degree of probability is in favor of this belief. But since the existence of this being goes no further than that of any other toward proving the need of worship, it is a theoretic truth with very little practical value. Therefore, since we may say, after such long experience, that religion does not imply exact honesty, we are authorized by the same reasons to think that atheism does not exclude it. Furthermore, who can be sure that the reason for man's existence is not simply the fact that he exists? Perhaps he was thrown by chance on some spot on the earth's surface, nobody knows how nor why, but simply that he must live and die, like the mushrooms which appear from day to day, or like those flowers which border the ditches and cover the walls.

Source: Julien Offray de La Mettrie, *Man a Machine*, translated by Gertrude Carman Bussey, revised by Professor M. W. Calkins, assisted by Mlle. M. Carret and Prof. George Santayana (La Salle, IL: Court Publishing Co., 1912).

V. The Philosophes: Views on Materialism

Document 20: Voltaire Discusses Free Will

Although not generally grouped with the materialist thinkers of the Enlightenment, Voltaire nonetheless expressed ideas that were materialist in nature. One example can be found in his article on "Free Will, in which he equated human liberty with conscious, deliberate choice—that is, with action, or rather the natural, almost mechanical function of the human mind through the exercise of reason.

> In what then consists liberty? In the power of doing what we will? ... Liberty ... on which so many volumes have been written, reduced to its proper sense, is only the power of acting.... A great passion, a great obstacle, may deprive [a man] of his liberty, or power of action. The words liberty and free-will are, then, abstractions, general terms, like beauty, goodness, justice.... Further, liberty being only the power of acting,—what is this power? It is the effect of the constitution, and the actual state of our organs.... Locke is then very right in calling liberty, power.

Source: Voltaire, "Free Will," in Franklin Baumer, ed., *Main Currents of Western Thought: Readings in the Western European Intellectual History from the Middle Ages to the Present*, 4th ed. (New Haven, CT: Yale University Press, 1978), 415.

Document 21: La Mettrie Views Man as a Machine

In his book, *Man a Machine* (1747), Julien Offray de La Mettrie developed a completely mechanistic and materialistic theory of the human mind and of the brain's functioning, though his extremist point of view—which equated man with the rest of the animal kingdom, and also embraced atheism—dismayed even some of the most irreligious members of the intellectual community.

> Man is so complicated a machine that it is impossible to get a clear idea of the machine beforehand, and hence impossible to define it. For this reason, all the investigations have been vain, which the greatest philosophers have made *à priori*, that is to to say, in so far as they use, as it were, the wings of the spirit. Thus it is only *à posteriori* or by trying to disentangle the soul from the organs of the body, so to speak, that one can reach the highest probability concerning man's own nature, even though one

can not discover with certainty what his nature is. Let us then take in our hands the staff of experience, paying no heed to the accounts of all the idle theories of the philosophers.... The human body is a machine which winds its own springs. It is the living image of perpetual movement. Nourishment keeps up the movement which fever excites. Without food, the soul pines away, goes mad, and dies exhausted. The soul is a taper whose light flares up the moment before it goes out. But nourish the body, pour into its veins life-giving juices and strong liquors, and then the soul grows strong like them, as if arming itself with a proud courage, and the soldier whom water would have made to flee, grows bold and runs joyously to death to the sound of drums. Thus a hot drink sets into stormy movement the blood which a cold drink would have calmed.... In general, the form and the structure of the brains of quadrupeds are almost the same as those of the brain of man; the same shape, the same arrangement everywhere, with this essential difference, that of all the animals man is the one whose brain is largest, and, in proportion to its mass, more convoluted than the brain of any other animal ... The transition from animals to man is not violent, as true philosophers will admit. What was man before the invention of words and the knowledge of language? An animal of his own species with much less instinct than the others.... nor was he distinguished from the ape ...

Source: Julien Offray de La Mettrie, *Man a Machine*, translated by Gertrude Carman Bussey, revised by Professor M. W. Calkins, assisted by Mlle. M. Carret and Prof. George Santayana (La Salle, IL: Court Publishing Co., 1912).

Document 22: Hume's Views on Religion

In his 1757 book *The Natural History of Religion*, Scottish thinker David Hume applied his philosophical skepticism to religious faith and the history of religion, the origins of which he expressed in materialist terms. In the process, he speculated on the psychology of religious experience.

We are placed in this world, as in a great theater, where the true springs and causes of every event are entirely concealed from us; nor have we either sufficient wisdom to foresee, or power to prevent, those ills with which we are continually threatened. We hang in perpetual suspense between life and death, health and sickness, plenty and want, which are distributed amongst the human species by secret and unknown causes, whose operation is oft unexpected, and always unaccountable. These *unknown causes*, then, become the constant object of our hope and fear; and while the passions are kept in perpetual alarm by an anxious expectation of the events, the imagination is equally employed in forming ideas of those powers on which we have so entire a dependence. Could men anatomize nature, according to the most probable, at least the most intelligible philosophy, they would find that these causes are nothing but the particular fabric and structure of the minute parts of their own bodies and of external objects; and that, by a regular and constant machinery, all the events are produced, about which they are so much concerned. But this philosophy exceeds the comprehension of the ignorant multitude, who can only conceive the *unknown causes*, in a general and confused manner; though their imagination, perpetually employed on the same subject, must labor to form some particular and distinct idea of them. The more they consider these causes themselves, and the uncertainty of their operation, the less satisfaction do they meet with in their researches; and, however unwilling, they must at last have abandoned so arduous an attempt, were it not for a propensity in human nature, which leads into a system that gives them some satisfaction.

Source: Isaac Kramnic, Isaac, ed., *The Portable Enlightenment Reader* (New York: Penguin, 1995), 113.

VI. The Philosophes: Man in the State of Nature

Document 23: Locke Describes Man in the State of Nature

In his great work *Two Treatises of Government*, John Locke offered a view of man in the state of nature altogether different from that of Hobbes. Men still congregated together to increase their chances for survival and to secure their property, and thus formed a social contract (or compact, as Locke put it) for that purpose. But nature was not as harsh as Hobbes depicted it; it was more benign, with men living simply in complete liberty, but generally at peace. There is also, according to Locke, a moral code dictated by Natural Law. Having formed a permanent social contract for civil society, however, men then created a second contract for the purposes of establishing government, but did not at the same time surrender their individual sovereignty. That second contract could be broken if the government were inadequate, without disrupting the social contract, thereby removing the fear of revolution from political action.

To understand political power right, and derive it from its original, we must consider what state all men are naturally in, and that is, a *state of perfect freedom* to order their actions, and dispose of their possessions, and persons as they think fit, within the bounds of the law of nature, without asking leave, or depending upon the will of any other man. A *state* also *of equality*, wherein all the power and jurisdiction is reciprocal, no one having more than another: there being nothing more evident, than that creatures of the same species and rank promiscuously born to all the same advantages of nature, and the use of the same faculties, should also be equal one amongst another without subordination or subjection ... but through this be a *state of liberty*, yet it is *not a state of licence*, though man in that State have an uncontrollable liberty, to dispose of his person or possessions, yet he has not liberty to destroy himself, or so much as any creature in his possession, but where some nobler use, than its bare preservation calls for it. The *state of nature* has a law of nature to govern it, which obliges every one: And reason, which is that law, teaches all mankind, who will but consult it, that being all equal and independent, no one ought to harm another in his life, health, liberty, or possessions. For men being all the workmanship of one omnipotent, and infinitely wise maker; All the servants of one sovereign master, sent into the world by his order and about his business, they are his property, whose workmanship they are, made to last during his, not one another's pleasure. And being furnished with like faculties, sharing all in one community of nature, there cannot be supposed any such *subordination* among us, that may authorize us to destroy one another, as if we were made for one another's use, as the inferior ranks of creatures are for ours. Every one as he is *bound to preserve himself*, and not to quit his station wilfully; so by the like reason when his own preservation comes not in competition, ought he, as much as he can, *to preserve the rest of mankind*, and may not unless it be to do justice on an offender, take away, or impair the life, or what tends to the preservation of the life, liberty, health, limb or goods of another.

Source: John Locke, *Two Treatises of Government*, http://www/gutenberg/org/dirs/etext05/trgov10h.htm

Document 24: Montesquieu's Views of Man in the State of Nature

In the *Spirit of the Laws*, the baron de Montesquieu also addressed the problem of man living in the state of nature, for which he defined a number of natural laws that guided man's actions. He also disagreed with Hobbes' depiction of the natural condition of men, while similarly refuting (without directly doing so) Locke's assertion that natural man regarded himself not as equal to others but inferior. That sense, he added, was the source of peace. Thus civil society resulted from the mutual fear and mutual attraction felt by men toward each other in a state of nature.

> Man in the state of nature would have the faculty of knowing, before he had acquired any knowledge. Plain it is that his first ideas would not be of a speculative nature; he would think of the preservation of his being, before he would investigate its origin. Such a man would feel nothing in himself at first but impotency and weakness; his fears and apprehensions would be excessive; as appears from instances ... of savages found in forests, trembling at the motion of a leaf, and flying from every shadow. In this state every man, instead of being sensible of his equality, would fancy himself inferior. There would, therefore, be no danger of attacking one another; peace would be the first law of nature. The natural impulse or desire which Hobbes attributes to mankind of subduing one another is far from being well founded. The idea of empire and dominion is so complex, and depends on so many other notions, that it could never be the first which recurred to the human understanding.... Next to his sense of weakness ... man would soon find that of his wants. Hence another law of nature would prompt him to seek for nourishment. Fear, as I have observed, would induce men to shun one another; but the marks of this fear being reciprocal, would soon engage them to associate. Besides, this association would quickly follow from the very pleasure one animal feels at the approach of another of the same species.... Besides the sense or instinct which man possesses in common with brutes, he has the advantage of acquired knowledge; and thence arises a second tie, which brutes have not. Mankind have, therefore, a new motive of uniting; and a fourth law of nature results from the desire of living in society.

Source: Montesquieu, *Spirit of the Laws* (1748), trans. and ed. by Anne M. Cohler, Basia Carolyn Miller, and Harold Samuel Stone (Cambridge: Cambridge University Press, 2000), 3–5.

Document 25: Rousseau Discusses Liberty

In several of his works, such as the following excerpt from *Emile*, Jean-Jacques Rousseau addressed the issue of man in the state of nature, too, and attributes the foundation of civil society—like other thinkers—to man's desire for self-preservation. In developing his ideas, however, Rousseau raised the important problem of

whether, and how, man could preserve his individual liberty and yet
live in a community of other men. His solution was, again, the social
contract, by which government is responsible to the governed, meaning that political authority is derived from popular sovereignty, and
that all members of society find their freedom in conforming to the
General Will. Rousseau also discussed the idea of progress and generally dismissed prevailing notions. For him the progress made in
the arts and sciences "has corrupted our morals."[1]

All things are good as their Author made them, but everything
degenerates in the hands of man. By man our native soil is forced
to nourish plants brought from foreign regions, and one tree is
made to bear the fruit of another. Man brings about a general
confusion of elements, climates, and seasons; he mutilates his
dogs, his horses, and his slaves; he defaces and confounds everything, and seems to delight only in monsters and deformity. He is
not content with anything as Nature left it; not even with man,
whom he must train for his service like a saddle horse, and twist
in his own particular way like a tree in his garden.

Yet without this interference matters would still be worse
than they are, for our species cannot remain half made over. As
things now are, a man left to himself from his birth would, in his
association with others, prove the most preposterous creature possible. The prejudices, authority, necessity, and example, in short,
the vicious social institutions in which we find ourselves sub-
merged, would stifle everything natural in him and yet give him
nothing in return. He would be like a shrub which has sprung up
by accident in the middle of the highway to perish by being thrust
this way and that and trampled upon by passers-by....

To form this rare creature, man, what have we to do?
Much, doubtless, but chiefly to prevent anything being done....
In the natural order of things, all men being equal, their common vocation is manhood, and whoever is well trained for that
cannot fulfill any vocation badly which demands manhood.
Whether my pupil be destined for the army, the Church, or the
bar, concerns me but little. Before he is called to the career chosen by his parents, Nature summons him to the duties of human
life. To live is the trade I wish to teach him.... All our wisdom
consists in servile prejudices; all our customs are but suggestion,
anxiety, and constraint. Civilized man is born, lives, dies in a
state of slavery. At his birth he is sewed in swaddling clothes; at
his death he is nailed in a coffin; and as long as he preserves the
human form he is fettered by our institutions. It is said that
nurses sometimes claim to give the infant's head a better form
by kneading it, and we permit them to do this! It would appear
that our heads were badly fashioned by the Author of Nature,
and that they need to be made over outwardly by the midwife

and inwardly by philosophers! The Caribbeans are more fortunate than we by half.... Observe nature and follow the path she traces for you!

Source: James Harvey Robinson and Charles A. Beard, *Readings in Modern European History* (New York: Ginn & Company, 1908), 188–9.

VII. The Philosophes and the Noble Savage

Document 26: Lahontan's Views of Native Americans

The baron de Lahontan journeyed to the French possessions in North America in 1687 through 1689 and published an account of his experiences, which was translated into English in 1703. During his travels, he encountered various Native American groups, which he described in such a sympathetic light some historians question their accuracy and suggest that they represent a deliberate depiction of the Indians as Noble Savages in the New World. Especially noteworthy in Lahontan's account are the Indians' disdain for money as the source of social ills and their contempt for privilege and social distinctions owing to birth or wealth—ideas that appealed to the *philosophes* in search of living examples to illustrate their points of view.

The *Savages* are utter Strangers to distinctions of Property, for what belongs to one is equally others. If any one of them be in danger in the Beaver Hunting the rest fly to his Assistance without being so much as ask'd. If his Fusee [musket] bursts they are ready to offer him their own. If any of his Children be kill'd or taken by the Enemy, he is presently furnish'ed with as many Slaves as he hath occasion for. Money is in use with none of them but those that are Christians, who live in the Suburbs of our Towns. The others will not touch or so much as look upon Silver, but give it the odious Name of the *French Serpent*. They'll tell you that amongst us the People Murther, Plunder, Defame, and betray one another, for Money, that the Husbands make Merchandize of their Wives, and the Mothers of their Daughters, for the Lucre of that Metal. They think it unaccountable that one Man should have more than another, and that the Rich should have more respect than the Poor. In short, they say, the name of Savages which we bestow upon them would fit our selves better, since there is nothing in our Actions that bears an appearance of Wisdom. Such as have been in *France* were continually teazing us with the Faults and Disorders they observ'd in our Towns, as being occasion'd by Money. 'Tis in vain to remonstrate to them how useful the Distinction of Property is for the support of a Society; They make a Jest of what's to be said on that Head. In fine, they neither Quarrel nor Fight, nor Slander one another. They scoff at Arts and Sciences, and laugh at the difference of Degrees which is observ'd by us. They brand us for slaves, and call us miserable Souls, whose Life is not worth having, alleging, That we degrade our selves in subjecting our selves to one Man who possesses the whole Power, and is bound by no Law but his own Will; That we have continual Jars among our selves; that our Children rebel against their Parents; that we Imprison one another, and publickly promote our own Destruction. Besides, they value themselves above any thing that you can imagine, and this is the reason they al Inways give for't, *That one's as much Master as another, and since Men are all made of the same Clay there should be no Distinction or Superiority among them.*

Source: Baron de Lahontan, *Voyages to North America*, Reuben G. Thwaites, ed., 2 vols. (New York: Lenox Hill Pub. & Dist. Co., 1905), vol. II, 420-1.

Document 27: Rogers Describes the Rescue of Selkirk

In 1712, the English privateer Woodes Rogers published an account of his voyage around the world between 1708 and 1711, during which he rescued the Scottish seaman Alexander Selkirk, who had been marooned on Juan Fernandez Island off the west coast of South America by his shipmates a few years before. Rogers' description provided Daniel Defoe with the inspiration for his 1719 novel *Robinson Crusoe*, a novel that also reflects many of Locke's ideas, such as the value theory of labor, by which Defoe was influenced deeply. What Rogers' account also depicts, however, is not a Noble Savage, but rather a civilized man forced to return to a life of solitude in an actual, not hypothetical, state of nature.

Immediately our pinnace return'd from the shore, and brought abundance of craw-fish with a man cloth'd in goat-skins, who look'd wilder than the first owners of them. He had been on the island four years and four months, being left there by Captain Stradling in the ship *Cinque Ports*. His name was Alexander Selkirk, a Scotchman, who had been master of the *Cinque Ports*, a ship that came her last with Capt. [William] Dampier.... The reason of his being left here was a difference betwixt him and his captain [Stradling]. When left, he had with him his clothes and bedding, with a firelock [musket], some powder, bullets, and tobacco, a hatchet, a knife, a kettle, a Bible, some practical pieces, and his mathematical instruments and books. He diverted and provided for himself as well as he could; but for the first eight months had much ado to bear up against melancholy, and the terror of being alone in such a desolate place. He built two huts ... cover'd them with long grass, and lin'd them with the skins of goats ... he got fire by rubbing two sticks of piemento wood together on his knees ... [For food he ate] goat's flesh, of which he made very good broth ...; he kept an account of 500 that he kill'd while there, and caught as many more, which he marked on the ear and let go. When his powder fail'd [i.e., ran out] he took them by speed of foot; for his way of living, and continued exercise of walking and running, clear'd him of all gross humours, so that he run with wonderful swiftness through the woods, and up the rocks and hills ... [He also had] plenty of good turnips which had been sow'd here by Captain Dampier's men, and have overspread some acres of ground.... When his clothes wore out he made himself a coat and cap of goat skins, which he stitch'd together with little thongs of the same that he cut with his knife.... At his first coming onboard us, he had so much forgot his language for want of use, that we could scarce understand him, for he seemed to speak his words by halves.... And by this we may see, that solitude and retirement from the world is not such an unsufferable state of life as most men imagine.... We may perceive also by his story the truth of the maxim "that necessity is the mother of invention," since he found means to supply his wants in a very natural manner, so as to maintain life.

Source: Robert C. Leslie, ed., *Life Aboard a British Privateer in the Time of Queen Anne. Being the Journal of Captain Woodes Rogers, Master Mariner* (London: Diploma Press, 1894), 57–65.

Document 28: Montesquieu Satirizes European Mores

The *Persian Letters* is another example of travel fiction, but in this case two Persian characters visit Europe. Montesquieu used this device as a means of satirizing irrational European customs, beliefs, government structures, etc., as seen through the eyes of non-Christian foreigners. In the following passage, the Persian Rica comments on the power of the French monarch, the absurdity of venality of office, and papal authority, in addition to some of the traditions associated with monarch—such as touching victims of the skin disease scrofula, which was supposed to cure them—and certain Christian doctrines.

The King of France is the most powerful ruler in Europe. He has no gold mines like the King of Spain, his neighbor, but his riches are greater, because he extracts them from his subjects' vanity, which is more inexhaustible than mines. He has been known to undertake or sustain major wars with no other funds but what he gets from selling honorific titles ... and by a miracle of human vanity, his troops are paid, his fortresses supplied, and his fleets equipped. Moreover, this king is a great magician. He exerts authority even over the minds of his subjects; he makes them think what he wants. If there were only a million crowns in the exchequer, and he needs two million, all he has to do is persuade them that one crown is worth two, and they believe it [manipulation of currency values]. If he is involved in a difficult war without any money, all he has to do is to get it into their heads that a piece of paper will do for money, and they are immediately convinced of it. He even succeeds in making them believe he can cure them of all sorts of diseases by touching them ... such is the force and power that he has over their minds. You must not be amazed at what I tell you about this prince: There is another magician, stronger than he, who controls his mind as completely as he controls other people's. This magician is called the Pope. He will make the king believe that three are one [the doctrine of the Trinity], or else that the bread one eats is not bread, or that the wine one drinks is not wine [the doctrine of Transubstantiation], and a thousand other things of the same kind.

Source: Baron de Montesquieu, *Persian Letters*, C.J. Butts, trans. and ed. (London: Penguin Books, 1973), 72–3.

Document 29: Voltaire Depicts the Mythical El Dorado

In the following passage, Voltaire's fictional characters Candide and his translator Cacambo reach the kingdom of El Dorado, where gold and gems are so plentiful that they are despised, where no one wants for the necessities of life, and where the Arts and Sciences flourish. At length the two travelers encounter a 172-year-old man, with whom they discuss the social structures before touring the capital city. For this section of his novel, Voltaire invoked the myth of El Dorado, the so-called "Golden Man," a ruler of fabulous wealth whose realm, according to legend, was located somewhere in South America, and prompted several Spanish and English expeditions to attempt to discover it during the sixteenth century.

Their conversation was a long one and covered the form of government in El Dorado, local customs, behavior towards women, public ceremonies, and the arts. At last Candide, whose taste for metaphysics was insatiable, told Cacambo to ask whether any religion was practiced in the country. The old many blushed slightly. "Religion!" he exclaimed. "Why, of course there's a religion. Do you suppose we are lost to all sense of gratitude?" ... Candide was curious to see some of their priests.... The old man smiled. "My friends," said he, "we are all priests; the King and the heads of each family perform solemn hymns of thanksgiving every morning...." "Do you mean to say you have no monks teaching and disputing, governing and intriguing, and having people burned if they don't subscribe to their opinions?" "We should be stupid if we had," said the old man; "we are all of the same opinion here, and we don't know what you mean by monks." ... To pass away the time before supper they were shown the sights if the city. The public buildings were so lofty that their roofs seemed to touch the sky, and the market-places wee adorned with endless colonnades. Fountains of pure water, rose-water, and sugar-cane liqueur played unceasingly in the public squares, which were paved with a kind of precious stone smelling of cloves and cinnamon. Candide asked to see the Law Courts and the Court of Appeal, but was told there were none; court cases, in fact, were unknown. He enquired whether there were any prisons, and his guide answered no. What surprised and delighted him most of all was the Palace of Sciences, where he saw a gallery two thousand feet long filled with mathematical and scientific instruments.

Source: Voltaire, *Candide or Optimism*, John Butt, trans. (London: Penguin Books, 1947), 79, 80, 81–2.

Document 30: Diderot Contrasts Natural Law with Christian Views

In 1771, Denis Diderot wrote a *Supplement to a Voyage of Bougainville*. It is a fictional story based upon the recently published account by Count Louis-Antoine de Bougainville, a famous French explorer of the Pacific Ocean. Diderot admired the easy-going sexuality reported by Bougainville and other mariners of the Tahitians, an attitude he contrasted with the sexually repressed Christian Europeans. The latter were represented by a young chaplain who, after a brief struggle with his conscience, falls into the arms of the voluptuous young daughter of his Tahitian host, crying, "My religion, my holy orders!" The next day, a native named Orou listens patiently to the corrupted young chaplain's explanation of Christian ethics. In the following passage, Orou contrasts in response the moral law of Nature with the Catholic emphasis on man's sinfulness.

You are mad if you believe that there is anything in the universe high or low that can add or subtract from the law of nature. Her eternal will is that good shall be chosen rather than evil, the general welfare rather than the individual's well-being. You may decree the opposite, but you will not be obeyed. By threats, punishment, guilt, you can only make wretches and rascals, more depraved consciences, more corrupted characters ... [Y]our society [western Europe] cannot be anything but a swarm of hypocrites who secretly trample the laws under foot, for a multitude of wretched beings who served as instruments for inflicting willing torture upon themselves, or of imbeciles in whom prejudice has utterly silenced the voice of nature, or ill-fashioned creatures in him nature cannot claim her rights.

Source: Denis Diderot, "Supplement to Bougainville's Voyage," in *Rameau's Nephew and Other Works* (1761), trans. and ed. by Jacques Barzun and Ralph H. Bowen (Indianapolis. The Bobbs-Merrill Company, Inc., 1956), 200–2.

VIII. The Philosophes: Views on Government and Law

Document 31: Montesquieu's Theory of the Three Powers (from *The Spirit of Laws*)

In the following section Montesquieu, who served as a judge in the *parlement*, addressed the question of power. For him power must be a check to power. Elimination of intermediary powers he thought would pave the way for despotism. Montesquieu was greatly admired by his fellow philosophes, especially Voltaire, by subsequent theorists, such as Alexis de Tocqueville, and by the American founders whom, according to Paul Rahe, Montesquieu was cited more and relied upon more than any of the other *philosophes*.

In every government there are three sorts of powers....

By virtue of the first, the prince, or magistrate, enacts temporary or perpetual laws, and amends or abrogates those that have been already enacted. By the second, he makes peace or war, sends or receives embassies, establishes the public security, and provides against invasions. By the third, he punishes criminals, or determines the disputes that arise between individuals....

The political liberty of the subject is a tranquility of mind due to the assurance each person has of his safety. In order to have this liberty, it is requisite that the government be so constituted that no man need be afraid of another.

When the legislative and executive powers are united in the same person, or in the same body of magistrates, there can be no liberty, because apprehensions may arise lest the same monarch or senate should enact tyrannical laws, and then execute them in a tyrannical manner.

Again, there is no liberty if the judiciary power be not separated from the legislative and executive. Were it joined with the legislative, the life and liberty of the subject would be exposed to arbitrary control; for the judge would be then the legislator. Were it joined to the executive power, the judge might behave with violence and oppression.

There would be an end of everything, were the same man, or the same body, whether of the nobles or of the people, to exercise those three powers,—that of enacting laws, that of executing the public resolutions, and that of trying the suits of individuals.

Most kingdoms in Europe enjoy a moderate government, because the prince who is invested with the two first powers leaves the third to his subjects. In Turkey, where these three powers are united in the sultan's person, the subjects groan under the most dreadful oppression.

In the republics of Italy, where these three powers are united, there is less liberty than in our monarchies. Hence their government is obliged to have recourse to as violent methods for its support as even that of the Turks; witness the state inquisitors, and the lion's mouth into which every informer may at all hours throw his written accusations.

In what a situation must the poor subject be, under those republics! The same body of magistrates are possessed, as executors of the laws, of the whole power they have given themselves in the quality of legislators. They may plunder the State by their general determinations; and, as they have likewise the judiciary power in their hands, every private citizen may be ruined by their particular decisions.

The whole power is here united in one body; and though there is no external pomp that indicates a despotic sway, yet the people feel the effects of it every moment.

Hence it is that many of the princes of Europe, whose aim has been arbitrary power, have constantly set out with uniting in their own persons all the branches of magistracy and all the great offices of State.

Source: James Harvey Robinson and Charles A. Beard, *Readings in Modern European History* (New York: Ginn & Company, 1908), 191–2.

Document 32: Cesare Beccaria, *Of Crimes and Punishments*

In his *Essay on Crimes and Punishments*, Beccaria addresses the question of what is a good law, what is the purpose of law, and why torture should be abolished. This work has been widely regarded as the most influential book on law ever written.

Introduction

In every human society, there is an effort continually tending to confer on one part the height of power and happiness, and to reduce the other to the extreme of weakness and misery. The intent of good laws is to oppose this effort, and to diffuse their influence universally and equally

Of the Origin of Punishments

Laws are the conditions under which men, naturally independent, united themselves in society. Weary of living in a continual state of war, and of enjoying a liberty which became of little value, from the uncertainty of its duration, they sacrificed one part of it, to enjoy the rest in peace and security. The sum of all these portions of the liberty of each individual constituted the sovereignty of a nation and was deposited in the hands of the sovereign, as the lawful administrator. But it was not sufficient only to establish this deposit; it was also necessary to defend it from the usurpation of each individual, who will always endeavour to take away from the mass, not only his own portion, but to encroach on that of others. Some motives therefore, that strike the senses were necessary to prevent the despotism of each individual from plunging society into its former chaos. Such motives are the punishments established, against the infractors of the laws.

Of the Right to Punish

Every punishment which does not arise from absolute necessity, says the great Montesquieu, is tyrannical. A proposition which may be made more general thus: every act of authority of one man over another, for which there is not an absolute necessity, is tyrannical. It is upon this then that the sovereign's right to punish crimes is founded; that is, upon the necessity of defending the public liberty, entrusted to his care, from the usurpation of individuals; and punishments are just in proportion, as the liberty, preserved by the sovereign, is sacred and valuable....

Of Torture

The torture of a criminal during the course of his trial is a cruelty consecrated by custom in most nations....

No man can be judged a criminal until he be found guilty; nor can society take from him the public protection until it have been proved that he has violated the conditions on which it was granted. What right, then, but that of power, can authorise the punishment of a citizen so long as there remains any doubt of his guilt? This dilemma is frequent. Either he is guilty, or not guilty. If guilty, he should only suffer the punishment ordained by the laws, and torture becomes useless, as his confession is unnecessary, if he be not guilty, you torture the innocent; for, in the eye of the law, every man is innocent whose crime has not been proved. Besides, it is confounding all relations to expect that a man should be both the accuser and accused; and that pain should be the test of truth, as if truth resided in the muscles and fibres of a wretch in torture. By this method the robust will escape, and the feeble be condemned. These are the inconveniences of this pretended test of truth, worthy only of a cannibal ...

Conclusion

I conclude with this reflection, that the severity of punishments ought to be in proportion to the state of the nation. Among a people hardly yet emerged from barbarity, they should be most severe, as strong impressions are required; but, in proportion as the minds of men become softened by their intercourse in society, the severity of punishments should be diminished, if it be intended that the necessary relation between the object and the sensation should be maintained. From what I have written results the following general theorem, of considerable utility, though not conformable to custom, the common legislator of nations:

That a punishment may not be an act of violence, of one, or of many, against a private member of society, it should be public, immediate, and necessary, the least possible in the case given, proportioned to the crime, and determined by the laws.

Source: Cesare Beccaria, *Of Crimes and Punishments*, translated from the French by Edward D. Ingraham (Philadelphia, Pa: Philip H. Nicklin, 1819). Found online at The Constitution Society, http://www.constitution.org/cb/crim_pun.txt.

IX. The Enlightened Despots in Their Own Words

Document 33: Frederick II Describes a King's Duties

In his "Essay on the Forms of Government," King Frederick II of Prussia described those attributes associated with Enlightened Despotism. As a monarch, he took very seriously his royal duties and obligations toward the state and his subjects, though he also never forgot that as the supreme authority his responsibilities were to centralize the government and expand both the territory and prestige of Prussia (as seen in his secret instructions)—goals that often contradicted the principles he outlined below. Despite his political maneuvers in Europe and occasional opportunism, Frederick was viewed by contemporaries as the epitome of the Enlightened Despot.

> Princes, sovereigns, and kings have not been given supreme authority in order to live in luxurious self-indulgence and debauchery. They have not been elevated by their fellow-men to enable them to strut about and to insult with their pride the simple-mannered, the poor and the suffering. They have not been placed at the head of the State to keep around themselves a crowd of idle loafers whose uselessness drives them toward vice. The bad administration which may be found in monarchies springs from many different causes, but their principal cause lies in the character of the sovereign. A ruler addicted to women will become a tool of his mistresses and favorites, and these will abuse their power and commit wrongs of every kind, will protect vice, sell offices, and perpetrate every infamy.... The sovereign is the representative of his State. He and his people form a single body. Ruler and ruled can be happy only if they are firmly united. The sovereign stands to his people in the same relation in which the head stands to the body. He must use his eyes and his brain for the whole community, and act on its behalf to the common advantage. If we wish to elevate monarchical above republican government, the duty of sovereigns is clear. They must be active, hard-working, upright and honest, and concentrate all their strength upon filling their office worthily. That is my idea of the duties of sovereigns.

Source: J. Ellis Barker, trans., *The Foundations of Germany* (New York: E.P. Dutton, 1916), 22–3.

Document 34: Secret Instruction of Frederick to His Envoy in France (June 1740)

> The pretext for your journey to the court of France is to present your compliments to the king as an ally of my deceased father and to notify him of my father's death, assuring him that I am much inclined to maintain the same attitude toward him as my father, provided that this is reconcilable with my best interests. I am sending Truchsess to Hanover. He is to exercise a check there on the policy of the Cardinal [i.e. Fleury, the French chief minister], and you must talk about Truchsess as a man for whom I have the highest esteem and who is in the secret of things. Emphasize this so that the French won't wish to let me escape them and will

make me better terms than they did the late king, my father. England wants me, that is sure, and it is certain that she will make me some advantageous propositions ...

The increase of my forces which will take place during your stay at Versailles will furnish you an excuse for talking of my lively and impetuous habits of mind. You can say that it is to be feared that this strengthening of my army may produce a fire which will sweep all Europe; that is the nature of young people to be rash, and you may recall the fact that the ambition to be a hero has caused, and may still cause, infinite disturbance to the repose of the nations. You may say that quite naturally I love France, but that if she neglects me now, that may settle the business once and forever; if, on the contrary, she conciliates me now, that I shall be in a position to render the French monarchy more important services than Gustavus Adolphus ever rendered it.

Frederick

Ruppin, June 11, 1740

Source: James Harvey Robinson and Charles A. Beard, *Readings in Modern European History* (Boston: Ginn & Company, 1908), 68–9.

Document 35: Catherine II's Views on Sovereignty and Law

Having consolidated her hold on the Russian throne after deposing her husband Peter III, Catherine II summoned an assembly in 1767 to draft a new law code for Russia and issued instructions that outlined the principles by which it was to be guided. Although nothing significant came of the endeavor, two things are noteworthy in the empress' instructions. First is her endorsement of absolute monarchy for Russia, and second is the Enlightenment notion of the rule of law, which she borrowed directly from Montesquieu's *Spirit of the Laws*, a book that had influenced her deeply.

The Sovereign is absolute; for there is no other Authority but that which centers in his single Person, that can act with a Vigor proportionate to the Extent of such a vast Dominion. The Extent of the Dominion requires an absolute Power to be vested in that Person who rules over it.... Every other Form of Government whatsoever would not only have been prejudicial to Russia, but would even have proved its entire Ruin.... What is the true End of Monarchy? Not to deprive People of their natural Liberty; but to correct their Actions, in order to attain the *supreme Good*. The Form of Government, therefore, which best attains this End, and at the same Time sets less bounds than others to natural Liberty, is that which coincides with the Views and Purposes of rational Creatures, and answers the End, upon which we ought to fix a steadfast Eye in the Regulations of civil Polity. The Intention and the End of Monarchy, is the Glory of the Citizens, of the State, and of the Sovereign. But, from this Glory, a Sense of Liberty arises in a People governed by a Monarch; which may produce in these States as much Energy in transacting the most important Affairs, and may contribute as much to the Happiness of the Subjects, as even Liberty itself.... The Laws ought to be so framed, as to secure the Safety of every Citizen as much as possible. The Equality of the Citizens consists in this; that they should all be subject to the same Laws. This Equality requires Institutions so well adapted, as to prevent the Rich from oppressing those who are not so wealthy as themselves, and converting all the Charges and Employments intrusted to them as magistrates only, to their own private Emolument.... In a State or Assemblage of People that live together in a Community, where there are Laws, Liberty can only consist *in doing that which every One ought to do,* and *not to be constrained to do that which One ought not to do* ... [Thus] *Liberty is the Right of doing whatsoever the Laws allow:* And if any one Citizen could do what the Laws forbid, there would be no more Liberty; because others would have an equal Power of doing the same. The political Liberty of a Citizen is the Peace of Mind arising from the consciousness, that every Individual enjoys his peculiar Safety; and in order that the People might attain this Liberty, the Laws ought to be so framed, that no one Citizen should stand in Fear of another; but that all of them should stand in Fear of the same Laws.

Source: Catherine II, "Proposals for a New Law Code," from *Documents of Catherine the Great: The Correspondence with Voltaire and the Instruction of 1767 in the English Text of 1768,* W.f. Reddaway, trans. (Cambridge: Cambridge University Press, 1931), excerpted in the Internet Modern History Source Book, http://www.fordham.edu/halsall/mod/18catherine.html.

Document 36: Joseph Explains His Goals as Ruler

Upon assuming the throne in 1765 on the demise of his[?] mother, Joseph II, who regarded himself as epitomizing the idea of the enlightened ruler, outlined his goals.

I determined from the very commencement of my reign to adorn my diadem with the love of my people, to act in the administration of affairs according to just, impartial, and liberal principles; consequently, I granted toleration [in 1781], and removed the yoke which had oppressed the protestants for centuries.

Fanaticism shall in future be known in my states only by the contempt I have for it; nobody shall any longer be exposed to hardships on account of his creed; no man shall be compelled in future to profess the religion of the state if it be contrary to his persuasion ...

Tolerance is an effect of that beneficent increase of knowledge which now enlightens Europe and which is owing to philosophy and the efforts of great men; it is a convincing proof of the improvement of the human mind, which has boldly reopened a road through the dominions of superstition ... and which, fortunately for mankind, has now become the highway of monarchs.

Source: "Letters of Joseph II," in *The Pamphleteer*, London, XIX (1822), 290.

Men, even when their aim is identical and their motives of the highest, see the same things from very different points of view. Some are charmed by everything that is new, while others remain blindly attached to the habits of their predecessors. The fault of the first is levity and their merit is their anxiety to make things better. The defect of the second class is their indolence of mind and their reluctance to look for anything that lies outside their range of knowledge. Their redeeming traits are prudence and confidence.... I do not belong to either party. I do not give expression forthwith to every whim that happens to come into my head, and, on the other hand, I do not ruminate on my ideas too long, lest I fall into a state of indecision and become a mere dreamer.

Our present situation demands, as I see it, our undivided attention and prompt measures of reform. Of course I am as yet a mere novice and can only express myself in accordance with general principles, relying upon hearsay and a little common sense. I am far from censuring what has been done, since I do not have such a high esteem for myself that I can believe that my wise predecessors would not have done the same thing as I, had they found themselves in the situation which prevails today, or had they seen things from the point of view that I regard them....

I may say that all that I have observed or learned has forced me to the conclusion that there is nothing so dangerous as cleverness and subtlety in discussion. I will not recognize the force of any argument derived from the ancient Greeks or the modern French. Reasons drawn from the past century or the customs of a hundred years fail to convince me, since the Austrian monarchy does not resemble any other and the year 1765 cannot be compared with any other since the birth of Christ. Let us act, then, according to the dictates of good sense and reflection, for we shall have done enough if we reach our decisions in the light of such talents as the Creator has vouchsafed us, and execute them with confidence and determination when once we have made up our minds....

To hold that everything that has been done before our time is good and unchangeable or, on the other hand, to believe that everything should be revolutionized, both these are prejudices which have serious consequences. The latter is particularly seductive, since we see that things are not going well, and we conclude that they formerly went even worse because what we now have was once itself regarded as a remedy. Everything in this world can be made good if we diminish its faults and increase its advantages. The greatest prejudice of all and the least excusable is not to dare to attack or emancipate one's self from prejudice. We must have a great deal of courage and still more love of country to be a reformer in this world. No form of evil instinct is easier to inculcate, adopt, and follow than that which encourages us to leave things where we find them without giving any thought to the matter. But we shall have one day to give an account of the good that we should have sought for and then accomplished.

Source: James Harvey Robinson and Charles A. Beard, *Readings in Modern European History* (New York: Ginn & Company, 1908), 213–6

X. The Enlightened Despots in Contemporary Eyes

Document 37: A French Diplomat Portrays Catherine II

The following letter (dated September 3, 1762) was written by Laurent de Bérenger, the French *chargé d'affaires* in St. Petersburg from 1762 to 1765, just scant months after Catherine II had usurped the Russian throne. Breteuil's appraisal of her qualities derived from experience in the stark world of *Realpolitik*, and portrays the monarch as ambitious, cunning, opportunistic, and determined in her efforts to consolidate her hold on power—attributes not usually associated with Enlightened Despotism, of which Catherine became one of the major exemplars in Europe.

This princes seems to combine every kind of ambition in her person. Everything that may add luster to her reign will have some attraction for her. Science and the arts will be encouraged to flourish in the empire, projects useful for the domestic economy will be undertaken. She will endeavor to reform the administration of justice and to invigorate the laws; but her policies will be based on Machiavellianism; and I should not be surprised if in this field she rivals the king of Prussia. She will adopt the prejudices of her entourage regarding the superiority of her power and will endeavor to win respect not by the sincerity and probity of her actions but also by an ostentatious display of her strength. Haughty as she is, she will stubbornly pursue her undertakings and will rarely retrace a false step. Cunning and falsity appear to be vices in her character; woe to him who puts too much trust in her. Love affairs may become a stumbling block to her ambition and prove fatal for her peace of mind. This passionate princess, still held in check by the fear and consciousness of internal troubles, will know no restraint once she believes herself firmly established.

Source: George Vernadsky, trans., *A Source book for Russian History*, 3 vols (New Haven: Yale University Press, 1972), vol. II, 398. Found online at http://www.fordham.edu/halsall/mod/18catherine.html.

Document 38: Casanova Criticizes Joseph II

Eventually, in 1783 to 1784, Casanova found himself back in the Austrian capital of Vienna, which he had first visited in 1753. By this time, Empress Maria Theresa was dead and her son and co-ruler since 1765, Joseph II, had been governing the Habsburg empire alone for two years. Casanova was impressed by monarchs and had met a number of so-called Enlightened Despots, from most of whom he sought unsuccessfully a government appointment. Of the monarchs he met, however, he disapproved of Joseph II. And although his disapproval was obviously subjective, as were his more positive depictions of Frederick II, Catherine II, and Stanislaus II Poniatowski, Casanova nevertheless sensed some of the Emperor Joseph's impatience with those who did not share his desire for rapid reform, his high ideals, his essential humanity, and his stubbornness in the face of opposition.

> ... [T]he knowledge which he believed himself to possess destroyed the learning which he had in reality. He delighted in speaking to those who did not know how to answer him, whether because they were amazed at his arguments, or because they pretended to be so; but he called pedants, and avoided all persons, who by true reasoning pulled down the weak scaffolding of his arguments. Seven years ago I happened to meet him at Luxemburg, and he spoke to me with just contempt of a man who had exchanged immense sums of money, and a great deal of debasing meanness against some miserable parchments, and he added,—

"I despise men who purchase nobility."

"Your majesty is right, but what are we to think of those who sell it?"

After that question he turned his back upon me, and hence forth he thought me unworthy of being spoken to.

The great passion of that king was to see those who listened to him laugh, whether with sincerity or with affectation, when he related something; he could narrate well and amplify in a very amusing manner all the particulars of an anecdote; but he called anyone who did not laugh at his jests a fool, and that was always the person who understood him best … but he had no idea whatever of the art of government, for he had not the slightest knowledge of the human heart, and he could neither dissemble nor keep a secret; he had so little control over his own countenance that he could not even conceal the pleasure he felt in punishing, and when he saw anyone whose features did not please him, he could not help making a wry face which disfigured him greatly.

Joseph II sank under a truly cruel disease, which left him until the last moment the faculty of arguing upon everything.… This prince must have felt the misery of repenting everything he had done and of seeing the impossibility of undoing it, partly because it was irreparable, partly because if he had undone through reason what he had done through senselessness, he would have thought himself dishonoured, for he must have clung to the last to the belief of the infallibility attached to his high birth, in spite of the state of languor of his soul which ought to have proved to him the weakness and the fallibility of his nature.… He must likewise have felt the misery of knowing that he would not be regretted after his death—a grievous thought, especially for a sovereign.

Source: Arthur Machen, trans., *The Memoirs of Jacques Casanova de Seingalt, 1725–1798* (London, 1894). Available through the University of Adelaide Library at http://ebooks.adelaide.edu.au/c/casanova/c33m/c33m.html.

Notes

1. Quoted in Paul Rahe, *Twilight of Liberty, Democracy's Drift to Soft Despotism* (New Haven, CT: Yale University Press, 2008), 265.

GLOSSARY OF SELECTED TERMS

Absolutism. The cult of unrestricted sovereignty located in the ruler, who monopolizes all legitimate power in the state. In the seventeenth and eighteenth centuries, absolutism referred generally to a form of centralized government in which the monarch (or monarchy, meaning the ruler and all branches of the royal administration directly under and responsible to monarchical authority) had unfettered power to make decisions, formulate policy, and create law. Because sovereignty resided solely in the person of the monarch, it was indivisible and could not be shared. Consequently, the monarch constituted at once the supreme executive, legislative, and judicial authority in the state, without constitutional limitations. The absolute monarch was expected nonetheless to uphold immutable, fundamental law, as derived from traditional practice and the custom of the people, as well as the law of God from whom the monarch also received his crown by divine right. Absolutism should not be confused with despotism, however, insofar as despotism implied the arbitrary exercise of political power irrespective of fundamental or divine law. Also the rationale for absolutism shifted in the eighteenth century from an emphasis on its sacred obligations to more secular, utilitarian ones associated with Enlightened Despotism.

Despotism. In general, this term applies to the progressive or "enlightened" monarchies of Western Europe during the eighteenth century. In theory, these monarchies were reform-minded, centralized, and absolutist in character, insofar as all sovereign power still resided in the person of the ruler. But where the absolute monarch of the seventeenth century saw as his primary duty the preservation of the divinely ordained order of the world together with fundamental law, the Enlightened Despot of the eighteenth century ruled theoretically in accordance with natural law, which did not necessarily proceed from God. This form of despotism was also considered to be "enlightened" because it sought through humanitarian and utilitarian reform to enhance the well-being of the subject, together with the prosperity and stability of the state, in accordance with ideas expressed by the *philosophes*.

Ancien Régime. This term, which translates as Old Regime, refers to the prevailing social and political order not just of France to which it is usually
applied, but to Europe as a whole prior to the French Revolution of
1789. That enduring order of things consisted in particular of monarchical, absolutist government supported by a corporate social order that
included the three estates of society (the clergy, nobility, and com-
mons), organizations such as guilds, universities, towns, and law
courts, in addition to numerous other institutions, groups, and vested
interests. According to these traditional structures, only corporate
rights and privileges, as opposed to individual entitlements, were recognized under the law in a society in which inequality was a legal principle and privilege was associated with hereditary status. Originally,
status and duty, or privilege and responsibility, were regarded as two
sides of the same social coin. But by the eighteenth century, that ancient
relationship had dissolved, and the remaining social and political structure became the object of criticism by the Enlightenment *philosophes*,
who regarded hereditary privilege as an obstruction to political justice
and progress in the human condition.

Deism. A form of natural religion that arose in the early eighteenth century
as an alternative to traditional Christianity and Christian theology
embodied in the Catholic and Protestant versions of the faith. It
stressed a belief in God as the creator of a mechanistic universe governed by immutable natural law. Deism rejected superstition and supernatural events, such as miracles, which were both unreasonable and
unscientific, but it kept the ethics as a necessary means of social control. Deism also seemed to offer a rational basis for religious belief that
could render obsolete the fervent doctrinal quarrels and sectarianism
that afflicted European society, promoted intolerance, and caused religious strife. Deism was also intensely anti-clerical, as it criticized in particular the sexual abuses of the Catholic clergy, the evident wealth of
the Catholic Church, and Catholic intolerance toward Protestants and
Jews.

Empiricism. This theory, which emerged most prominently during the Scientific Revolution of the seventeenth century, asserted that all knowledge
is derived from experience. Accordingly, ideas develop through the
process of induction, as the mind accumulates and then transforms the
information gathered through the senses through the active agency of
human reason. During the eighteenth century, empiricism also suggested to some Enlightenment thinkers that because the human mind
changes over time with experience, human development could be
shaped by controlling that experience; hence the contemporary emphasis on education as a process, as well as a specific body of knowledge.

Individualism. In Enlightenment philosophy, this category of thought focused
on the individual human being as the basic building block of civil society,
and therefore includes economic, political, and ethical facets of human

conduct, as well as issues related to justice. Prior to the eighteenth century, the social group or community took the center of attention in both thought and practice, for the very simple reason that the precariousness of human life rendered the individual a poor foundation upon which to build a philosophical, let alone an actual, political or social structure. Consequently, all privileges, rights, and obligations under the law were defined according to one's membership in a specific group or caste, but because individuals belonged to several groups at the same time (e.g., towns, trades, social orders, etc.), their entitlements varied from context to context. In any case, specific groups were distinguished differently under the law, creating a system of legalized inequality, and the role of law and government lay largely in preserving the entitlements of all the groups. With improvements in the quality of human life during the eighteenth century, Enlightenment thought began to stress the basic equality of all men, whose nature was universal throughout the world, an idea derived from the philosophy of John Locke. Building on that foundation, the *philosophes* emphasized the need to preserve individual rights and liberty, while endeavoring to resolve issues related to the relations between individuals and civil society in which the individuals needed to live. Individualism in political philosophy thus developed as the doctrine that the state exists for the welfare of the individual citizen, and not *vice versa.*

Materialism. According to the theory of materialism, the functions of the human body, including those of the mind, all derive from the material substances of which the body is composed. The theory gets its name from the concept developed during the seventeenth and eighteenth centuries that life was nothing more than matter acting according to natural physical laws. In a secular sense, materialism also denies the idea of a spiritual soul, because it has no corporeal existence. The theory of materialism was especially prominent in the French Enlightenment, and played a major part in the development of contemporary psychology and moral philosophy.

Mechanical Philosophy. A form of natural philosophy that developed in the opening decades of the seventeenth-century Scientific Revolution. It was based upon two related intellectual foundations. First, that all natural phenomena could be reduced to problems of matter in motion; and second, that simple cause-and-effect governs the relations between and among all natural phenomena. Mechanical philosophy was frequently explained through the metaphor of the machine as a model for the structure of both the universe and of living beings. Also, because matter was considered to be inert, motion came from the action of external causes. The ultimate cause was God, the creator of all things. Once matter had been set in motion, however, inertia took over and motion could be stopped thereafter only if it was impeded by some external body of force. Mechanical philosophy sometimes resulted in accusations of atheism toward its adherents, because it implied a universe regulated by natural laws and forces without the need for God. It also directly contradicted biblical authority and Church doctrine.

Moral Philosophy. Also known as ethics, moral philosophy is that study or discipline which concerns itself with judgments of moral approval and disapproval, judgments as to the rightness or wrongness, goodness or badness, virtue or vice, desirability or wisdom of human actions, dispositions, objectives, or states of affairs. Prior to the eighteenth century, all discussion of moral knowledge and ethical behavior relating to mankind in society fell within the sphere of Christian theology and its assumptions about the relationship among man, God, and the universe, as revealed through scripture and Providence. With the Scientific Revolution beginning in the sixteenth century, however, the religious foundation of knowledge began to shift away from revelation to reason and empiricism, which compelled European thinkers to reconsider the relationship between man and God. A body of universal, immutable, natural laws—discernible through man's reason—was now seen to control the ordinary operations of the physical world, without any need for divine intervention. During the Enlightenment, European thinkers therefore began to reconsider the origins of good and evil not from a religious but from a temporal perspective. That perspective sought answers in human nature, and those answers stressed the duties and obligations owed by individuals to their fellow human beings in civil society. Thus, the moral philosophy of the eighteenth-century Enlightenment studied the secular, as opposed to the sacred, foundations of man's understanding about morality and ethical behavior.

Natural Philosophy. This broad discipline, which had its roots in the medieval university curriculum, encompassed in the seventeenth and eighteenth centuries what is now known as the natural sciences. Hence, natural philosophy may be defined as the study of the natural world, and more specifically of the philosophical principles and first causes that operate in nature. Originally included in the course of study associated with aspects of mathematics during the late Middle Ages, the subsequent association of mathematics and various mixed sciences during the Scientific Revolution of the sixteenth and seventeenth centuries resulted in the grouping together of these various fields of study under the category of natural philosophy; hence, those who studied the sciences during this period were also called natural philosophers.

Natural Rights. This concept, which was central to Enlightenment thought, was derived from seventeenth-century theories of natural law as applied to human society and the developing notion of individualism. In civil society, natural laws are considered to be a higher form of law than the positive law of the state, because the rules of natural law that govern relations in nature were derived from nature itself. Moreover, those rules were believed to be ordered, rational, self-evident, and discernible through human reason. Natural rights, as developed from natural law, prescribed certain fundamental relations and entitlements for mankind, including individual rights to liberty, equality, property, and the pursuit of happiness. As the Enlightenment unfolded, these rights came to include also the right to personal security and freedom from political oppression. The primary responsibility of government, however constituted, and society as a whole was to safeguard the natural rights of all individuals.

Philosophe. This is a French term meaning "philosopher," and it is generally used to denote the various intellectuals and free-thinkers associated with the eighteenth-century Enlightenment. The *philosophes* were not, however, professionally trained, systematic philosophers. On the contrary, they were critics of the prevailing social, political, and cultural order of contemporary Europe, and they used reason as a primary tool for evaluation, analyzing and satirizing the problems that faced European society under the Old Regime. They also proposed a utilitarian, as opposed to theoretical, agenda for moral and social reform; they were secularists, for the most part, who viewed the established Church and organized religion as an impediment to human progress; and they popularized many of the ideas of the Scientific Revolution of the previous century.

Salons. The salons constituted a social institution most commonly associated with the eighteenth-century Enlightenment. They were popular gatherings of aristocrats and educated commoners held in private homes, where wealthy, educated, and often powerful women usually presided as hostesses. These meetings helped many *philosophes* by providing them with a ready-made audience that was both receptive to, and critical of, their ideas. The salons also provided Enlightenment thinkers with opportunities to make important connections with prominent people; at the same time, the salon hostesses, especially those in Paris, frequently used their status to intervene on behalf of their intellectual protégés to secure appointments to the royal academies and other prestigious positions. Though the most important and notable salons were held in Paris, they could be found in other cities across Europe, where they served the additional function of popularizing the ideas of the Enlightenment.

ANNOTATED BIBLIOGRAPHY

Surveys and General Histories of Europe and the Enlightenment

Adams, Geoffrey. 1991. *The Huguenots and French opinion, 1685–1787: The Enlightenment debate on toleration.* Waterloo, Ont.: Wilfred Laurier University Press. Beginning with the Revocation, this is an intellectual history of the Huguenots, their relationship to the Enlightenment, and the development of ideas of toleration among the *philosophes.*

Anderson, M.S. 1987. *Europe in the eighteenth century, 1713–1783.* 3rd ed. London: Longman. An excellent survey of European life in the eighteenth century, covering political, intellectual, economic, and social issues on the continent, the British Isles, Eastern Europe, and the European colonial empires.

Baumer, Franklin, ed. 1978. *Main currents of Western thought: readings in the Western European intellectual history from the middle ages to the present.* 4th ed. New Haven, CT: Yale University Press. An excellent collection of great works of intellectual history, organized chronologically and thematically with interpretative essays by the editor. Covers Western thought from the Middle Ages through the latter twentieth century and topics such as philosophy, cosmology, religion, the Scientific Revolution, man, nature, and society.

Borchert, Donald M., ed. 2006. *Encyclopedia of philosophy.* 10 vols. 2nd ed. Farmington Hills, MI: Thomson Gale. One of the best and most comprehensive reference works on philosophy, taking a global perspective and covering such topics as bioethics, aesthetics, epistemology, metaphysics, and including useful biographies of major philosophers.

Brinton, Crane. 1963. *Ideas and men: the story of Western thought.* 2nd ed. Englewood Cliffs, NJ: Prentice Hall, Inc. A survey of intellectual history in the Western tradition, from ancient times to the mid-twentieth century, focusing on cosmological, theological, metaphysical, ethical, and aesthetic questions.

Caponigri, A. Robert. 1963. *Philosophy from the Renaissance to the Romantic Age*. Notre Dame: University of Notre Dame Press. An introductory survey of philosophy from the Renaissance to Hegel, with a significant portion devoted to Enlightenment thought.

Cassirer, Ernst. 1968. *The philosophy of the Enlightenment*. Edited by James P. Pettegrove. Translated by Fritz C.A. Koelin. Princeton: Princeton University Press. A classic history of Enlightenment thought in which the author demonstrates how the ideas of the period were unified despite their embracing no particular system of philosophy.

Craig, Edward, ed. 1998. *Routledge encyclopedia of Philosophy*. 10 vols. London: Routledge. A comprehensive encyclopedia of philosophy and theology that covers individuals, issues, and theories from a global and multicultural perspective.

Fitzpatrick, Martin, Peter Jones, Christa Knellwolf, and Iain McCalman. 2004. *The Enlightenment world*. London: Routledge. A comprehensive analysis of the Enlightenment that examines its intellectual origins and includes the views of both contemporary and modern critics of the Enlightenment.

Gay, Peter. 1967. *The Enlightenment: an interpretation*. 2 vols. New York: Alfred A. Knopf. A comprehensive examination of the Enlightenment in two volumes. Volume one analyzes the *philosophes'* critique of Christianity and appeal to pre-Christian thought. Volume two examines the economic and cultural effects of the Enlightenment. Each volume includes a comprehensive bibliographic essay.

Goldie, Mark, and Robert Wokler, eds. 2006. *The Cambridge history of eighteenth-century political thought*. Cambridge: Cambridge University Press. One of the most comprehensive overviews of European political thought during the Enlightenment. Includes essays on major themes of the period, along with biographical sketches and excerpts from the writings of the principal thinkers of the era.

Goodman, Dena, and Kathleen Wellman, eds. 2004. *The Enlightenment*. Boston: Houghton Mifflin Company. A good, general introduction to the conflicting views among some writers from the eighteenth century to the present.

Haakonssen, Knud, ed. 2006. *The Cambridge history of eighteenth-century philosophy*. 2 vols. Cambridge: Cambridge University Press. An invaluable resource for scholars of eighteenth-century philosophy within the historical context. The work focuses on human nature while exploring the connections between philosophy, science, and theology.

Hampson, Norman. 1968. *The Enlightenment*. Harmondsworth, Middlesex: Penguin Books. A good, concise survey of certain dominant themes of the Enlightenment from 1715–1789.

Hazard, Paul. 1964. *The European mind, 1680–1715*. Translated by J. Lewis May. Harmondsworth, Middlesex: Penguin Books Ltd. First published under the title, *La Crise de la conscience européene*. Paris, 1935. Excellent survey that captures the shift in outlook that occurred during the Enlightenment with the works of Newton, Locke, and others.

Hyland, Paul, Olga Gomez, and Francesca Greensides. 2003. *The Enlightenment: a sourcebook and reader*. London: Routledge. A rich collection of the works of major Enlightenment thinkers, gathered thematically into sections on such aspects of the Enlightenment as political theory, religion and belief, art, and nature.

Melton, James Van Horn. 2001. *The rise of the public in Enlightenment Europe*. Cambridge: Cambridge University Press. A cogent analysis of the place of the public sphere in eighteenth-century Europe, examining politics and the rise of public opinion in England and France, as well as print culture, literacy, and the popularity of salons and taverns.

Merriman, John. 1996. *A history of modern Europe, from the Renaissance to the present*. New York: W.W. Norton & Company. Comprehensive survey of European history from 1300 to the collapse of the Soviet Union, emphasizing political events.

Moote, A. Lloyd. 1970. *The seventeenth century: Europe in ferment*. Lexington, Mass.: D.C. Heath and Company. An excellent general survey of seventeenth-century Europe.

Munck, Thomas. 2000. *The Enlightenment: a comparative social history, 1721–1794*. London: Hodder Arnold. Examines the impact of Enlightenment ideas on a broad range of social groups apart from the intellectual elites, drawing comparisons across Europe.

Randall, J.H. 1940. *The making of the modern mind*. Revised ed. New York: Houghton Mifflin. An outstanding and sweeping intellectual history of the main currents in Western thought, bringing together religion, philosophy, politics, science, economics, literature and the arts, and the social and behavioral sciences.

Reill, Peter Hanns, and Ellen Judy Wilson. 1996. *Encyclopedia of the Enlightenment*. New York: Facts on File. Covers such key subjects as education, science, natural law, and the social contract to provide a concise survey of the Enlightenment. Biographies of the major figures of the period form a large part of the entries, and an extensive bibliography of both primary and secondary sources is a great resource for students.

Rothrock, George A., and Tom B. Jones. 1975. *Europe: a brief history*. 2 vols. 2nd ed. Chicago: Rand McNally College Publishing Company. An excellent survey of European history from the ancient world through the latter twentieth century.

Schmidt, James. 2000. "What Enlightenment Project?" *Political theory*. 28.6:734–757. Examines postmodern critics of the Enlightenment, arguing that their objections to Enlightenment ideas stem from a flawed understanding of what the Enlightenment was and what the *philosophes* were trying to do.

Enlightened Despotism

Beales, Derek. 2005. *Enlightenment and reform in eighteenth-century Europe.* London: I.B. Tauris. A collection of articles examining Enlightened Despotism in Europe, but focusing primarily Joseph II and the Habsburg monarchy.

Bernard, Paul B. 1979. *The limits of Enlightenment: Joseph II and the law.* Urbana: University of Illinois Press. A study of the administration of criminal justice under Joseph II in relation to his professed ideas of enlightened rule.

Blanning, T. C. W. 1994. *Joseph II.* London: Longman. An excellent study of Joseph II that examines his attempts to consolidate territories and to impose reform on a diverse population that was deeply resistant to reform.

Bruun, Geoffrey. 1967. *The enlightened despots.* New York: Holt, Rinehart and Winston. Classic study of the rulers whose absorption of Enlightenment ideas led them, with various degrees of success, to attempt to put those ideas into practice.

Catherine II. "Proposals for a New Law Code." Online. In Modern History Sourcebook. Available http://www.fordham.edu/halsall/mod/18catherine.html. Drafted in 1767, but never enacted, Enlightenment ideas are evident throughout this new code of law (e.g., "What is the true End of Monarchy? Not to deprive People of their natural Liberty; but to correct their Actions, in order to attain the supreme Good.").

Duffy, Christopher. 1988. *Frederick the Great: a military life.* London: Routledge. A biography of the Russian Czar, emphasizing his accomplishments as a military leader who transformed Russia into a formidable power and increased the size of his territory significantly.

Gagliardo, John G. 1967. *Enlightened despotism.* New York: Thomas Y. Crowell Co. A concise analysis of the Enlightened Despots that focuses on the relationship of their reforms to the Enlightenment ideas of the *philosophes*.

Harris, R. W. 1964. *Absolutism and Enlightenment.* London: Blandford Press Ltd. Discusses the monarchies and empires of Europe in the context of the shifts in social and political thought during the Enlightenment.

Hubatsch, Walther. 1975. *Frederick the Great: absolutism and administration.* London: Thames and Hudson. An excellent biography of Frederick II that focuses on the political administration of his reign rather than his personal life and relationships. The development, problems, and achievements of his administrative system are examined in detail.

Krieger, Leonard. 1970. *Kings and philosophers, 1689–1789*. New York: W.W. Norton & Company. A study of the development of European monarchy during the Enlightenment, examining in particular the "philosopher kings," the enlightened absolutists.

MacDonogh, Giles. 2001. *Frederick the Great: a life in deed and letters*. New York: St. Martin's Press. This biography reveals a contradictory ruler whose conquests made him one of the most formidable leaders of the eighteenth century, while his patronage of the arts and intellectual community contributed to his rank as one of the Enlightened Despots.

Madariaga, Isabel de. 1990. *Catherine the Great: a short history*. New Haven, CT: Yale University Press. An informative and balanced biography of Catherine II and her reign in the context of the social, political, and cultural history of Russia in the eighteenth century.

Ritter, Gerhard. 1968. *Frederick the Great: a historical profile*. Translated by Peter Paret. Berkeley: University of California Press. A critical examination of Frederick II, his ideas, his domestic and foreign policies, and his military endeavors.

Scott, Hamish M., ed. 1990. *Enlightened absolutism: reform and reformers in later eighteenth-century Europe*. Ann Arbor: University of Michigan Press. A collection of essays examining such topics as the Danish reformers, Catherine the Great, Italy and Spain, and the Habsburg Monarchy.

The Enlightenment and Revolution

Commager, Henry Steele. *The empire of reason: how Europe imagined and America realized the Enlightenment*. New York: Anchor Press, 1977. Examines European Enlightenment thought and its practical application in America.

Foner, Eric. 1977. *Tom Paine and revolutionary America*. Oxford: Oxford University Press. This work examines the impact of Enlightenment thinker Thomas Paine on the American Revolution, and suggests why he failed to have a similar impact during his career in revolutionary France.

McDonald, Joan. 1965. *Rousseau and the French Revolution, 1762–1791*. London: University of London Athlone Press. A study of the impact of Rousseau's thought on the French Revolution, examining published pamphlets and debates in which *The Social Contract* was cited.

Palmer, Robert R. 1959–1964. *The age of the democratic revolution: a political history of Europe and America, 1760–1800*. 2 vols. Princeton: Princeton

University Press. A comprehensive history of the American War of Independence, the French Revolution, and the beginnings of the parlia-
mentary reform movement in Great Britain, as well as other countries
of continental Europe during the revolutionary era.

The Counter-Enlightenment: Criticism of Enlightenment Thought

Berlin, Isaiah. 2000. *Three critics of the Enlightenment: Vico, Hamann, Herder.*
Edited by Henry Hardy. Princeton: Princeton University Press. This
collection of essays is an important study of three contemporary figures the Counter-Enlightenment and their place in the history of
ideas.

Bradley, Owen. 1999. *A modern Maistre: the social and political thought of Joseph
de Maistre.* Lincoln: University of Nebraska Press. An account of the
social and political thought of Joseph de Maistre, a contemporary critic
of the Enlightenment whose insisted upon the central and inevitable
place of violence, irrationality, and disorder in human experience.

Herzog, Don. 1998. *Poisoning the minds of the lower orders.* Princeton:
Princeton University Press. A detailed examination of England's
responses to the French Revolution, and the conservative reaction to
the public's imbibing of Enlightenment ideas and their perceived
threat to the social hierarchy.

McMahon, Darrin. 2001. *Enemies of the Enlightenment: the French counter-
Enlightenment and the making of modernity.* Oxford: Oxford University
Press. A study primarily of Catholic and extreme conservative opposition to the Enlightenment, arguing that it was inseparable from opposition to revolution.

The *Philosophes*—Their Works and Related Scholarship

Cambridge Texts

A fine place to begin any examination of the ideas of the *philosophes*
is the excellent series "Cambridge Texts in the History of Political
Thought" (edited by Raymond Geuss and Quentin Skinner) and
"Cambridge Texts in the History of Philosophy" (edited by Karl
Ameriks and Desmond M. Clarke), both published by Cambridge
University Press. Nearly all of the major Enlightenment thinkers are
represented in these series, and wherever possible, their works are

published in their entirety. Furthermore, each volume contains a concise critical introduction together with chronologies, biographical sketches, and guides to further reading.

Readers and General Works

Brinton, Crane, ed. 1956. *The portable Age of Reason reader*. New York: Viking Press. Excellent collection of representative works of the Enlightenment that includes lesser known writers as well as those better known.

Cranston, Maurice W. 1986. *Philosophers and pamphleteers: political theorists of the Enlightenment*. Oxford: Oxford University Press. A good introduction to eighteenth-century French political literature, with chapters focusing on major figures of the French Enlightenment.

Gay, Peter. 1959. *The party of humanity: essays in the French Enlightenment*. New York: W.W. Norton & Company, Inc. A collection of essays on three major figures of the French Enlightenment, Voltaire, Rousseau, and Diderot, that portrays them as serious thinkers whose ideas were inseparable from the social and cultural contexts in which they emerged.

Havens, George R. 1955. *The age of ideas: from reaction to revolution in eighteenth-century France*. New York: Henry Holt & Company. A useful introduction to the French Enlightenment that presents the ideas of the Enlightenment through biographical sketches of some of the major French political and literary figures of the time.

Kafker, Frank A., and Serena L. Kafker. 1988. *The encyclopedists as individuals: a biographical dictionary of the authors of the Encyclopédie*. Oxford: Oxford University Press. A useful collection of biographical sketches of the 139 men who contributed articles to Diderot's *Encyclopédie*.

Kramnic, Isaac, ed. 1995. *The portable Enlightenment reader*. New York: Penguin. A diverse collection of Enlightenment works that emphasizes the impact of the "Age of Reason" on conceptions of God, humanity, and nature.

Rahe, Paul. 2008. *The twilight of liberty: democracy's drift to soft despotism*. New Haven, Conn.: Yale University Press. An important new study of Montesquieu, Rousseau, and Alexis de Tocqueville that examines their concerns about the potential problems inherent in the emerging egalitarian order, and the potential for democracy to become tyrannical.

Torrey, Norman L., ed. and trans. 1960. *les philosophes: the philosophers of the Enlightenment and modern democracy*. New York: Capricorn Books. Translations of important sixteenth- and seventeenth-century works, along with interpretive essays and an introduction that places them within historical context in order to show how Enlightenment thought proceeded from earlier philosophical and theological ideas to form the basis for modern democracy.

Jean le Rond d'Alembert

d'Alembert, Jean-le-Rond. 1821–1822. *Oeuvres*. 5 vols. Paris. The complete works of d'Alembert collected in five volumes, including his philosophical and mathematical writings and *Encyclopédie* articles.

————. [1751] 1995. *Preliminary discourse to the Encyclopedia of Diderot*. Translated by Richard N. Schwab and Walter E. Rex. Chicago: University of Chicago Press. The definitive English translation of the *Preliminary Discourse*, along with a good sketch of Jean le Rond d'Alembert's career and background on the *Encyclopédie*.

Grimsley, Ronald. 1963. *Jean d'Alembert, 1717–1783*. Oxford: Clarendon Press. A biography of d'Alembert that places his work within the context of the larger European Enlightenment. Includes material on his early years and a treatment of his philosophy of science.

James Boswell

Boswell, James. 1998. *Life of Johnson*. Edited by R. W. Chapman, J. D. Fleeman, and Pat Rogers. Oxford: Oxford University Press. This classic biography of Samuel Johnson also reveals the vivid writing and humor of the biographer, who was singularly devoted to his subject and whose observations are exemplary of the best of eighteenth-century literature.

————. 1994. *The journals of James Boswell: 1762–1795*. Edited by John Wain. New Haven, Conn.: Yale University Press. A fine selection of James Boswell's writings, together with an informative introductory essay by the editor.

Boswell, James, and Samuel Johnson. 1996. *Journey to the Hebrides: a journey to the Western islands of Scotland and the journal of a tour to the Hebrides*. Edited by Ian McGowan. Edinburgh: Canongate Books. An account of Boswell's and Johnson's tour of the Highlands and Western Islands of Scotland during the autumn of 1773. Their vivid accounts illustrate a society very different from the Europe of the Enlightenment.

Edmund Burke

Burke, Edmund. [1790] 1986. *Reflections on the revolution in France*. Edited with an introduction by Conor Cruise O'Brien. Reprint, London, Penguin Books. Written before the radical phase of the French Revolution, Burke predicted that it would result in terror and tyranny.

————. 1981. *The writings and speeches of Edmund Burke*. 9 vols. Edited by Paul Langford and William B. Todd. New York: Oxford University Press. Comprehensive collection of Burke's works from his early years until the French Revolution, organized chronologically and thematically into nine volumes.

Kramnick, Isaac. 1977. *The rage of Edmund Burke: portrait of an ambivalent conservative.* New York: Basic Books. An important biography of Burke, "the father of modern conservatism," that underscores the many ambiguities in his thinking.

Lock, F. P. 1999. *Edmund Burke.* Vol. 1: *1730–1784.* Oxford: Clarendon Press. A collection of Burke's early writings with a biographical sketch. It focuses on Burke as a writer and private individual rather than a political thinker and public persona.

Denis Diderot

Diderot, Denis, and Jean-le-Rond d'Alembert, eds. 1751–1772. *Enclyclopédie, ou dictionnaire raisonné des sciences, des arts et des métiers.* 17 vols. Online in French and in English translation. Available http://www.lib.u-chicago.edu/efts/ARTFL/projects/encyc/. An important work that helped to disseminate Englightenment ideas about science and the arts.

Diderot, Denis. [1761] 1956. *Rameau's nephew and other works.* Translated and edited by Jacques Barzun and Ralph H. Bowen. Indianapolis: The Bobbs-Merrill Company, Inc. A satirical criticism of the enemies of the Enlightenment that was not published until after Diderot's death.

———. 1992. *Political writings.* Edited by J. H. Mason and R. Wokler. Cambridge Texts in the History of Political Thought. Cambridge: Cambridge University Press. A collection of the most important of Diderot's articles for the *Encyclopédie,* a substantial number of his contributions to the *Histoire des Deux Indes,* and many others. The editors' introduction sets these works in their context, and the volume includes a chronology of events and a bibliography.

Bremner, Geoffrey. 1983. *Order and chance: the pattern of Diderot's thought.* Cambridge: Cambridge University Press. A study of Diderot's way of thinking that argues he never strayed far from Cartesian philosophy in his discussions of both physical matter and political systems.

Darnton, Robert. 1979. *The business of enlightenment: a publishing history of the Encyclopédie, 1775–1800.* Cambridge, Mass: Belknap Press of Harvard University Press. A history of the publication of the *Encyclopédie,* both early and later editions, including an examination of the book's origin, manufacture, marketing, and influence.

Furbank, Philip Nicholas. 1992. *Diderot: a critical biography.* New York: Alfred A. Knopf. An incisive study of Diderot's private life, public career, and his literary and philosophical works.

Thomas Hobbes

Hobbes, Thomas. [1651] 1997. *Leviathan.* A Norton Critical Edition. Edited by Richard E. Flathman and David Johnston. New York: W.W. Norton & Company. This is the most complete expression of Hobbes's philosophy.

He famously posited that the state of nature in human beings is one of struggle for survival, and that the best solution to the problem is the formation of a commonwealth under the authority of an absolute sovereign.

————. 1998. *On the citizen*. Edited and translated by Richard Tuck and Michael Silverthorne. Cambridge Texts in the History of Political Thought. Cambridge: Cambridge University Press. Hobbes's first extended effort to discuss the political ideas that would be developed more fully in *Leviathan*. This is the first modern English translation of the work.

Bagby, Laurie M. Johnson. 2007. *Hobbes's Leviathan: reader's guide*. New York: Continuum International Publishing Group. A good guide for students that offers a look at the context and themes of *Leviathan* and takes the reader through the text systematically.

Cranston, Maurice William, and Richard Stanley Peters. 1972. *Hobbes and Rousseau*. New York: Anchor Books. A collection of essays on Hobbes and Rousseau (nine devoted to each *philosophe*, and one that links the two) and address both the philosophical and political aspects of their works.

Strauss, Leo. 1963. *The political philosophy of Hobbes: its basis and its genesis*. Chicago: University of Chicago Press. An analysis of the political philosophy of Thomas Hobbes that argues that his ideas arose not from tradition or science but from his own deep knowledge and experience of human nature.

David Hume

Hume, David. [1779] 1948. *Dialogues concerning natural religion*. Edited by Henry D. Aiken. New York: Hafner Publishing Co. Considered by some to be the greatest philosophical work of one of Europe's greatest philosophers, Hume uses the device of a dialogue to examine whether or not the existence and nature of God can be proved rationally.

————. 1994. *Political essays*. Edited by Knud Haakonssen. Cambridge Texts in the History of Political Thought. Cambridge: Cambridge University Press. A fully annotated collection of twenty-seven of Hume's most important political essays, reflecting the entire range of his intellectual engagement with politics.

Norton, D. F., ed. 1993. *The Cambridge companion to Hume*. Cambridge: Cambridge University Press. A comprehensive overview of Hume's work that includes not only his contributions to epistemology, metaphysics, and the philosophy of religion, but also to many other disciplines.

Immanuel Kant

Kant, Immanuel. [1781] 1998. *The critique of pure reason*. Translated and edited by Paul Guyer and Allen W. Wood. Cambridge Edition of the Works of Immanuel Kant. Cambridge: Cambridge University Press.

An authoritative translation that includes a useful introduction summarizing Kant's main arguments.

———. 1964. *Perpetual peace and other essays on politics, history, and morals.* Edited by Ted Humphrey. Indianapolis: Hackett Publishing Co. A collection of essays detailing Kant's views on politics, history, and ethics.

———. 1991. *Political writings.* Edited by Hans Reiss. Translated by H. B. Nisbet. Cambridge: Cambridge University Press. An important collection of Kant's political writing, together with an expository essay examining recent development I Kant scholarship.

———. [1793] 1960. *Religion within the limits of reason alone.* Translated by T.M. Greene and H. H. Hudson. New York: Harper. Illuminates Kant's understanding of man's moral life and some of the fundamental beliefs of Christianity.

Allison, Henry E. 1996. *Idealism and freedom: essays on Kant's theoretical and practical philosophy.* Cambridge: Cambridge University Press. Collection of essays on Kant's theoretical and practical philosophy, along the author's interpretation of transcendental idealism and other aspects of Kant's moral philosophy.

Guyer, Paul. 2006. *Kant.* New York: Routledge. An introduction to Kant's metaphysics and epistemology, explaining his arguments about the nature of space, time, and experience in his most influential but difficult work, *The Critique of Pure Reason.* Includes an overview of Kant's life and times.

Kuehn, Manfred. 2002. *Kant: a biography.* Cambridge: Cambridge University Press. A comprehensive biography of Kant that examines his life from childhood through his years as a university professor and traces the development of his philosophical thought.

Scruton, Roger. 1983. *Kant.* Oxford: Oxford University Press. An excellent, concise biography that examines Kant's moral, aesthetic, and political philosophy, as well as his relations with and responses to Descartes, Leibniz, and Hume.

Sullivan, Roger J. 1989. *Immanuel Kant's moral theory.* A detailed, authoritative account of Kant's moral philosophy, including his ethical theory, his philosophy of history, his political philosophy, his philosophy of religion, and his philosophy of education.

Wood, Allen W. 2005. *Kant.* Malden, Mass: Blackwell Publishing. A thought-provoking biographical study of Kant that examines his life and philosophical thought and provides an exposition of Kant's major philosophical works, including *Critique of Pure Reason.*

John Locke

Locke, John. [1689] 1955. *A letter concerning toleration.* Indianapolis: The Bobbs-Merrill Company, Inc. An important document arguing the case for religious toleration and liberalism in general. A religious counterpart to Locke's political writings.

————. 1997. *Political essays*. Edited by Mark Goldie. Cambridge Texts in the History of Political Thought. Cambridge: Cambridge University Press. A comprehensive collection of Locke's writings on politics and society that includes over a dozen of his major and minor essays together with a biographical introduction and suggestions for further study.

————. [1689] 2000. *Two treatises of government*. Edited by Peter Laslett. Cambridge: Cambridge University Press,. The best edition of Locke's classic works on civil government, which includes a scholarly introduction on Locke, the historical context of his political treatises and their relation to Hobbes's theories.

Cranston, Maurice William. 1957. *John Locke: a biography*. London: Longmans. This biography of Locke is not an analysis of Locke's philosophy, but rather an account of his life and career, revealing a man of remarkable versatility who was at once philosopher, diplomat, economist, and theologian.

Dunn, John. 1984. *Locke*. Oxford: Oxford University Press. An excellent introduction to the work of Locke that focuses on his public life and career, his many friendships with political figures and thinkers from all over Europe, and his years of political exile in which he wrote *An Essay on Human Understanding*.

————. 1969. *The political thought of John Locke: an historical account of the argument of the "Two Treatises of Government."* Cambridge: Cambridge University Press. A comprehensive study of Locke's political thought, stressing the predominantly theological character of all Locke's thinking about politics.

Thomas Paine

Paine, Thomas. 1945. *The complete writings*. 2 vols. Edited by Philip S. Foner. New York: Citadel Press. A collection of Paine's most important writings, together with a lengthy biographical sketch that examines whether Paine's political thoughts grew out of his religious ideas.

————. 2000. *Political writings*. Edited by Bruce Kuklick. Cambridge Texts in the History of Political Thought, ed. Raymond Geuss and Quentin Skinner. Cambridge: Cambridge University Press. Contains the full texts of *Common Sense, The Rights of Man, The Age of Reason*, and other works, along with a biographical introduction and chronology.

————. "Of the Religion of Deism compared with the Christian Religion." Online. Internet Modern History Sourcebook. Available http://www.fordham.edu/halsall/mod/ paine-deism.html. A short treatise in which Paine posits the ideas of religious toleration, freedom of conscience, and the importance of rational inquiry in all matters, including religion.

Aldridge, A. Owen. 1984. *Thomas Paine's American ideology.* Cranbury, N.J.: Associated University Presses. Analyzes the entirety of Paine's intellectual work between 1775 and 1787, not merely his attitude toward American independence. The author explains Paine's major philosophical doctrines in the context of earlier ideas.

Claeys, Gregory. 1989. *Thomas Paine: social and political thought.* Oxford: Routledge Press. A comprehensive study of the social and political thought of Thomas Paine, concentrating on his tract *The Rights of Man.*

Keane, John. 1995. *Tom Paine: a political life.* New York: Grove Press. A definitive biography of Thomas Paine, examining his reputation as a notorious pamphleteer and one of the greatest political figures and writers of his day.

Jean-Jacques Rousseau

Rousseau, Jean-Jacques. [1781] 1996. *The confessions.* Ware, Hertfordshire: Woodsworth Editions Ltd. A memoir of Rousseau's life that serves as a detailed glimpse of life in the eighteenth century, from the more pleasurable recollections of his youth through his darker latter years.

———. [1751] 1992. *Discourse on the sciences and arts, and polemics.* Translated and edited by Roger D. Masters, Christopher Kelley, and Judith R. Bush. Hanover, N.H.: University Press of New England. A fresh translation of Rousseau's controversial first discourse and contemporary responses to it.

———. [1762, 1754] 1967. *The social contract and discourse on the origin of inequality.* Translated and edited by Lester G. Crocker. New York: Pocket Books. Rousseau's classic study of the foundations of political society and the importance of developing virtue within civilized society.

Cobban, Alfred. 1964. *Rousseau and the modern state.* Hamden, Conn.: Archon Books. A thorough analysis of Rousseau's work, which argues that while Rousseau rejected philosophical systems, there was nevertheless a fundamental unity about his thought.

Cranston, Maurice. 1982. *Jean-Jacques: the early life and work of Jean-Jacques Rousseau, 1712–1754.* Chicago: University of Chicago Press. The first volume of Cranston's definitive biography of Rousseau, covering his early life from his birth in Geneva, his youthful wanderings, and his return to his birthplace in 1754 as a celebrated writer and composer.

———. 1991. *The noble savage: Rousseau, 1754–1762.* Chicago: University of Chicago Press. The second volume of Cranston's biography of Rousseau offers an exposition of his life and works, offering a vivid history of his most eventful and productive years.

Launay, Michel. 1971. *Jean-Jacques Rousseau: écrivain politique (1712–1762).* Cannes: C.E.L. A careful and thorough study of the main themes of Rousseau's political writings, placing them within both the political and social contexts.

Starobinski, Jean. 1988. *Jean-Jacques Rousseau: transparency and obstruction.* Translated by A. Goldhammer. Chicago: University of Chicago Press. One of the most comprehensive studies ever written on Rousseau, placing his work into the context of his personal life.

Charles de Secondat, baron de Montesquieu

Montesquieu, Charles de Secondat, baron de. 1998–2007. *Oeuvres complètes de Montesquieu.* 18 vols. Edited by J. Ehrard and C. Volpilhac-Auger. Oxford: Voltaire Foundation. Comprehensive collection of Montesquieu's works in the French language. Volumes 1–2, 8–9, 11–13, 16, and 18 are available now, with other volumes to come.

———. [1721] 1973. *Persian Letters.* Translated by C. Betts. London: Penguin. Controversial in its day, *The Persian Letters* is novel, philosophical treatise, and "travelogue." It is a collection of fictional letters between two Persian brothers roaming Europe, and some of the most thrilling satire on Western European idiosyncrasies.

———. [1748] 2000. *Spirit of the laws.* Translated and ed. by Anne M. Cohler, Basia Carolyn Miller, and Harold Samuel Stone. Cambridge Texts in the History of Political Thought. Cambridge: Cambridge University Press. A treatise on political theory that influenced Enlightenment thinkers, including Catherine II and the framers of the United States Constitution. It was subject to censorship in France and was banned by the Catholic Church.

Carrithers, David W., Michael A. Mosher, and Paul A. Rahe, eds. 2001. *Montesquieu's science of politics: essays on* The Spirit of Laws. Lanham, Md.: Rowman & Littlefield Publishers. A collection of essays dedicated to the analysis of Montesquieu's contributions to political science, paying careful attention to the historical, political, and philosophical contexts of Montesquieu's ideas.

Shackleton, Robert. 1970. *Montesquieu: a critical biography.* Oxford: Oxford University Press. An important biography of Montesquieu that explores his life, scholarship, relationships, and political activity and public concerns.

Shklar, Judith N. 1987. *Montesquieu.* Oxford: Oxford University Press. Examines Montesquieu's purpose by exploring the range of his literary output, focusing on his scandalous novel, *The Persian Letters*, his philosophical writings, and his magnum opus, *The Spirit of the Laws*.

Abbé Emmanuel Joseph Sieyès

Sieyès, Abbé Emmanuel Joseph. [1789] 1963. *What is the third estate?* Translated and edited by M. Blondel and S.E. Finer. London: Pall Mall Press. A short but profoundly important work that provided the revolutionaries in eighteenth-century France with both inspiration and method for attacking the privileged class by calling for civil equality and equating the people with the nation.

Forsyth, Murray. 1987. *Reason and revolution: the political thought of the Abbé Sieyès*. Leicester: Holmes & Meier. A study of Sieyès and his political writings that reveals him to be a brilliant political theorist.

Van Deusen, Glyndon G. 1932. *Sieyès: his life and his nationalism*. New York: Columbia University Press. A well-researched study of Sieyès that examines his revolutionary career.

Voltaire (François-Marie Arouet)

Voltaire. [1759] 1947. *Candide or optimism*. Translated by John Butt. London: Penguin Books. A classic eighteenth-century satire criticizing optimism and the idea of a good and all-powerful God as wholly inadequate responses to human suffering.

———. [1733] 1980. *Letters on England*. Translated by Leonard Tancock. London: Penguin Books. Banned in France for its critical view of French institutions, Voltaire praised English tolerance, freedom, and progress while at the same time satirizing their illogical aspects.

———. [1764] 1972. *Philosophical dictionary*. Translated and edited by Theodore Besterman. London: Penguin Books. Though taking the alphabetical arrangement of a dictionary, this work is a series of essays promoting the revolutionary cause, and was roundly condemned by civil and religious authorities in France.

———. 1755. "Poem on the Lisbon Disaster, or: An Examination of that Axiom 'All is Well.'" Online. Available http://geophysics.tau.ac.il/personal/shmulik/LisbonEq-letters.htm. Satirical poem criticizing the idea that "a free and good God" was at work in the face of the human suffering after the Lisbon earthquake.

———. 1973. *The selected letters of Voltaire*. Translated and edited by Richard A. Brooks. New York: New York University Press. An excellent collection that weaves Voltaire's letters with events of his life and highlights Voltaire's epistolary talents.

Gay, Peter. 1988. *Voltaire's politics: the poet as realist*. New Haven: Yale University Press. An important study of Voltaire that places his political ideas in the context of eighteenth-century history, establishing the writer as practical political theorist.

Howells, R. J., A. Mason, and D. Williams, eds. 1985. *Voltaire and his world: studies presented to W.H. Barber*. Oxford: The Voltaire Foundation. A fascinating collection of twenty-six essays dealing with various aspects of the life and work of Voltaire: his political thought, his literary works, and the controversies surrounding him.

Wade, Ira O. 1969. *The intellectual development of Voltaire*. Princeton: Princeton University Press. An important intellectual history of Voltaire, analyzing the development of his philosophical ideas both chronologically and topically.

Other Philosophical and Literary Works of the Enlightenment

Beaumarchais, Pierre-Augustin, Caron de. [1773, 1778] 1964. *The barber of Seville and the marriage of Figaro*. Translated by John Wood. London: Penguin Books. These plays were censored for many years by the French government for their critique of the nobility and the provocative ideas expressed memorably in the monologues of the character of Figaro.

Fielding, Henry. [1749] 1963. *The history of Tom Jones, a foundling*. New York: The New American Library. An epic novel that provides an excellent view of eighteenth-century society at all levels.

Fox-Genovese, Elizabeth, trans. and ed. 1984. *The autobiography of Du Pont de Nemours*. Delaware: Scholarly Resources Inc. The autobiography of a French gentleman of royalist sympathies, which he wrote during the French Revolution while hiding out in the French countryside. Includes extensive notes by the translator.

Hardy, J. P. 1968. *The political writings of Dr. Johnson*. London: Routledge and Kegan Paul. A collection of some lesser-known works of Samuel Johnson, which reveal his lifelong interest in politics and political history, spanning the years 1756 to 1775.

Holbach, Paul-Henri Thiry, baron d'. 1774. *La système de la nature ou des loix due monde physique & du monde moral*. 2 vols. London. Nicknamed "the atheist's Bible" and considered radical even in its own day, this philosophical work describes a purely materialist world in which there is no power outside of nature itself.

Montaigne, Michel de. [1580] 1958. *Essays*. Translated by J. M. Cohen. London: Penguin Books. Remarkable for their modernity, these influential essays exhibit many characteristics of Enlightenment thought, such as skepticism, cultural relativism, and a preference for experiential over abstract knowledge.

Newton, Sir Isaac. [1687, 1729] 1934. *Principia, or mathematical principles of natural philosophy and his system of the world*. Translated by Andrew Motte, edited by Florian Cajori. Berkeley: University of California Press. One of the most important scientific works ever written, it describes Newton's laws of motion and law of universal gravitation and was a principle work of the scientific revolution.

Pope, Alexander. 1972. *Selected poetry and prose*. Edited by William K. Winsott. 2nd ed. New York: Holt, Rinehart and Winston, Inc. A good selection of work from arguably the greatest English poet of the eighteenth century.

Smollett, Tobias. [1753] 1990. *The adventures of Ferdinand Count Fathom*. Edited by Paul-Gabriel Boucé. London: Penguin Books. A novel that examines with comic irony the more notorious characters of eighteenth-century England.

Sterne, Lawrence. [1768] 1967. *A sentimental journey through France and Italy*. Edited by Graham Petrie. Harmondsworth, Middlesex: Penguin Books. Engaging account of a tour through France and Italy that includes thought-provoking anecdotes and philosophical musings.

Wain, John, ed. 1976. *Johnson on Johnson: a selection of the personal and autobiographical writings of Samuel Johnson (1709–1784)*. New York: E.P. Dutton & Co. Excellent anthology that reveals the character and greatness of this eighteenth-century writer.

INDEX

absolute monarchy, 33–34, 77–78, 79–80, 81–82, 167 *See also* "Enlightened Despots"

abstract mathematics, 29–30

Academy of Dijon, 105, 106

The Adventures of David Simple (S. Fielding, 1744), 41

The Adventures of Ferdinand Count Fathom (Smollett, 1748), 90–92

Alworthy, Squire, 61

American Constitution, 101, 102, 136

"An Answer to the Question: What is Enlightenment" (Kant, 1784), 75

Anderson, M. S., 75–76

aristocracy, 10, 47, 78–81, 90–93

Arouet, François-Marie. *See* Voltaire

Atheism, 18, 66, 70

Austria. *See* Joseph II, Emperor

Avril, Philippe, 13–14

Baumer, Franklin, 76–77

Beccaria, Marchese di Cesare Bonesana, 116–17, 171–72

Bérenger, Laurent de, 177–78

biblical scrutiny, 11

Boswell, James, 5, 69–70, 153; biography of, 117–18; on happiness, 871; on *philosophes*, 39, 128, 149, 151–52

Bougainville, Count Louis-Antoine de, 15

Bourg-en-Forêt, 1

bourgeois, 9–10, 90–92. *See also* *philosophes*

Breteuil, Gabrielle Émilie Le Tonnelier de, marquise du Châtelet, 50; biography of, 120–21

Brinton, Crane, 64, 82

Burke, Edmund, 7, 40, 78

Calas Affair, 65

Cambridge University, 136

Candide (Voltaire, 1759), 2, 59, 84, 86, 167–68

Caponigri, Robert, 16, 25

Cartesian rationalism, 29–30, 49–50, 50–51

Casanova, Giacomo, 113–14, 148, 178–79

Catherine II "the Great," 75, 93, 94–95, 114, 126, 177–78; biography of, 118–20; writings of, 174–75

Catholic Church, 2, 10, 54, 58, 131

censorship, 43, 49

checks and balances, 102–104

Christianity, 2, 35, 50–70; antipathy for, 56–57, 66–70;

Christianity (*continued*)
  declining authority of, 10–12;
  developments in, 47; dogma
  and, 55–56, 62, 63, 84;
  hypocrisy of, 53–54, 60. *See also*
  Catholic Church; clergy; Deism;
  God; faith; *philosophes*,
  Christianity and; religion;
  religious authority; toleration,
  religious
Christianity Not Mysterious
  (Toland, 1696), 56
civil society, 105, 106, 107,
  162–64
clergy, 53–54
Condillac, Abbé Étienne Bonnot
  de, 83
Condorcet, Marquis de, 18
The Confessions (Rousseau, 1782),
  106, 139–40
The Conscious Lovers (Steele,
  1722), 90
*Considerations on the Causes of the
  Greatness of the Romans and
  Their Decline* (Montesquieu,
  1734), 135
constitutional monarchy, 103–104
cultural relativism, 12–16, 25

d'Alembert, Jean-le-Rond, 43, 76,
  146, 150; biography, 123–24
Declaration of Independence,
  American, 92
Deism, 62–66, 69
De l'Esprit (Helvétius, 1758),
  68–69
Deleyre, 70
Della Mirandola, Pico, 10
democracy, 104–105, 108–109
Democratic Revolution, 47
Dempster, George, 153
Descartes, René, 12, 29–30, 50
D'Holbach, Baron, 67–68, 76, 84
Diderot, Denis, 5, 6; biography of,
  125–26; on Christianity; on

natural law, 168–69; on
  philosophes, 26, 144–46; political
  thought and, 83, 93, 96; on
  reason, 36–37; 41, 42, 43
Discourse on Inequality (Rousseau,
  1754), 108, 138–39
Discourse on Sciences and Arts
  (Rousseau, 1750), 138
Dumarsais, Chesneau, 147–48

economic stability, 9–10
educated class. *See philosophes*
education, 59
Elementi di Economica Pubblica
  (Beccaria, 1804), 117
*The Elements of Newtonian
  Philosophy* (Le Tonnelier &
  Voltaire, 1738), 50–51, 122
Émile (Rousseau, 1762), 108,
  162–64
Encyclopedia (Diderot ed., 1750–
  1765), 6, 67, 113, 125, 139
England. *See* Great Britain
"Enlightened Despots," 4, 19, 80–
  82, 92–96, 105, 119–21, 126–
  28; contemporary views of,
  177–79; writings of, 172–77. *See
  also* Catherine II "the Great";
  Fredrick II "the Great"; Joseph II
Enlightenment: definition and
  historical debate, 3–4, 25;
  disunity, 5–6; fundamental
  principles, 2–3, 6–7, 16–17, 76;
  geography of, 4–5, 19, 38, 47–
  48; intellectual preconditions,
  27–44 (*see also specific
  philosophers and scientists*);
  material preconditions, 8–10,
  37; phase one (1700–1748), 17;
  phase two (1748–1778), 17–18;
  phase three (post-1778), 18–19;
  religion and, 10–12, 18 (*see also*
  Christianity; *philosophes*,
  antipathy for Christianity and;
  philosophes, Christianity and;

religion); socio-political reality,
8–9, 9–10, 19, 39–40, 47,
77–78, 79–80, 133. *See also*
"Enlightened Despots"; natural
law; *philosophes*; *philosophes*,
writing on the Enlightenment
and *philosophes*; reason
equality, 89–90, 106–107; lack of,
152–53. *See also* political
structure, liberal
*Essay Concerning Human
Understanding* (Locke, 1690),
31, 133–34
Essay on Man (Pope, 1733–1734),
27
Essays Moral and Political (Hume,
1741–1742), 128
"Essays on Forms of Governments"
(Frederick II of Prussia), 172–73
exile, 49, 51, 115, 116, 132–33
experimental philosophy/
psychology, 28–29, 30–31,
43–44, 50, 134
experimental science, 40–41,
43–44, 51, 137

faith, 51–52. *See also* Catholic
Church; Christianity; Deism;
God; religion
fanaticism, 35, 38, 55, 57–58, 61,
64, 65, 157
fiction, 167–69. *See also* travel
literature, fictional
Fielding, Henry, 40–41, 61
Fielding, Sarah, 1, 41
France, 4, 7, 38, 40, 47–48, 65, 79,
102–103, 117, 104; clergy of, 54.
See also Paris; *philosophes*,
French; salon culture
Fredrick II "the Great," 19, 93, 94–
95, 116; biography of, 126–28;
writings of, 172–74
freedom, 6–7, 75–76, 87, 89; of
expression, 42. *See also* political
structure, liberal

free will, 38, 85, 106. *See also*
freedom, human agency;
"General Will"; political
structure, liberal
French Revolution, 7

Galileo, 11, 12
Gay, Peter, 7, 16, 25, 35, 81
"General Will," 108–109, 163–64.
See also free will
German states, 4
"Glorious Revolution," 133
God, 35, 57–58, 60, 61–62, 62–63,
70. *See also* Optimism
Godwin, William, 101
government. *See* political structure
Great Britain, 4, 38, 39, 47, 103–
104, 115. *See also philosophes*,
English; *philosophes*, praise for
Great Britain
Guiffardière, Charles de, 39–40
Gulliver's Travels (Swift, 1729), 15

happiness, 26, 37, 87, 92
Harris, R. W., 76
Helvétius, Claude-Adrein, 68–69,
104
Henriade (Voltaire, 1724), 54–55
Henry IV, 55
"high Enlightenment," 17–18
history, students of, 52, 54–55,
77–78, 79–80, 85–86
Hobbes, Thomas, 32, 87
human agency, 3, 75–76. *See also*
reason
humanism, 10, 11
humanitarianism, 26–27, 79
human nature, 31–32, 41–42, 82,
85, 158–59; political systems and,
86–87, 106, 107–108, 109–110
human rights, 81, 87, 88, 92
Hume, David, 83, 149–50; on
Christianity, 57, 58–59, 59–60,
62, 66, 159–60; biography of,
128–29

Idées républicains (Voltaire, 1765), 82

Il Caffè, 118

individualism, 89–90

industrialism, 47

An Inquiry into the Wealth of Nations (Smith, 1776), 141

Johnson, Samuel, 35–36, 89, 119, 153

Joseph II, Emperor, 93–94, 94–95, 178–79; biography of, 129–31; writings of, 175–77

Kant, Immanuel, 18, 75, 83, 143–44; biography of, 131–32

Kings and Philosophers: 1689–1780 (Krieger, 1970), 77, 78

Krieger, Leonard, 77, 78, 79

Lahontan, Baron de, 164–65

"*laissez-faire*," 18, 141

La Loubère, Simon de, 13

La Mettrie, Julien de, 68, 157, 158–59

La Nouvelle Héloïse (Rousseau, 1761), 108

language, 39–40

Las Casas, Father Bartholomé de, 15

La Système de la Nature (D'Holbach, 1770), 67–68

laws, 51, 52, 87, 88, 101, 107, 171–72; English, 103–104; French, 102–103; Russian, 94, 174–75. *See also The Spirit of the Laws* (Montesquieu, 1748)

Leibniz, Gottfried Wilhelm, 84–87, 116

Lespinasse, Mlle. Julie de, 123

Letter Concerning Toleration (Locke, 1685), 51–52

Letters on England. See Philosophical Letters

Letters Writ by a Turkish Spy (Marana, 1684), 15

Letter to Voltaire on Providence (Rousseau, 1756), 108

L'Homme Machine (La Mettrie, 1748), 68

The Life of Samuel Johnson (Boswell, 1791), 119

Locke, John, 8, 27, 31–32, 32–34, 35, 51–53; biography of, 132–34; natural law and, 160–61; political thought and, 87, 88, 92

Louis XIV, 8, 9

Louis XVI, 19

Man a Machine (La Mettrie, 1747), 158–59

Marana, Giovanni, 15

maritime commerce and exploration, 9, 12–16, 47

materialism, 56, 66–70, 157; views of *philosophes* on, 158–60

mathematics, 113

miracles, 56, 58, 60, 65–66

monarchy. *See* absolute monarchy; constitutional monarchy; "Enlightened Despots"

money, 164–65

Montaigne, Michel de, 15

Montesquieu, 17–18, 34; biography of, 134–36; natural law and, 161–62; political thought and, 83, 95–96, 101, 102–104, 110, 166–67, 169–70

nation-state, 8–9, 47

The Natural History of Religion, (Hume, 1757), 159–60

natural law, 3, 8, 11, 26, 27–28, 88–89; Locke and, 31, 33; materialism and, 56; Newton and, 28–29, 30; *philosophes* and, 160–64; religion and, 60–62, 64, 65–66, 157; social standards and, 36. *See also* human nature; human rights; "Rules of Reasoning"; universal gravitation nature of man, 1–2

Newton, Sir Isaac, 12, 27–29, 30, 35, 49–50, 61–62; biography of, 136–37. *See also* universal gravitation

"noble savage," 14–15, 32; *philosophes* and, 164–69

On Crimes and Punishments (Beccaria, 1764), 117, 171–72

Optimism, 84–87

Oration on the Dignity of Man (Della Mirandola, 1486), 10

Oroonoko (Behn, 1688), 15

Paine, Thomas, 63

Paris, 38, 39. *See also* salon culture

The Persian Letters (Montesquieu, 1721), 15, 135, 166–67

Peter I "the Great," 120

Pétrouille de la Live, Madame d'Epinay, 121, 122–23

philosopher-kings. *See* "Enlightened Despots"

philosophers. *See philosophes*

philosophes, 2, 3; antipathy for Christianity and, 56–57, 66–70; Austrian, 129–31; Christianity and, 57–70 (*see also* Deism); criticism of philosophers, 83–87; division among, 149–52; English, 132–34, 136–37; Enlightenment phases and, 17–19; French, 48, 113–17, 122–24, 134–36; geography and, 4–5; goals of, 35–36, 78; ideology of, 5–6, 7–8, 25–27, 36; individuality of, 5–6; materialism and, 158–60; "noble savage" and, 164–69; political thought and, 78–87, 87–96, 101–110; position in society, 77, 78–79; praise for Great Britain, 39–40, 49, 87, 103, 115; Prussian, 119–21, 126–28;

rationalism of, 41; Russian, 119–21; Scottish, 118–19, 128–29, 140–41; Swiss, 137–40; tradition and, 76–77; violence upon, 48–49; writing on the Enlightenment and *philosophes*: Casanova, 148; D'Alembert, 146–47; Dederot, 144–46; Dumarsais, 147–48; Kant, 143–44. *See also* "Enlightened Despots"; *specific individuals*

"philosophical anarchism," 101

Philosophical Dictionary (Voltaire, 1752), 65–66, 155–56

Philosophical Letters (Voltaire, 1734), 49–50, 53, 122

philosophy, eighteenth century, 25–27, 83–88. *See also* Enlightenment; *philosophes*

Poem on the Lisbon Disaster (Voltaire, 1756), 86

Political Justice (Godwin, 1793), 101

political structure, 8–9, 77–78, 79–80 (*see also* Enlightenment: socio-political reality); "Enlightened Despots" and, 172–73, 174–77; intellectual theory and, 32–43; liberal, 101–110 (*see also* checks and balances; constitutional monarchy; democracy; "philosophical anarchism"; popular sovereignty); *philosophes* and, 169–72. *See also* "Enlightened Despots"; *philosophes*, political thought and; social contract theory

Pope, Alexander, 25, 27

popular sovereignty, 104–107

primary documents, 143–79

Principia Mathematica (Newton, 1687), 27, 28–29, 136

print culture, 17. *See also* publication

privilege, 2, 90–92
property, 32, 33, 106–107
Prussia. *See* Fredrick II "the Great"
publication, 42. *See also* print
　culture
public opinion, 17
Pugachev Rebellion, 95, 120
punishment, 171–72

Raleigh, Sir Walter, 15
Rasselas, Prince of Abyssinia
　(Johnson, 1759), 15
"rational-classical," 18
rationalism, 26–31, 41. *See also*
　Cartesian rationalism;
　experimental philosophy/
　psychology; experimental
　science; reason
reason, 7, 8, 16, 27, 38; application
　of, 2, 75–76; religion and, 58,
　59–61; Voltaire and, 53, 54. *See*
　also experimental philosophy/
　psychology; rationalism
The Reasonableness of Christianity
　(Locke, 1695), 56, 133
the Reformation, 7
religion, 18, 35, 51–54, 154–57.
　See also Atheism; Christianity;
　Deism; Enlightenment, religion
　and; faith; God; toleration,
　religious
religious authority, 10, 167
the Renaissance, 7
Rodet, Marie-Thérèse, Madame
　Geoffrin, 121, 122, 123
Rogers, Woodes, 165–66
Rohan, chevalier de, 48–49
Roland, Madam, 26, 40, 156–57
Rousseau, Jean-Jacques, 5, 6, 149,
　152; biography of, 137–40; on
　inequality, 152–53; natural laws
　and, 162–64; on *philosophes*, 26,
　83, 129, 150–51; political
　thought and, 83, 95, 104–110;
　on reason, 41, 42

Royal Society of London, 136, 137
"Rules of Reasoning," 28–29, 30.
　See also natural law
Russia, 95, 174–75. *See also*
　Catherine II "the Great"

salon culture, 17, 113–14, 114,
　115, 121, 122, 123–24, 126,
　129, 135, 139
satire, 16, 17, 86
scientific discovery, 11–12
scientists, 11–12. *See also specific*
　scientists
Secondat, Charles-Louis de, Baron
　de Brède et de Montesquieu.
　See Montesquieu
secularization 10–12, 27. *See also*
　Christianity, declining authority
　of; tradition, erosion of
"sentimental-romantic," 18
Smith, Adam, 140–41
Smollett, Tobias, 5–6, 90–92
The Social Contract (Rousseau,
　1762), 6, 108, 139
social contract theory, 6, 52–53,
　108–109, 160–61
Some Thoughts Concerning
　Education (Locke, 1693), 134
The Spirit of the Laws
　(Montesquieu, 1748), 17, 34,
　102, 110, 135–36, 161–62,
　169–70, 174
Stanislaus II Poniatowski, King,
　105
Steele, Richard, 90
Sterne, Lawrence, 13
Supplement to a Voyage of
　Bougainville (Diderot, 1771),
　168–69

Theory of Moral Sentiments (Smith,
　1752), 140
Toland, John, 56
toleration, 49, 51–52, 55; religious,
　53, 56, 134, 154–57

Tom Jones (H. Fielding, 1749), 61
torture, 171–72
tradition: antipathy for, 36–37;
    erosion of, 2, 7–8, 10–12, 75–76
travel literature, 12, 13–15, 165–
    66; fictional, 15–16, 168–69
Treatise on Human Nature (Hume,
    1739), 128
Treatise on Systems (Condillac,
    1749), 83
Treatise on Tolerance (Voltaire,
    1763), 65
The Two Treatises of Government
    (Locke, 1690), 32–33, 88, 133,
    160–61

"universal good," 6–7, 75. *See also*
    Enlightenment: fundamental
    principles
universal gravitation, 27, 28, 50
University of Edinburgh, 128

Van Paassen, Pierre, 1
Vernes, Jacob, 154

Vichy-Chaumond, Marie de,
    Marquise du Deffand, 121,
    122–23
The Village Fortune Teller
    (Rousseau. 1752), 138
Voltaire, 2, 5, 17, 149, 150–51,
    152; biography of, 113–16, 121–
    22; on Christianity, 53–55, 57,
    60, 61, 62; on Deism, 64–65;
    "Enlightened Despots" and, 81–
    82, 93; on materialism, 158; on
    Newtonian science, 29, 50–51
    (*see also The Elements of
    Newtonian Philosophy* (Voltaire
    & Le Tonnelier); on Optimism,
    85–87, 154; on *philosophes*, 6,
    41, 42–43, 83, 129, 134, 150;
    political thoughts and, 19,
    78–79, 82, 104, 107–108; on
    reason, 1, 26; satire and, 4, 53;
    on toleration, 47, 48–50; 53; 59,
    155–56, 167–68

warfare, 47

About the Author

RONALD S. LOVE was Associate Professor of History at the University of West Georgia, Carrollton, GA. His many published works include *Maritime Exploration in the Age of Discovery, 1415–1800* (Greenwood, 2006) and *Distant Lands and Diverse Cultures: The French Experience in Asia, 1600–1700* (co-edited with Glenn J. Ames, Praeger, 2002).